Retrieving Nature

Retrieving Nature

Education for a Post-Humanist Age

Michael Bonnett

Blackwell
Publishing

First published as a special issue of *the Journal of Philosophy of Education, 2003*

BLACKWELL PUBLISHING
350 Main Street, Malden, MA 02148-5020, USA
108 Cowley Road, Oxford OX4 1JF, UK
550 Swanston Street, Carlton, Victoria 3053, Australia

First published 2004 by Blackwell Publishing Ltd

Library of Congress Cataloging-in-Publication Data has been applied for

ISBN 1-4051-0883-5

A catalogue record for this title is available from the British Library.

Set by Macmillan India Ltd

For further information on
Blackwell Publishing, visit our website:
http://www.blackwellpublishing.com

Contents

Preface

A concern for the environment is evident in educational policy and practice in many countries, at all levels, and in a variety of ways. This is welcomed alike by teachers and pupils, many of whom are moved by the urgency of repairing the ozone layer, cutting greenhouse gas emissions and saving the whale. At stake ultimately, they realise, is the Earth itself – at least, the Earth insofar as it is a place for human beings to live. What could be more serious? The argument seems to be clear. But while it is true that 'the environment' is the *sine qua non* of all that we do, these matters are fraught with a potential for evasion and sentimentality, and for confusion and misunderstanding – over key concepts and the language in which they are expressed, over the nature of the ethical issues that are raised, over the metaphysical perspectives within which they come to light, and over what a fitting (non-tokenistic) educational response might be. In this monograph, Michael Bonnett addresses the challenge of these matters in such a way as to offer not only clarity of insight into the very nature of the problems but also a vision of how education might rise to meet them. This has, as we shall see, pervasive significance for the principles that inform policy and important implications for practice itself. We are grateful to Michael Bonnett for this rich contribution to understanding and addressing these complex problems.

Paul Standish

Acknowledgements

I am indebted to many people for the opportunities they have given to discuss the ideas in this volume, but I would like to acknowledge particular debts of gratitude to Ian Frowe and David Whitley for their encouragement and helpful comments on early drafts of a number of chapters, and to Andrew Light and Heeson Bai for their help in relating ideas broached in Chapter One to environmental education in North America. The volume as a whole has also benefited immensely from numerous helpful suggestions made by the series editor, Paul Standish. I would like to thank him for his patience and the sensitivity of his editing.

Some of the arguments in this book draw upon and rework material that has previously appeared in article form. I am grateful for permission to draw on material from the following sources: 'Education for sustainable development: a coherent philosophy for environmental education?', *Cambridge Journal of Education* (1999) 29.3; 'Education for sustainability as a frame of mind', *Environmental Education Research* (2002) 8.1. (The website for these two Taylor & Francis journals is: http://www.tandf.co.uk.) Also: 'Environmental education and beyond', *Journal of Philosophy of Education* (1997) 31.2; 'Environmental concern and the metaphysics of education', *Journal of Philosophy of Education* (2000) 34.4.

Michael Bonnett

Chapter 1. Introduction: a Tangled Web

Humanity is facing its greatest challenge in the course of its long and troublesome evolution. Through their tool-making genius, humans have transformed the earth, and no part, however deep in the ocean or high in the sky, does not reveal their imprint. Their numbers have swelled to more than five billion, and they multiply in an ever-increasing scramble. They drag out the entrails of the earth for metals and minerals, they sweep the seas for food, they turn the forests into swathes of short-lived pasture and destroy the sheltering sky. They are on the threshold of disaster, and nothing short of a fundamental change in consciousness and society can prevent them from careering towards ecocide. (Peter Marshall, *Nature's Web*, 1995, p. 448).

At this stage in its history it is difficult to identify an issue of greater importance for humankind than its relationship with its environment, nor one that is more fraught. It must be a unique phenomenon—on Earth at least—for a species to be contemplating the possibility of its self-extinction. Yet as evidence mounts daily to confirm that human action is affecting the environment in ways that are both unprecedented and unsustainable, the issues raised appear ever more complex and the way ahead far from straightforward. Given that the consequences of this situation are having to be faced in increasingly acute forms by the citizens of the early twenty-first century, clearly it would be irresponsible for education somehow to attempt to remain aloof from the issues that this state of affairs throws up. And, of course, 'officially' it does not. There have been numerous international initiatives to promote environmental education—most notably those arising from the 1992 Rio Earth Summit Agenda 21—and most European countries incorporate it into the school curriculum in some way. It has a particularly strong presence in the education systems of countries such as Norway, Sweden, Germany, Austria and Switzerland. In the USA the situation is complicated, as responsibility for public education is at state level and in some states local governments or school districts play a substantial role in curriculum development. Nonetheless, the US Environmental Protection Agency is active in initiating and supporting environmental and sustainability education in many states.[1] Similarly, recommendations to integrate environment and sustainability themes into the curriculum are found in Canadian states such as British Columbia.

At the time of writing, in England and Wales environmental education is represented in the National Curriculum (QCA, 1999) from its earliest levels of Key Stages One and Two. Here the stated aims include that the curriculum 'should develop [pupils'] awareness and understanding of and respect for, the environments in which they live, and secure their commitment to sustainable development at a personal, local, national and global level' (p. 11). 'Education for sustainable development' is to be an aspect of pupils' 'learning across the curriculum' within the school, particularly in their work in geography, science, personal, social and health education, and citizenship (p. 23). Thus in the relevant programmes of study pupils are to learn to 'care for the environment', to recognise how it can be 'improved', 'damaged' and 'managed sustainably', and 'to identify opportunities for their own involvement'. While there are, of course, issues to be resolved over what counts as 'improved' and being 'involved', etc., at least environmental concern is formally acknowledged in the curriculum.[2]

Given this apparent attention to environmental issues in formal education and the undoubted sensitivity to them of society at large as evidenced by the degree of media attention they attract, the efforts of large industrial corporations to portray themselves as deeply concerned for the environment, the formulation of social policies and the assessment of new projects in terms of their environmental impact, it may well be asked: just what is the problem? Why should we not simply go along with the enlightened attitude towards the environment that it appears is currently abroad? As one commentator, Kate Rawles, has put it, 'The declarations of governments and institutions across the world on the subject of sustainable development would, if taken at face value, leave us assured in the belief that our environment and social problems are on the brink of final resolution' (Rawles, 1998, p. 132).

However, as the irony in this observation suggests, it may be that any such view that all is basically well is as deceptive as it is comforting. And should this be true, there are grounds for suspicion that the kind of environmental education supported by current policy may be largely cosmetic when measured against the depth and complexity of the issues at stake. For example, the political consequences of certain interpretations of our environmental problems are highly uncongenial to consumerist market orientated economies and on these views their long-term resolution will require a radical overhaul of such systems. As Williams Ophuls starkly put it, 'liberal democracy as we know it . . . is doomed by ecological scarcity; we need a completely new political philosophy and set of institutions' (Ophuls, 1977, p. 3). While, undoubtedly, this view lies at one extreme of the spectrum of debate, it indicates something of its scope and more modestly, many writers detect an incompatibility between sustainability and capitalism (see, for example, Kovel, 2002; de-Shalit, 2000). In addition, the very notion of environmental imperatives can be taken as challenging the foundational principle of liberal democracy that individuals decide their own view of the 'good life'.

Something of this underlying antagonism between some expressions of environmental concern and what is currently politically congenial is indicated by the singular lack of alacrity with which more radical policies—policies that may nonetheless still appear modest enough when compared with the problems they attempt to address—have been taken up in practical terms; indeed sometimes they have been ignored altogether.

(For an example, see John Elliott's (1995) illuminating case study of the UK Government response to the OECD initiative to develop pilot schools that give a high profile to education for sustainability.) Such tardiness does not augur well for the prospect of implementing the more extensive changes in society that an adequate response to environmental problems seems likely to demand. 'Solutions' that require relatively minor adjustment rather than major change are understandably attractive, and certainly the suggestion that we may need to relinquish deeply entrenched conceptions of economic development, that arguably have driven Western-style societies throughout the modern era, is not to be easily acquiesced in—particularly when alternatives sometimes take the form of the extreme and unsubstantiated visions of self-appointed ideologues. And there seems little sign that any Western government is on the brink of grasping the consequences of the fact that the Earth, as, effectively, a closed system, cannot sustain unlimited economic growth and the exuberant high-consumption lifestyles to which its population has become accustomed. If attempts to modulate environmental concern in ways that do not disturb the inertia of current social arrangements and expectations seem ever less credible, their short-term political attractiveness remains high.

'In our attempt to make conservation easy, we have made it trivial' (Leopold, 1993, p. 337). For some, Aldo Leopold's assessment of the expression of an earlier generation of environmental concern has strong resonances today. Against this backcloth one thing is clear: we must be wary of environmental education simply endorsing naïvely overconfident versions of environmental issues. And despite the truistic ring today of admonishments to take account of the environmental consequences of our actions, the way to achieve this is often bedevilled by highly contentious matters both of fact and of value and consequently by diverse views on how to proceed and what our ultimate goals should be.

Against such a backcloth, some important questions clearly are raised for environmental education in the context of state schools. Should it attempt to instruct pupils in specific ways on how to treat the environment? Should it attempt to instil a basic 'environmental ethic' in a way that, say, parallels its aim of conveying a basic human ethic? If so, how is this ethic to be characterised and justified? What stance should environmental education take towards current, deeply embedded social practices that are viewed as harmful from an environmental perspective and towards the claims of 'underdeveloped' societies and related issues of global justice? To what extent should it 'stray' into controversial value issues at all, rather than confining itself to teaching the 'scientific facts', where these are known, about nature, the global ecosystem and the effects of human action upon it? And how possible is this? When the causes of something as potentially profound as global warming are heavily disputed, what *are* the scientific facts, and how are educators—let alone pupils—to set about evaluating them and to judge and frame appropriate action?

Clearly, these questions about underlying educational purposes raise important questions for pedagogy, the curriculum and the school as an institution. As we shall see, there may be strong arguments to suggest that environmental education, properly conceived, requires a radical transformation of the nature of schooling and a re-examination of the idea of education itself.

But, for the issues involved to be properly understood, any focus on schooling needs to be set on a larger stage. Several thinkers have claimed that the ramifications of environmental issues are becoming fundamental in shaping human society and consciousness. For example, Ulrich Beck (1992, 1994) has developed the thesis that environmental issues are redefining modernity and that a new political order is required to deal with them. He argues that environmental hazards such as pollution and depletion are now so transgressive in their effects as to undermine the notion of a welfare state in which risks can be identified, attributed, calculated and compensated for, and that the 'social explosiveness' of environmental hazards, which break through a thin veneer of tranquillity and normality with increasing frequency, is leading to a rather stark political choice. Society will respond to such explosiveness by reorganising itself either as an 'authoritarian technocracy' in which the issues are rigorously managed by technocrats, or as an 'ecological democracy' in which power hierarchies are dissolved and the issues are subject to open public debate with the onus on the potential polluter to prove that their proposals are harmless.

In a related if somewhat less stark interpretation of the situation, Charles Taylor has suggested that the generalisation of environmental concern in society may be creating a common understanding that can challenge one of the great motives of modern Western culture: the unbridled dominance of instrumental reason. It may prove to have the potential to break the 'iron cage' of technology (Taylor, 1991, p. 98). He suggests that, hitherto, the situation has largely been one of local communities and fragmented groups of concerned citizens expressing concern for some bit of their environment and standing over against the vast majority of the public by demanding a sacrifice in development in the name of what appears as their minority interest:

> So formulated, the case seems hopeless: it is a politically lost cause, and it doesn't even seem to deserve to win. The mills of democratic politics ineluctably grind such small islands of resistance into powder . . . But once a climate of common understanding comes to be created around the threat to the environment, the situation changes . . . some local battles come to be seen in a new light, they come to be differently enframed . . . they come to be seen as part of a new common purpose (p. 100).

Taylor holds that in thus disturbing the unexamined dominance of instrumental reason, environmental concern may be catalytic in bringing into question many aspects of its character and influence (such as the disengaged model of rationality and the human subject (pp. 101–103)), that could result in technological activity becoming re-enframed in an ethic of caring (p. 106). Such an outcome would presage a major reorientation in the political climate and in social arrangements at every level.

I intend to explore some of the key elements expressed in such views in later chapters of this volume. At present, I simply present them as illustrative of the extent of what might be at stake for us in the pursuance of environmental concern and to make the point that the importance of getting environmental education 'right' is underlined not simply by the increasingly manifest consequences to humans of mistreating their physical environment, but by the potential influence of environmental consequences and concern on the nature of society itself. This in turn will condition how we view and attempt to resolve seemingly more specific problems, such as those raised by new technologies in biological (including genetic) engineering and medicine.

But there is another dimension to all of this that is highlighted in the aphorism 'nature has no problems'. P. Fleischman (1969), for example, has observed that there is no *biological* reason for conservation—it is based on human value systems: 'Nature will not miss whooping cranes or condors or redwoods any more than it misses the millions of other vanished species. Conservation is based on human value systems. Its validation lies in the human situation and the human heart' (cited in O'Riordan, 1999, p. 35).

The general argument here appears to be that nature's history has been one of constant change and upheaval—one state of relative equilibrium succeeding another. Oceans and continents form and fragment, species of living beings arise, become extinct and are replaced; no one moment in this flux of change is more natural—a truer expression of nature, one might say—than any other. It matters nothing to biophysical nature whether the earth is dominated by dinosaurs, human beings or nematodes—or, indeed, if there is life at all. A new equilibrium will simply be set up with or without us. In nature *per se* there are environmental *changes*, but not environmental *problems*. How things are with nature and the world can matter only to self-conscious beings. Only such beings can recognise value and this, in an important sense, places them outside nature.

This leads us up against a set of very profound issues that lie at the kernel of any approach to environmental education: what *is* nature and—crucially—what should be our relationship to it? This immediately raises the question: in what sense does nature have value? Can it have intrinsic value or is it only to be valued instrumentally in terms of its potential to serve human needs (including aesthetic and spiritual needs)?[3] Arguably, the stance that one adopts on this issue has profound implications for how to educate pupils to address environmental problems, especially if we acknowledge as a part of their education not only formal pedagogy but the powerful influence of the attitudes embedded in the culture and practices of the school. For example, our underlying stance on nature's value will determine how environmental problems will be conceived and the *kinds* of answers that will be sought, that is, what will *count* as an answer. It will thus determine the kinds of knowledge and understanding to be considered relevant, and, fundamentally, what the ethical basis for judging policy and action will be. It will clearly be decisive on issues where the perceived interests of humans and nature are in conflict such as, perhaps, in the case of battery farming, or deforestation to provide for local human needs, but even on issues where such conflict is less overt, it will determine the procedures and weightings that go into decision-making. It raises starkly the pressing question of what our basic environmental ethic should be (for there is an important sense in which we—and a school community— cannot avoid having one, however tacit) and how it should be taught.

This recognition of the ethical constituent to environmental issues in turn raises another set of issues, heightened by the views of postmodernists. For them, the environment can be understood from a variety of perspectives, and there is neither one grand narrative that will harmonise all of these, nor some point of ultimate authority from which to make judgements about which are true or superior in any objective sense. It all depends on the historico-cultural framework within which one is situated.

Now whether or not one finally accepts this postmodernist assessment of the situation, it does alert us to the need to be aware of the values that inform the frameworks for understanding nature and the environment that we employ, and also to evaluate the adequacy of the concepts that constitute them. For everything *could* be seen differently—and on occasion perhaps it *should* be. Thus we need to ask: how does a particular perspective pre-dispose us to view matters? What does it assume to be valuable, important, true? What does it disclose and what does it make invisible? There is here, then, an admonishment to investigate, amongst other things, the values, motives and inherent understandings that structure the disciplines of knowledge through which we investigate and describe nature and the environment. There are strong arguments to suggest that understanding, reasoning and knowledge are never neutral; they always have their own motives and aspirations, giving rise to their own procedures and standards for truth, which colour how they invite us to perceive the world. In the same way that, say, describing commerce between the developed and undeveloped world as 'trade' or 'exploitation' invites quite different value orientations, so does viewing nature as, say, a machine, or as an organism, or as the creation of a divine being. Given the complexity and diversity of views that are characteristic of environmental issues, it is particularly important to examine the adequacy and value implications of the metaphors and the conceptual schemes that we use for articulating them. And, of course, central to all of this will be our understanding of the concept of 'nature' itself. Just what sort of 'thing' do we take nature to be? For example, is it to be conceived essentially as the physical world, as revealed by science—or does it have other, even more fundamental, aspects and significances? What, indeed, are the connotations of referring to something as 'part of nature' or 'natural', and what logical or emotional force should such ascriptions have in the way we understand our environmental situation and develop responses to it?

The issues at stake here are brought into stark relief by those who see ideas of nature and what is natural as serving political ends. Ulrich Beck observes that 'The meanings of nature do not grow on trees, but must be constructed' (Beck, 1994, p. 39). And their construction reflects the interests of those in power. Thus the traditional notion of nature as an underlying reality becomes conceived as tyrannical, imposing on us a conception of ourselves—an 'essence'—that cabines our ability to think of ourselves and our choices in new ways and implicates us in certain power relationships. The ways in which our ideas of nature form a naturalised matrix that categorises and distributes power have perhaps been most keenly felt by certain feminist writers such as Donna Haraway (1991), who elaborate how such basic 'natural' categories as 'man' and 'woman' are far from politically innocent—just naturally given and beyond challenge—but are constructed as part of a political matrix. Acknowledging this 'denatures' them and frees us from their totalising influence. Thus for her it is imperative that we 'self-consciously construct a space that cannot affirm the capacity to act on the basis of natural identification, but only on the basis of conscious coalition, of affinity, of political kinship' (Haraway, 1991, p. 156).

Alongside the charge of the tyranny of nature sits the charge that it is non-existent. Bill McKibben (1989) has argued that, because of the pervasive effects of human activity, Nature is at an end and we live in a 'post-natural world'; Anthony Giddens (1994) declares that, in our 'post-traditionalist' culture, 'Nature no longer exists!' (p. 11), has become 'socialised' (p. 208), has 'dwindled away' (p. 223); and Andrew Stables has summed up the predicament of environmental education as relying on 'a conception of nature which has little cultural and historical stability' (Stables, 2001, p. 245). In undermining the idea of nature as some shared underlying reality, each of these views throws up serious problems for the very attempt to characterise or identify 'our' environmental situation, environmental problems, environmental solutions on anything other than a very local basis, and this has to be a matter of supreme concern to those, such as the authors of Agenda 21, who speak of global dimensions requiring global responses.

So, again, the issues that emerge are complex. Issues of fact and issues of value interweave. Issues of perspective colour issues of validity, and issues of validity affect our ability to evaluate differing perspectives. At first blush we seem to be confronted by a tangled web of competing interests and beliefs, and such entanglement brings unavoidable frustration on two counts. First, environmental issues demand *action*—and with a sense of ever-increasing urgency. Seemingly ever-proliferating and evolving strands of concern and debate are hardly conducive to mounting decisive action strategies, yet a rush to simplify and act decisively is hardly conducive to their thoughtful disentanglement. Given the possible scale of the future consequences of ill-considered responses—such as, say, a reversion to nuclear power sources to reduce carbon gas emissions— such haste is to be contemplated with foreboding.

Second, arguably the recognition of environmental issues turns us into a global community with a force that is potentially greater than any that we have yet experienced. Certainly, such ideals as universal human rights, or, say, the current pragmatics of world trade—extensive and insidious as the latter, in particular, may be—pale into insignificance in comparison. For there is a sense in which they remain *optional* for the human race. The world could go on—and has previously done so—in a way that turns its back on them, or at least gives them relatively low levels of attention. (Indeed, some Green thinkers advocate precisely a dismantling of world trade through a focus on significantly independent 'bio-regions' as a way of forcing communities to live within their environmental means.) But the need for attention to burgeoning environmental problems is gaining the force of *necessity*. The result is that a global community is being forged that is based on a new and more powerful kind of interdependence than was formerly the case. One in which different traditions, which previously—and not withstanding the ever-increasing incursions of global capitalism—were able to maintain a fair degree of cultural and spiritual autonomy, are now thrown together to seek to achieve solutions to urgent and ever-growing problems—problems that promise to affect us all on a scale, the extent and depth of which, the human race has not previously experienced. Here then is a powerful impulse for education for global citizenship, and for the identification of the values that should underpin it.

In the face of this wealth—not to say tangle—of complexity, the seductiveness of apparently simple solutions is wholly understandable, and, because of the repercussions of a general point that it raises for the view to be developed in this volume, I would like briefly to consider one illustration of such a 'solution' here. As previously mentioned, in recent years much of the discussion of environmental action and education has taken 'sustainable development' as a key guiding notion. I shall be discussing the possible contribution of this notion in more detail in a later chapter, but at this point I wish to consider what I believe to be the shortcomings of a view that is not infrequently offered as a contribution to practical issues of sustainability, namely the example provided by certain indigenous cultures.

While there is no space to develop the argument here, I suggest that there is limited point in industrial cultures looking to non-industrial cultures for indications of practical solutions to their environmental problems. Apart from the fact that the benevolent image of some native cultures is somewhat tarnished when we learn that their talk was not matched by their practice (Smithson, 1997), the chief reasons why they lived in a more 'sustainable' way with the environment were: 1) a very low population density; 2) a very low level of technological development. It seems reasonable to suppose that, if either of these factors had reached anything like the current levels in Western society, some of the attitudes and practices of these cultures (such as some forms of shifting agriculture) would have had catastrophic consequences for the environment.

I think this point is instructive in a number of ways. First, it illustrates the pretty obvious but sometimes insufficiently recognised point that the conditions to which such cultures were attuned—and in terms of which their practices were in some sense sustainable—were very different to the conditions that currently face us. This itself is a stark illustration of an important general sense in which environmental problems and sustainable solutions are indeed historically, geographically and culturally *local*.

Second, while it is undoubtedly beneficial to have one's conceptions of possible responses to the environment broadened by an awareness of the possibilities expressed in the practices and rhetoric of other cultures, there is a level at which it remains necessary for Western society (like any other) to produce its own solutions. This is because no other society has precisely *its* capacities, faces *its* problems, nor has the same possibilities for 'internal' insight into them. The point has been well made, by, for example, David Cooper (1992), that one's primary understanding of the environment derives from one's ongoing involvement in one's own life world, and by implication in Michael Oakeshott's remarks (1962) to the effect that attempts simply to import the principles and formal procedures of one culture into another are doomed to failure because their meaning and influence derive from their being embedded in a set of grown social practices. Thus, ultimately we must look to our own cultural resources and the possibilities of innovation that grow out of them in order to understand the way forward, for they represent the only authentic horizon of intelligibility for such an endeavour. (Naturally, this argument can be made in converse form about Eurocentric approaches to 'development' in the southern hemisphere.) And despite its bad image, modern Western culture is not devoid of intellectual and emotional resources for beginning to articulate and address these issues. If, as will be argued, an adequate response to our environmental predicament requires a transformation at the metaphysical level, it nonetheless can only be accomplished from within the horizons of significance—and thus the metaphysical space— with which our culture provides us and opens up.

Having said this, Western culture is caught up in a tangled web in a variety of respects. Its impact on nature has often brought disruption and confusion to the web of natural processes—quite literally, one might say, in the instance of the population of polar bears who have become hermaphrodite as a result of the accumulation in their tissues of pesticides used in the 1950s. Many have argued that our relationship to nature has become challenging, manipulative and arrogant as a result of the Enlightenment project of setting everything up as susceptible to the ordering of human reason and in the service of human utility. In the modern era respect for nature has declined and the dominant social paradigm is, according to Hillier, to treat nature either as an externality or as a set of infinitely exploitable resources (Hillier, 1998, p. 80; see also, Katz, 1996).

And nature is being disrupted not only physically but *metaphysically*. As an idea—and thus as an area of experience—intellectually influential views have arisen that question its innocence and existence, fragmenting its sense of organic holism if not condemning it outright as an anachronistic or dead metaphor. At the very least, then, it has to be acknowledged that, for us, appeals to nature are not unproblematic. All this precisely at the time when, as Anthony Giddens observes, we are trying to recapture or reinvent a nostalgic sense of nature with which to protect and deceive ourselves in the face of the relentless reflexive demands of modernity (Giddens, 1994, Chapter 8). The once authoritative substratum of 'nature' and the 'natural' is now no more than a chimera of sanctuary from the angst of choice in our lives. Yet, I will argue, a right relationship with nature lies at the heart of environmental education—and indeed education as a whole, for there is an important sense in which nature *does* constitute our primordial reality, setting the standard for our sense of 'the real'—and therefore for truth, knowledge, understanding and value.

It must therefore be the task of this volume to retrieve an understanding of nature that will allow a view of that right relationship to appear. It seems clear that, amongst other things, this will involve challenging the hubris of modern humanism, not least in its particularly inflated 'postmodern' guise in which nature is ultimately construed as a mere product of optional human narratives.[4] But at the same time it must beware a retrieval that reinstates simply and uncritically those ideological aspects of the cultural concept of nature that postmodernist critiques have helped to foreground and that have historically enabled it to be enlisted to authenticate a conventional order that does violence to certain groups in society.

We have now perhaps achieved a sufficient vantage point from which to discern and summarise some of the main issues for environmental education:

(1) What understanding of nature and our relationship with nature and the environment should we invite pupils to participate in?
(2) What (environmental) ethic should inform our approach?
(3) What kinds of knowledge and understanding best illuminate our relationship with nature or the environment and the environmental consequences of our actions, including their ideological content?
(4) What kinds of knowledge and pedagogy are appropriate in an area where many of the issues are considered controversial and yet where we are seeking to influence pupils' actions?
(5) How might any of the above require a redefinition of roles and ethos within the school as an institution and in its dealings with the community outside itself?
(6) By what standards should schools judge their success: what qualities of learning should they promote?

It is clear that each of these interrelated issues has strong philosophical elements, raising fundamental questions about the nature of ethics, knowledge and our relationship to the world. Indeed, environmental issues raise in a most powerful way the issue of the quality of our psychological space—the space of consciousness. In so doing they may well have implications for how we should educate in a *general* sense. It is not simply, then, that, as some have put it, 'all education is environmental education' because everything we learn can affect how we think and behave towards the environment, but that environmental issues, because of the depth of reflection on human consciousness and awareness that they provoke, raise the question of the nature of education itself. Indeed, it will be one of the themes of this volume to suggest that they invite us to consider a new *metaphysics* of education. That is to say, the exploration of issues raised by environmental education invites a radical re-interpretation of the philosophical groundwork and first principles of education: the nature, structure and constitution of *educational space, its reality*. This involves a reconsideration not only of what the central purpose(s) of education should be but of the kinds of knowledge and values around which it should be orientated, and thus of the fundamental attitude towards the world that it should convey. This in turn may have radical consequences for the methods and procedures of teaching and learning, and for social relationships both within the school and between it and the society it serves.

One further point in connection with the idea of the *general* impact that the study of environmental issues may have on education as a whole: quite apart from arguments for the necessity of environmental education on the grounds that our historical situation now requires it, there are other less dramatic but possibly equally compelling considerations when viewed from the standpoint of intrinsic educational values. Much of the foregoing has emphasised the way in which environmental issues are not straightforward and involve an intimate interweaving of facts and values, a close connection between learning and action and a sense of how conflicting demands have to be weighed and compromises struck. In this sense environmental issues are *par excellence* representative of real life. Addressing them requires pupils to engage with complexity and uncertainty, to live with provisionality, to develop their own views and to draw on things learnt both from life outside school and from many different aspects of the formal school curriculum. This thoroughly *integrative* potential of environmental education is one that some educational thinkers have valued highly and that has been reflected in the practices of so-called 'ecological schools', whose rationale will be examined in a later chapter. Certainly there is emerging evidence to suggest that students of all ages can be stimulated by the quality of learning and the level of personal significance that engagement with environmental issues provokes, and that it can provide a rich vein for re-vitalising education for previously disaffected students.

If the issues surrounding environmental education are difficult, there is also an assurance that they are worth grappling with.

Finally, I would like to suggest that the metaphor of a web—or webs—is a singularly appropriate one when thinking about nature, our relationship with it and the issues that are raised. Just as it is clear that nature itself is composed of highly complex interrelationships that extend organically throughout time and space, so it is clear that understanding nature and our relationship to it will not permit of a straightforward linear investigation. Rather we must expect to revisit ideas in differing contexts and from differing viewpoints if we are to take account of the reality with which we are dealing.

NOTES

1. Provision is inconsistent. For an official account of the recent history of environmental education in the US, see the report prepared for Congress by the National Environmental Education Advisory Council (December 1996): *Report Assessing Environmental Education in the United States and the Implementation of the National Environmental Education Act of 1990.*
2. There is also a growing theoretical literature on environmental education which includes, for example, Joy Palmer and Philip Neal (1994) and a number of special editions of academic journals such as *The Cambridge Journal of Education*, 29.3 (1999) and *Educational Philosophy and Theory*, 33.2 (2001). In the USA the work of David Orr is prominent (see, for example, Orr, 1992, 1994).
3. For a useful summary of the current state of the debate by Anglo-American philosophers on this topic, see Andrew Light's 'Contemporary Environmental Ethics: From Metaethics to Public Philosophy' (2002).
4. A collection of essays responding to this kind of postmodernism can be found in the collection edited by Michale Soule and Gary Lease, *Reinventing Nature: Responses to Postmodern Deconstruction* (1995).

Chapter 2. Metaphysics, Education and Environmental Concern

I suggested in the previous chapter that the issues raised by taking environmental concern seriously may turn out to be fundamental for the whole enterprise of education—indeed that they may invite a reorientation at the *metaphysical* level. By way of preface to more detailed argument to be developed in subsequent chapters, I will attempt here to set out the general nature and significance of this claim, including some of the main issues that it raises for education as a whole. First, I will say something about the sense in which education is to be construed as metaphysical.

METAPHYSICS AND EDUCATION

If, initially, we take metaphysics as in some sense concerned with the character of first principles and underlying reality, it is clear that the idea of education is metaphysical in a number of interrelated ways. First, it is rooted in certain fundamental notions such as knowledge, truth, morality and personhood, which have deeply metaphysical aspects. To transform the understanding that we have of the underlying nature of these, their character and purpose, would be to transform our notion of what it would be to educate someone. For example, if someone were to re-conceive knowledge as residing in our empirical transactions with the world rather than some extra-sensory realm accessed by pure reason, their view of the curriculum and teaching would be radically transformed. Second, and following from this, the way in which education construes such fundamental concepts creates a certain underlying reality in which it operates, that is to say it creates a certain metaphysical space within which its activities are performed and interpreted. This is experienced in the ethos or 'feel' of participating in education, living in this space. It configures one's sense of the spirit in which the enterprise is undertaken—for example, one's sense of the value and place of one's own beliefs and reason. Third, it invites pupils to participate in certain understandings of the 'real' world by initiating them into a certain form, or forms, of sensibility in terms of which what is truly significant—'real'—is to be identified and comprehended. For some pupils this may seriously conflict with the sensibility with which they first embarked on the educational enterprise, and, in any case, education proper is always concerned not with indulging pre-existing sensibilities, but with their development and refinement.

But now I must be more explicit about what I take 'metaphysics' to mean in this context, for clearly I do not intend this term to be construed in the way that has sometimes been the case in the Anglo-Saxon tradition of thinking. Here metaphysics has not infrequently been regarded as the most abstract—not to say empty—domain of philosophical thinking. On this view the business of metaphysics is with highly speculative and theoretical models of reality that have little or nothing to do with everyday life and experience. The study of first principles and underlying reality becomes interpreted as the production of abstract *constructions*— sets of high order general categories that illuminate experience, if they do so at all, *post hoc* and that therefore tend to be regarded as of merely 'academic' interest. They reflect the view of classical logic that meaning is achieved by definition in terms of a series of broader genera, the widest and broadest of which assume the countenance of the most profound. These are not part of experience, but rather a spectatorial embellishment. Worse, they are perhaps pre-eminently subject to Nietzsche's vehement rejection, in *Twilight of the Idols*, of the twin idiosyncrasies of a certain breed of philosopher:

> There is their lack of historical sense, their hatred of even the idea of becoming, their Egyptianism. They think they are doing a thing *honour* when they dehistoricise it, *sub specie aeterni* – when they make a mummy of it. All that philosophers have handled for millennia has been conceptual mummies; nothing actual has escaped their hands alive. They kill, they stuff, when they worship, these conceptual idolaters – they become a mortal danger to everything when they worship. Death, change, age, as well as procreation and growth, are for them objections – refutations even. What is, does not *become*; what becomes *is* not . . . Now they all believe, even to the point of despair, in that which is (Nietzsche, 1990, p. 45).

> The other idiosyncrasy of philosophers is no less perilous: it consists in mistaking the last for the first. They put that which comes at the end – unfortunately! for it ought not to come at all! – the 'highest concepts', that is to say the most general, the emptiest of concepts, the last fumes of evaporating reality at the beginning *as* the beginning (p. 47).

But there is another interpretation which sees the metaphysical not as some ultimate abstract classification of entities or processes—Nietzsche's 'last fumes of evaporating reality'—but as a vital influence that, for example, *leads* us to understand the world in the ways that we do, *provokes* the constructions—theoretical and abstract or otherwise—that we might make (for clearly understanding is bereft without *some* kind of conceptualisation). Metaphysics in *this* sense seeks not to set up ossified fixtures, but to reveal the primal motives and relationships which are working themselves out in the various epochs of human existence and which therefore shape our lives—the complexion of our lived relationships and understandings—in the most fundamental of ways. The working out of these motives provide the realities in which we exist, for there is an important sense in which reality—our understanding of it—is thoroughly conditioned by our projects towards (and within) the world. As was noted in the previous chapter, in the context of environmental concern one such motive that is foregrounded by many commentators is an overweening desire for mastery of nature. Some of the myriad manifestations that this finds will be explored in more detail in later chapters, but that at the general level such a motive would heavily colour our understanding of, and intercourse with, the world hardly needs to be laboured. And if true, it will of course spawn its own philosophies and sets of underlying explanatory and justificatory categories, of which those associated with pragmatism might be an exemplar—whether it be the objectivist version proposed by Pierce or the subjectivist interpretation given by James, and subsequently Rorty.

Thus there is a certain sense in which the working out of such motives in our lives may be properly thought of as constituting our *destiny*. This latter is not perhaps a notion that enjoys high degrees of credibility outside the 'dark arts' of astrology and other forms of fortune-telling, and elsewhere it is apt to be interpreted as implying some rigid (causal or logical) determination of the future. Yet in human affairs we can speak of things as having been set in train without implying this degree of immutability and it is in the sense of experience being fundamentally *conditioned* rather than exclusively *determined* that I use the term here. The ascendance of certain cultural motives opens certain possibilities that dress the stage upon which our lives will be lived out. Which of these possibilities we take up and in what precise manner, either at the individual or societal level, to a degree remain matters of choice and chance, but the ambience that they establish for our lives is not easily escaped, if at all. For example, as Heidegger (1977) rightly points out, however critical we may be of the technological motive, we cannot simply absent ourselves from it. We are thoroughly implicated in the world of modern technology and it is as plausible to suppose that an individual could simply live a life innocent of it as to suppose that they could live the life of a mediaeval bishop or a samurai warrior—our society simply cannot confirm such identities.

Straightforward rejection of such a motive therefore remains essentially cosmetic in the sense both that it is now deeply inherent in our way of seeing the world, implicitly colouring what we mean by 'rejection', and that any such rejection is overtly a reaction to it—thus its essence still motivates us. There are many ways in which we are thrown into a world not of our choosing, and metaphysics, now construed as an elucidation of such motivational currents, can properly be taken as the study of human destiny. Far from being exclusively concerned with abstractions that are removed from 'real' life, the metaphysical can be seen as inherent in real life in the most profound way, contributing to the ever-evolving structure of its interplay.

Let me now refer this conception of metaphysics back to the idea of education. This can be done in two complementary ways.

First, as mentioned above, there is the claim that all learning and teaching in an educational context is based upon assumptions about the nature of truth, knowledge and understanding, morality, personhood and human consciousness. This is clearly reflected in all serious contemplation of the concept of education from Plato to Richard Peters and thereafter. For example, in his essay on the justification of education, Peters (1973) argues for the pursuit of truth as not only having intrinsic value in human life, but as, in important senses, being *constitutive* of it. Now from the understanding of metaphysics being developed here, it is important to note that this invites a view of truth that sees it not simply as an abstract idea, but as an ideal in which we are imbricated. That is to say, it is a *power*, the draw of which leads us to live a certain kind of life. For Peters (and many others) respect for, and pursuit of, truth are fundamental to education, and while he has been taken by some of his critics to be preoccupied with a cold abstract intellectual analysis of educational concepts, on the present interpretation implicit in his view is an apprehension of a formative metaphysical dynamic of education. Thus an understanding of such ideals constitutes, as it were, the underlying domain of meaning in which the idea of education is located, and provides the sense of reality in terms of which its meaning is realised. Understanding such basic concepts in this way can properly be seen as constituting a metaphysics of education that reveals underlying realities not as a set of dead abstractions, but as a play of powers. Their identity lies not in the immutable definition of specific properties, but in their genealogical relationships and the way they are experienced in different contexts—the differing quality of their draw upon us.

Second, and coming from the opposite direction as it were, particular versions of educational practice refract metaphysical motives in particular ways, revealing particular instantiations of underlying realities to us—'underlying reality' now being taken not in the sense of some pure overarching logical order, but in the sense of the play of a motivational (and therefore connative and affective) order, of which we may not be immediately aware and yet that is being expressed through us. Such practices provide particular spaces or 'clearings' in which the play of such motives shows up. In doing this, the contingencies of different educational practices condition the ways in which truth, knowledge, morality and personhood appear—their fundamental character in their appearing—while at the same time being conditioned by them. Such ideas are what they are in this space which in part they themselves make possible, open up. Here then, through this reciprocity between contingent educational situations and metaphysical impulses, something is being said not simply about educational reality, but about the way in which we can construe metaphysics itself: namely, again, that it is not merely an academic study of the highly abstract, but itself *participates in reality*. Different metaphysics hold sway in different realities and are mirrored by them.

So, in what senses might environmental concern affect or disturb our current metaphysics of education? I will argue that it does so in a particularly trenchant way by raising fundamental questions concerning a now often overlooked, but hugely formative metaphysical relationship— our relationship with nature. For this is in constant interplay with those elements that I have identified as constituting the metaphysical space of education: knowledge, truth, morality and personhood.

EDUCATION AND NATURE

Education and nature were once perceived to be very closely and overtly allied. The educational romantic movement initiated by Rousseau and sustained by the likes of Froebel, Holmes and Gessell, emphasised both that nature was a source of knowledge and virtue and accordingly that education should be in harmony with the essential nature of the child; it should bring it out and follow its contours and natural stages. This view was given a particular metaphysical consolidation by Froebel in the *Education of Man*:

> Everything has a purpose, which is to realise its essence, the divine nature developing within it, and so to reveal God in the transitory world. Man has a special purpose. As a perceptive and rational being, he is intended to reach full awareness of his essential nature. He is meant to reveal the divine element within him by allowing it to become freely effective in his life (Froebel, 1967, p. 49).

Rousseau's claim that everything is good as it comes from nature led to an education that was concerned not just to follow the child's inner nature, but was also physically close to and mentally engaged with the natural world. For Emile, in his early years, 'nature was to be his teacher' because what were taken to be the necessities of the natural world constituted reality proper, in contrast to the abstracted and artificial world of aristocratic and emerging bourgeois society. Thus Emile's understanding was to be developed through the senses, careful observation of nature and pondering for himself the puzzles that he encountered there (if often prompted by his tutor). In this way, through first-hand experience, he would come to assimilate the natural laws that govern life, and to appreciate nature as a source of truth and perfection. Thus, too, Rousseau's disdain for what he perceived as the artificial alternative of an education abstracted from nature: 'What is the world? It is a cardboard globe. There you have the child's geography' (Rousseau, 1970, p. 49).

Here, then, was a metaphysic that flowered into the whole child-centred educational movement with its vocabulary of 'self-expression', 'readiness', 'innate interests', 'play', 'growth', 'nurturing', and various other horticultural analogies, and more latterly 'autonomy' and 'authenticity' when augmented by strands from other philosophies such as liberalism and existentialism. (For accounts of such interrelationships see Bonnett, 1986; Bonnett and Cuypers, 2003; Dearden, 1968, chapters 2 and 3.)

Of course, this approach to education was an articulation of a more general mood that arose in the eighteenth century, in which Peter Marshall suggests: 'Apart from the Great Chain of Being, the key concept of the eighteenth century was 'Nature', and nearly all thinkers urged their readers that if only they were to "follow Nature" all would be well. Nature became the touchstone of beliefs in religion and politics' (Marshall, 1995, p. 222). But the long, if chequered, history of child-centred education met its 'nemesis' materially in failing to meet the needs defined by a burgeoning, highly competitive, technologically based global economy and philosophically in the critical analysis of its central tenets by rationalist philosophers such as Richard Peters, Paul Hirst, Robert Dearden and Israel Sheffler, who found it confused and wanting in many ways. It is not so much that they simply upheld the traditionalist evaluation that it was irredeemably pernicious, but that in their rationalist re-articulation of some of its underlying values (such as the pursuit of personal understanding and the development of the individual) they emptied it of vitality. Severed from its metaphysical base—that is, essentially de-motivated—child-centred education was turned into a philosophical and political toy. Now it is regarded by many as anachronistic in the extreme, allowed to continue only in the role of suitably enervated *bête noire* of the curious alliance of traditionalist and managerial/technicist reaction that currently holds the field in education.

Yet if explicit talk of 'nature' in educational discourse has faded, this does not mean that its influence is entirely dissipated. Possibly, quite the reverse. For, on the view of metaphysics outlined above, in some ways ideas of nature may be as influential in their overt demise as in their flowering; all of the views that have 'replaced' it, or substantiate themselves in reaction to it, posit at their heart a certain relationship to it that, as a source of their sense, affirms its potency.

This may be illustrated by returning to the broader front. The general point is well made by Martin Heidegger in his essay on Aristotle's concept of 'nature' (Heidegger, 1998), where he argues that the notion of nature has become a fundamental pole for defining the relationship that the West has to the world, including humanity itself. The word 'nature', as he puts it, 'harbours within itself decisions about the truth of beings' (p. 185). It seems to me that Heidegger's observation rings true in a number of ways. To start with, it is surely true that our sense of nature—what it is and our position with regard to it—conditions our understanding of ourselves and of our place in the greater scheme of things. In this sense the term 'nature' is not merely a noun, but a regulatory principle operating at a number of levels and in a variety of ways. For example, whether nature is conceived (at whatever level of consciousness) as, say, some essentially mechanical system or as the living expression of divinity has large implications for our attitudes towards the world as a whole, including ourselves. The conception of nature that we hold is therefore constitutive of the human spirit in the sense of conditioning some of our most profound intuitions, and, it will be argued, gives us our primordial feel for, and frame of reference for appraising, the situations in which we find ourselves. It defines, as it were, central elements of the posture of our vitality, and, as such, must lie at the heart of any idea of education as preparation for life.

If we no longer explicitly subscribe to the eighteenth-century admonition to 'follow nature in all things', it is still the case that much of what we do is understood against an (often implicit) set of socially shared assumptions about what is 'natural' and what is in keeping with nature. Such notions condition what is perceived as fitting, determining what counts as harmony or discord, reciprocity or exploitation, truth or untruth, perhaps beauty or ugliness. To call something 'unnatural' is still generally to censure it. That our view of nature has powerful consequences is amply illustrated by Peter Singer's characterisation of one of the major features of nature as understood in what he describes as the 'dominant Western tradition':

> According to the dominant Western tradition, the natural world exists for the benefit of human beings. God gave human beings dominion over the natural world, and God does not care how we treat it. Human beings are the only morally important members of this world. Nature itself is of no intrinsic value, and the destruction of plants and animals cannot be sinful, unless by this destruction we harm human beings ... Harsh as this tradition is, it does not rule out concern for the preservation of nature, as long as that concern can be related to human well-being. Often, of course, it can be (Singer, 1993, pp. 267–268).

This assessment of the influence of the Judaeo-Christian tradition is stark and heavily contested (for example, see Attwood, 1995; Hertzberg, 1998; Passmore, 1995), but its implications for how we may treat the natural world hardly need to be spelt out. And arguably we see the exploitation of nature that this view legitimises holding sway all around us—there may be that much truth in Singer's claim. Of course, there are other powerful views of nature at work in society which continue to lend it a more exalted—and sometimes highly romanticised—status.

To acknowledge this variation of attitudes is to identify a reason why our understanding of 'nature' has such wide influence: it is the sheer ubiquity of the concept in its many nuances. Some clarification of these nuances is the task of the next chapter. But there is another, related, aspect to this to which I alluded in Chapter 1. The point is often made that the concept of nature is historically variable and based on changing metaphysical assumptions which mean that it cannot be defined *a priori*. While acknowledgement of this element of relativism in the concept draws attention to the provisionality of any analysis of it, it also underlines the importance of any such analysis: analysis of *our* (current) concept reveals *our* (current) metaphysical assumptions—the assumptions that most fundamentally shape our perception of, and attitudes towards, the world. And this is why the concept of nature that cumulatively we initiate pupils into—no matter how tacitly and how piecemeal—is so formative and so important.

THE IMPACT OF ENVIRONMENTAL CONCERN

Previously, I have noted how as the consequences of human exploitation of the planet manifest themselves in myriad disturbing ways some commentators have not been slow in pointing out their extensive repercussions not just for the peripheral details of human life, but for the very structure of society and our social institutions. The sheer scale and profundity of ecological catastrophes, and the complexity and sometimes invisibility of their direct causes has been held to be precipitating a new social ambience of fragility. To the extent that such claims (and they proliferate almost daily) have to be taken seriously, we have indications that something profound may be afoot—if not yet quite at the metaphysical level, at least suggestive of some movement at that level. I will now tease out some strands of this 'movement' with particular reference to our relationship with nature.

For many, a growing awareness of our environmental situation has provoked not simply a re-assessment of certain kinds of human activity in the light of its effects on the natural world, but an investigation of, and re-appraisal of, our basic stance towards that world. Throughout the modernist epoch of Western civilisation runs a fundamental motive to subjugate and exploit nature. This is reflected in both our actions and our ascendant forms of knowledge, such as science and technology. The characterisation of modern empirical science by Francis Bacon at its inception provides stark illustration of this. Fritjof Capra observes that

> The terms in which Bacon advocated his new empirical method of investigation were not only passionate, but outright vicious. Nature, in his view, had to be 'hounded in her wanderings', 'bound into service' and made a 'slave'. She was to be put in 'constraint' and the aim of the scientist was to 'torture nature's secrets from her' (Capra, 1982, pp. 40–41).

Some feminist writers have suggested that this essentially aggressive attitude was underwritten by the way the concept was gendered in language. They claim that feminised nature invokes qualities of passivity, yet also of uncontrollable 'animal wildness', which legitimises motives of penetration, exploitation and bringing to order by 'masculine' culture (see Merchant, 1992, Chapter 2). The drive in modern rationalism to explain, predict and control nature through the elevation of the general and universal over the immediate and the particular, the logical and calculative over the emotional and empathetic, serves only to corroborate this characterisation.

It needs to be emphasised here that it is not being claimed that all science—and much less, all rationality—is aggressive towards nature in the same way and to the same degree. Indeed, because of its comparatively passive stance, some enthusiasts of experimental science have disparagingly likened the science of natural history to mere 'stamp collecting'. Furthermore, it is undoubtedly true that scientific knowledge frequently has evoked and enhanced our respect, even reverence, for nature. As we learn of the sheer magnitude, and the infinite diversity, complexity, integrity and subtlety of the cosmos, and encounter the beauty of its forms and processes through the ongoing revelations of many areas of science, admiration for nature can feel to be the only fitting response.

The point that is being made here concerns the *growing ascendancy* of instrumental motives in modern rationality and how these characterised the 'new' science of the seventeenth century which set the tone for much that has followed. Bacon was not alone. For example, Descartes, Joseph Glanville and Robert Boyle all advocated science as a means of mastering nature (see Merchant, 1992, pp. 46–47), and, of course, the great European Enlightenment project of progress was founded upon the application of disengaged reason in the service of human utility. Today, of course, in terms of science as a social practice one can add to this the massive growth of commercial corporate influence on scientific research expressed in relative resources invested in highly instrumental, profit-motivated research as against 'open' enquiry, and the commercial patenting of aspects of nature such as the human genome. Although, as we shall see, there is a significant sense in which all rationality is aggressive, there is an important area of the argument that centres on the qualitatively different motives that can inform it. And in his critique of what he calls 'the rage against reason', Richard Bernstein (1991, pp. 45–50), for example, is no doubt right to draw attention to significant differences between 'purposive rationality' and the kind of open 'communicative rationality' identified by Habermas.

Nonetheless, the issue of the growing cultural ascendancy of instrumentalism and its effect on the character of our intercourse with nature, is perhaps nicely illustrated by the modern way of producing things. This occurs largely according to blueprints that pre-specify all the relevant qualities of the product and of the process of its manufacture, leaving to nature the role of either supplying whatever this blueprint demands, or of being re-engineered so to do. As it were, nature has less and less 'voice' in determining either product or process. Even in agriculture where a certain contact with nature remains, the modern attitude is essentially one of challenging rather than waiting upon, and the inclination and opportunity to 'listen' to nature can be highly attenuated. Here, we might contrast Van Gogh's evocation of the relationship between farming and nature in his picture of *The Sower* with its modern counterpart. In the former the immediate contact with land and weather, the necessary attention to the proper distribution of the seed, the immediate consequences of a failure of the crop and so forth, hold open the possibility of an attendance on nature which is not invited by the modern tractor driver encased in his cab, with earphones tuned to some radio station or music tape, while the business of sowing is pre-calculated, handled automatically and at a distance by the machinery in tow. This is not to deny, of course, that the peasant sower may well be mentally preoccupied with things other than his immediate task, but it remains the case that he is not *removed* from this task by the nature of his equipment and the motives it expresses.

Aggressive science, nature gendered as feminine, the attempt of technology to turn the whole of nature into a resource, the challenging quality of modern manufacturing and agriculture, the emphasis on consumption: arguably to an ever-increasing degree, such attitudes characterise the underlying motivational framework through which, as a culture, we understand and interact with the world around us. And just at the point when they have come to dominate in our definition of the 'real' in everyday experience, they are now being called into question by some strands of environmental concern. For example, the bio- or ecocentric reaction to current basically humanistic utilitarian approaches to the setting-up of environmental problems challenges not just these manifestly aggressive and exploitative aspects of modernism towards nature, but also the anthropocentrism that grounds it. Thus Paul Taylor (1986) seeks to champion the 'rights' of non-human nature and sets human needs strictly on a par with the needs of all other members of 'the great community of life', while David Foreman (1993), founder of the 'Earth First!' movement, subordinates them to the well-being of the biosphere.

Such views will be explored in more detail when we come to consider the issue of founding an environmental ethic. For present purposes they illustrate how environmental concern can act as a catalyst for re-examining such basic elements in our understanding of reality and provoke us to confront a fundamental question: *What constitutes a right relationship with nature?* Such a question not only raises issues of basic attitudes towards nature, both current and potential, but also the significance of our relationship with nature for the constitution of *our own identity*—our sense of place and purpose in the greater scheme of things. How we regard and treat nature says a great deal about the kind of beings that *we* are. As Capra (1975, p. 77) points out, 'We never speak about nature without at the same time speaking about ourselves'.

A characteristic of the way that we define ourselves in relation to nature has been taken up by several eco-feminists (for example, Plumwood, 1995) who observe that under the rationalistic impulse, human nature is defined *against* nature. Precisely those qualities such as freedom, rationality and the transcendence of nature which we take to differentiate ourselves from the rest of nature have become definitive human virtues. In many ways, as Kate Soper rightly notes, through its definitions of the human and the non-human, Western configurations of nature 'function as a register or narrative of human self-projections' (Soper, 1995, p. 10). And we and nature in turn—the limits of community—are defined in our imaginations by our ideas of monsters, whose rehabilitation is the ultimate challenge to naturalised boundaries (Haraway, 1991, p. 180).

Thus environmental concern brings to the surface the issue of our primal relationship with nature, illustrates its importance and invites us to explore alternatives to the *status quo*. In so doing it invites us to acknowledge and overcome the metaphysics that holds sway in our time; it invites us to reconstitute reality and with it, just as surely, our sense of our own identity. Such an enterprise cannot fail to have substantial implications for the metaphysics of education, clearly raising issues for some of its basic metaphysical notions. Perhaps most fundamentally, coming to terms with environmental issues ultimately requires us to reconsider the nature of things themselves and how they are known, and to contemplate some views on this that are different from those that standardly underpin education today.

For example, amongst other things, we may be drawn to consider that traditional subject knowledge is born of a social history that was not only largely innocent of the environmental issues that now trouble us, but, it has been argued, whose central motive was the subjugation and exploitation of nature. In such a cultural milieu things themselves get set up in a certain way, namely, primarily as a resource. Thus environmental concern alerts us to the possibility of certain aggressive motives holding sway within traditional subject knowledge. It thereby raises fundamental educational questions not only about what kinds of knowledge will best illuminate environmental problems, but also about the nature of educational knowledge itself—the spirit in which it is acquired and how it conditions our outlook. In seeking to make explicit the tacit projects towards reality which energise different kinds of knowledge—and the corresponding pictures of reality which they hold up to us and sustain—the possibility is opened up that we may reveal some ways of knowing as being more seminal, fundamental, humanly relevant, than others which currently set the standard for knowledge in education and/or what is considered to be relevant to 'real life'. Indeed, one of the central issues at stake, of course, is precisely that of what should *count* as '*real* life'. Such a review may lead us, for example, to seek a reconstruction of that great paradigm of the rationalist project, scientific knowledge, by imbuing it with more receptive-responsive motives towards nature. Similarly, we may seek to reveal and re-appraise the metaphors of nature that different kinds of knowledge assume and employ, and to ponder the epistemological foundations of a curriculum germane to a genuinely 'organic' conception of reality.

Importantly, such issues can be extended into considerations concerning the generation and 'ownership' of knowledge in the educational context. If the academic canon can be held suspect, whose interpretations and explorations of the nature of things are to be the arbiter of knowledge? Should radical alternatives be presented and on what basis should they be selected?

Environmental concern also raises issues for traditional conceptions of morality and perhaps personhood. In particular it poses the question of how the moral community is constituted: to whom or to what do we have moral obligations? Consider the following rewriting of *Robinson Crusoe*:

> 19. Sept. 1685. This day I set aside to devastate my island. My pinnace being now ready on the shore, and all things prepared for my departure, Friday's people also expecting me, and the wind blowing fresh away from my little harbour, I had a mind to see how all would burn. So then, setting sparks and powder craftily among certain dry spinneys that I had chosen, I soon had it ablaze, nor was there left, by the next dawn, any green stick among the ruins (Midgley, 1995, p. 89).

Mary Midgley suggests that no matter how one worked on the style, the above paragraph can never become convincing because Crusoe, just like the rest of us, would feel an invincible objection to senseless destruction. 'Yet the language of our moral tradition has tended strongly, ever since the Enlightenment, to make that objection unstateable'. This, she holds, is true because the whole idea of moral obligation is enframed by the notion of a social contract that can only hold between free and rational agents. Similarly, Robin Attfield claims that traditional ethics cannot readily accommodate environmental issues because the former requires identifiable human legatees or recipients for duties, whereas the latter involves either no such human recipients or ones who cannot yet be identified (future generations). 'So a different understanding of duty (and of responsibility) is clearly needed' (Attfield, 1995, p. 332).

The fact that, as we have seen, some strands of environmental concern raise the notion of the worth of non-human nature in such a way as to *at the least* invite the extension of the idea of intrinsic moral standing to some, if not all, aspects of non-human nature can, then, be seen as a challenge to undertake some reconsideration of the metaphysical basis for ethics. It is true that there may be good reasons for supposing that any environmental ethic cannot be *simply* human ethics by extension; for example, as Holmes Rolston III (1997, p. 60) points out, the integrity of wild animals is under the forces of natural selection and therefore we necessarily treat such animals differently from humans, not interfering in the pain and fate of the former. Yet it may be that acknowledgement of the possibility of nature having a moral standing will open a new metaphysical landscape which invites us to go beyond what morality is traditionally taken to signify to a more primordial and inclusive apprehension of our relationship with the world around us.

It has been suggested that this stance may be neither anthropocentric nor biocentric and may be best described as human-related but not human-centred (see Taylor, 1992). Our awareness of things necessarily occurs in the context of human concerns and involvements, but that does not make our stance towards them exclusively human-centred. For example, we are capable—at least to some degree—of the *dis*interested pursuit of truth and of attention dedicated to the object of our interest. Though there can be the suspicion that such disinterested enquiry merely suspends full human sensibility in order to substitute a sometimes highly instrumental and constructing set of standards and procedures derived from an academic discipline which has its own tacit non-object orientated motives, this certainly need not always be the case. Also we believe ourselves capable of a sensitivity to the otherness of the other, of, for example, ecstatic and rapturous experience in which we are held in the sway of the other, ourselves deeply influenced or even inspired by it. On such occasions self-centred motives seem to be either much diminished or completely suspended.

To summarise: in the context of environmental concern, the most fundamental questions to ask of an era are metaphysical, where to ask a metaphysical question is primarily to ask after the primal motives that are holding sway—that is to say, holding sway in the space that is inter-subjective or cultural consciousness. This is a space more fundamental than the 'pure' physical space of the physical sciences, for it is the space that constitutes our form of sensibility, from which all else is abstraction. Education, too, unavoidably participates in this space and selectively so. It reflects and transmits ways of relating to the world—of being in it and of interpreting it—and this preliminary sketch of some of the issues raised by environmental concern invites us not only to recognise, but to *rethink*, for example, the conceptions of truth, knowledge, morality and personhood that underpin our understanding of education and constitute the metaphysical space in which it is currently practised. Environmental issues can disturb the traditional contours of educational space and produce a landscape of a different complexion and ambience whose internal quality reverberates to a different set of motives, a different metaphysics. This means that raising the question of environmental education is to raise questions about the nature of educational learning, knowledge and understanding in ways that will challenge many recent and current conceptions of education itself, such as liberal-rationalist, managerial and market orientated. I will argue that there is an important sense in which each of these in its own way evinces motives that derive from a modernist humanism that needs to be overcome.

Chapter 3. Notions of Nature

Nature ... the power that creates and regulates the world ... the power of growth ... the established order of things ... normal feeling ... conformity to truth or reality (*Chambers 20th Century Dictionary*).

In recent years it has been a sense of environmental crisis in terms of resource depletion, pollution and the disruption of natural systems that has motivated the concern for environmental education and thus placed at its kernel a concern to preserve or conserve nature in some way or another. It is this sense of crisis, too, that provokes what I have argued to be the pivotal underlying question for environmental education: what constitutes a right relationship with nature? But what is it, exactly, that we are to conserve, to have a right relationship with? To make progress in understanding what should constitute environmental education we need to address the question: What *is* nature?

Yet, and notwithstanding the above, to many this last may seem to be an odd and perhaps eminently unnecessary question to ask. Certainly many current schemes for environmental education do not pursue it with any great vigour. Perhaps the answer seems too obvious to warrant attention and in any case at first blush its direct contribution to the furtherance of environmental education may appear less than clear. 'Nature': is it not simply the world of animals and plants—and hills, mountains, rivers and clouds—which we happily think of quite straightforwardly as the world of 'natural' things? We know that our own survival is dependent upon the continued smooth functioning of this world. We know also that human activity is increasingly disrupting this functioning, resulting in 'environmental problems'. And so the task is essentially to learn more about how the natural world functions so that we can then find ways of either ameliorating the effects of human action upon it or modifying those actions themselves. None of this seems overtly to require any extensive conceptual investigation into the idea of 'nature'. We simply need to know what it is that we do to the environment that will have adverse effects on us either now or in the future.

There is a certain down-to-earth practicality to such a view that appeals to common sense, and its perspective has been a strong influence in traditional conceptions of environmental education where it has been felt that success can be directly and sufficiently measured in terms of overt results, such as students demonstrating knowledge of natural processes and the inculcation of behaviours that lead to reduced pollution and resource consumption.

But things are not this straightforward—at least not if we wish to become aware of dimensions and possibilities which common sense largely leaves out of view. And arguably when confronted with a problem of such magnitude as to involve the possibility of our own extinction, we should be concerned to evaluate as many perspectives that can contribute to our understanding of our situation as possible. We need to be in the business of revealing issues rather than covering them over, and in particular to question current common sense, for this itself is necessarily imbricated in our present environmental predicament. For example, the assumptions expressed in identifying 'adverse effects' referred to in the previous paragraph will need to be examined. These are intimately related to the whole set of criteria that we customarily employ to judge quality of life, some of which, again, appeal to ideas of what is 'natural'. In such ways, it will be argued that there are issues of the highest importance to environmental concern implicit in the concepts of nature that inform our thinking—particularly if we wish both to understand what may be at stake when we attempt to weigh up the effects of our actions in anthropocentric terms of the value and significance of nature *for us*, and at least to entertain the possibility of non-anthropocentric dimensions to environmental issues.

One such set of issues is raised by posing the following question: 'Are *we* part of nature?' Even at the level of common sense, the answer to this is not entirely straightforward. Sometimes we think of our lives as intimately bound in with, or characterised by, a range of natural processes and phenomena such as birth, growth, ageing and death, and all sorts of natural features of the immediate physical world such as the presence of solid objects and gravity. But sometimes we may think of ourselves as somehow separate from—possibly 'above'—nature by contrasting the bruteness of nature with our own civilisation. We can be reluctant to think of ourselves as members of the same 'great family' as nematodes and Assassin Bugs, and Hegel's reference to the 'unhappy consciousness' involved in the mediaeval rejection of the animal part of our own nature still resonates in aspects of our self-images—varying re-accommodations to natural appetites in our 'more permissive' society, not withstanding.

Such ambiguities concerning their relationship with nature were revealed in a study into 10-year-old children's perceptions of nature and the environment in which I was involved (Bonnett and Williams, 1998). While recognising a high degree of dependence on nature, some children were highly equivocal about whether people were *part* of nature, which they tended to associate primarily with plants and (non-human) animals. And those who argued that 'people are animals too' because they have similar basic needs as animals nonetheless also tended to think of nature as something set apart from their everyday lives, often as a place of refuge, operating at a quite different pace and according to a quite different agenda and 'moral code' to the social world in which they for the most part saw themselves as living.

Many of the children were also sensitive to another dimension of complexity: they recognised different *degrees* of naturalness, ranging from what they took to be wild 'untouched' places such as forests, to cultivated fields, to towns and motorways (the last being for several, the epitome of 'not nature'). Again, there is ambiguity about the relationship to nature of what might be taken at one level as perfectly natural human activities such as home building and travel. Two important points arise here. First, there are clearly different *senses* of 'nature' and 'natural' operating in these children's thinking, between which tensions can arise. This, in turn, can bring about a certain vagueness and confusion when it comes to addressing environmental issues; indeed, this was the case with the majority of the children in the study, there being very limited translation of their generalised and highly charged emotional *simpatico* with nature into thought and action in the context of the everyday. Second, while the issue of their sense of place in relation to nature was far from unequivocal, it was also central to their attitude towards environmental problems. It seems to me that such responses echo a number of ambiguities that commonly pervade this area of adults' thinking, as, for example, when they come to value their weekend rural retreat to refresh them for a renewed assault on the environment on Monday morning, or when they participate in environmentally destructive mass air-travel tourism to wilderness sites. Or, indeed, at another level, when they collude in the deceit of copywriters who portray margarine as coming from dew-bedecked pastures (see Soper, 1995, p. 194).

Environmentally appropriate thought and action require a clear and steady understanding of what is to be valued or respected and in what senses. If, as has been argued, our ideas of nature are fundamental in conditioning our outlook in this area, the task of clarifying our understanding of the concept would seem to be a critical first step to an effective examination of environmental issues and to the proper characterisation of environmental education. Related to this, the point was made in Chapter 1 that for modern Western culture to address effectively the environmental issues that confront it, it needs to develop its own authentic understanding of its situation. This will require *inter alia* the marshalling of its own intellectual and emotional resources for understanding the matters at stake. Part of this will involve retrieving understandings that were perhaps explicit in the past, yet continue to shape our relationship towards nature and the environment, if now more implicitly. Thus, as part of this gathering of intellectual and emotional capital, I intend now to recall three broad conceptions of nature and our relationship to it which have been prominent in the Western tradition, post antiquity.

But first a health warning! Though what I will have to say clearly draws in some sense on the historical development of the Western view of nature, in what follows I neither wish, nor pretend, to give an historical account of this development. This has been done in numerous places elsewhere. (See for example, Glacken, 1967, and also Marshall, 1995, whose account I draw upon in my sketch of Romanticism.) My intention here is limited to providing something of a general backcloth of influential ideas that may help in locating and understanding certain more contemporary views that will be examined in later chapters of this volume. Thus my focus here is to sketch, as it were, certain ideal types based on logical and emotional relations between key ideas that have been highly influential in shaping our relationship with nature. In this way, I hope to present not historical (over-) generalisations, but frames of mind which to varying degrees continue to vie with each other today. So though, for convenience, sometimes I use labels that can, and elsewhere often are employed to, denote loose historical periods, I am not essentially attempting to offer historical descriptions—and in particular, I am not saying that the views I describe do justice to the subtlety and diversity of thought that actually occurred at any historical point.

NATURE AS MOTHER

Harking back to the metaphysical theme of the previous chapter, it is salutary to recognise just how much our conception of nature has changed over the last 500 years and therefore just how different is the underlying character of the world that we now inhabit compared with the mediaeval or early Renaissance world. The understanding of the earth as a living, conscious organism whose processes and moods could in some respects be viewed as human nature writ large, demanded ways of interaction with our natural surrounds and a societal structure which are difficult to psychologically re-enter, so profound is the difference. Miners observing strict cleanliness and sexual abstinence out of respect for the Mother Earth whose womb they were about to enter, smiths accorded the status of shaman because of the awesome responsibility they assumed in precipitating the birth of metals, thus aborting their natural growth cycle in the artificial womb of the furnace (see Merchant, 1992, pp. 42–44)—these are expressions of a relationship to nature capable of pervading all aspects of life and of rooting humankind in the great scheme of things in a way that overtly and profoundly defines the shape of people's lives and their conceptions of themselves. To view the earth as a person requiring respect, whose ways and moods dictated human affairs and had to be propitiated and accommodated to, clearly required a basically subservient attitude towards nature and certainly served as a cultural constraint on the actions of human beings. As Carolyn Merchant observes: 'One does not readily slay a mother, dig into her entrails for gold, or mutilate her body' (p. 43). Rather one must attempt to live in harmony, shunning any disruption of nature's ways.

   In any case, dominance was not an option. Most everyday natural processes and phenomena such as birth, growth, disease, death, remained mysterious—often arbitrary—or were perceived as fulfilling their own inscrutable purposes. There were of course intellectual and religious systems that attempted to explain natural phenomena, sometimes to predict or even to influence them, but not to directly control them. One went against nature at one's peril. To live with nature was to engage in a relationship with an all-powerful other. Nature could be studied and described, aspects increasingly assigned to natural categories, but wisdom consisted in attempting to go with the flow of what was natural and in some sense predestined by natural powers. Awe, wonder, reverence, might characterise such consciousness of nature, but so too might fear and abject resignation when the harvest failed or the plague struck.

This essentially organismic conception of nature in which all things are regarded as integral parts of a living unity was melded to some degree with another cosmological synthesis: the long-evolving integration of Aristotelian with Judaeo-Christian world views. Here the cosmos was understood teleologically: all events worked towards fulfilling a distant purpose—a perfection—implicit in God's design. Physical laws were a function of this and in the imperfect terrestrial zone of random change and non-circular motion, all objects were understood as attempting to fulfil God's desire to restore perfection. Thus gravity could be explained as the desire of, say, a stone to get to its natural place at the centre of the earth, and nature itself could be regarded as a book in which, along with the Bible, God's design could be studied and his purposes read. Thus theology becomes the great university discipline that also sets the paradigm for science; scientific knowledge could be divorced neither from human values nor analogies with human experience. Again this strand of mediaeval cosmology was heavily anthropomorphic, but now also on some readings anthropocentric to a higher degree, since the earth was provided by God for the use of man.

It is worth drawing out of the above sketch two particularly significant features for later thinking. First, this view of nature securely roots individuals in nature as a greater whole that sustains them, requires them to be attentive to its ways and to work *within* it, that is, respectfully and in keeping with their place. There are strong echoes of this in much current ecological thought, particularly in some strands of the resurrected Gaia motif. Second, nature is seen as a living source of values. From such a perspective it is not that what is sensed as being in keeping with the natural order is *assessed* as valuable as through some process of rational scrutiny, but that the natural order and the moral order are experienced as *synonymous*. To work in harmony with the natural order is the tacit *criterion* of moral value. Thus to speak, as moderns may, of nature as having intrinsic value is to misrepresent the quality of consciousness in question, for in this frame of mind the separation of nature's 'value' from nature is unintelligible—they do not exist separately in this metaphysical landscape. They are directly intuited as a naïve, innocent oneness—not a reconstructed whole, as in a sense was necessarily the case with Romanticism, which had to reintegrate what had been sundered by modernism.

NATURE AS MACHINE

It was Francis Bacon in the early seventeenth century who criticised the traditional Aristotelian sciences for having done nothing to relieve the condition of humankind. In positing instrumental efficacy as the underlying motive in science, he both inserted a vigorous humanist impulse into the nature of enquiry and set in train the modern experimental interventionist model of science that reigns today. As previously observed, this conception of science is inclined to view natural history as mere 'stamp collecting'—passive and essentially unthoughtful. In very broad terms, two related things happen to our understanding of nature with the burgeoning of modern science. First, with Descartes' view of the human subject as defined by its immaterial soul, humans are increasingly seen as no longer part of nature in the inclusive way that they were conceived to be on the organismic view. Second, nature comes to be viewed as a machine—a great clockwork—which consists of inert particles driven mechanically by external and impersonal forces (such as gravity). The combined result of these two thrusts is that nature ceases to have its own moral status; it no longer possesses moral power or authority. It is soulless, to be investigated and exploited in whatever ways best meet human needs and purposes. As mentioned in Chapter 2, it has been claimed by some that this exploitative attitude towards nature was encouraged further by the gendering of nature as feminine.

While it has been argued that there is a sense in which initially science helped to *divinise* nature—for the Great Machine presupposed a Divine Mechanic whose thought and purpose imparted order and law to the cosmos—this presents a cabined and sanitised view of nature's 'soul'. For if the argument from design was the mainstay of those deists who rejected the 'superstition' of the Middle Ages, but could not accept a world of accidental atoms (Marshall 1995, p. 223), arguably at this point nature's divinity was reconstructed in a strong sense: it was a conscious attempt to overcome the rupture of the more primal association between nature and divinity that the new science had itself precipitated. It was a view of a nature *designed*, and a view congenial to the rationalist humanist outlook, for a designed universe is a rational universe, and a rational universe is a predictable universe and thus one most susceptible to instrumental investigation and manipulation.

The net result of the expansion of this attitude is that ultimately nature becomes conceived of as a *resource*—at the disposal of humankind, and ideally infinitely switchable and manipulable, any resistance on nature's part becoming viewed as a challenge to be overcome, no matter what the cost to nature itself. There are strong resonances of this in the technocratic approach to environmental problems that predominates today. The idea that nature needs managing—to be set in order by man for her own and the general good—is perhaps the completion of that long-gestating motive to dominate and to control.

NATURE AS POEM

In keeping with the general tenor of modernism, the classicism that underwrites it sees nature as inferior to art and in need of being perfected by man. A rather different view of matters is presented by the Romantic sentiment. Although more directly affiliated to neo-classicism, Alexander Pope, in a proto-Romantic moment, famously put it thus:

> First follow NATURE, and your Judgement frame
> By her just Standard, which is still the same:

Unerring Nature, still divinely bright,
One clear, unchang'd, and Universal Light,
Life, Force, and Beauty, must to all impart,
At once the Source, and End, and Test of Art.
(*An Essay on Criticism*, lines 68–73, in Butt, 1963, p. 146)

Greg Garrard has described Romantic writing as a spiritual resource for Western ecological world views—'a wellspring of love for, sympathy with and confidence in the natural world' that represents the first steps beyond human chauvinism (Garrard, 1998, p. 115). We should note the self-confidence implied here and how this differs from the way nature was experienced by mediaeval consciousness whose receptiveness was born out of a certain servitude. With the Romantics, despite their claims to the contrary, there is a strong sense of their *conferring* value on nature from a position of relative strength. Nature's beauty is more apparent when one is not threatened by it and, interestingly, confidence in the natural world and positive feelings of identity with it come more easily with a degree of felt independence.

As Peter Marshall puts it,

Romantics like modern ecologists revelled in the idea of diversity and difference. They believed that diversity itself is the essence of all excellence and sought the fullest possible realization of difference in nature and human nature. They rejected the classical idea of single perfection for a multiplicity of forms; they looked for the individual and the particular rather than the universal and the general (Marshall, 1995, p. 283).

In particular, Romanticism rejected the movement of Renaissance scientists and Enlightenment philosophers to reduce nature to mathematics, and to conceiving its sensory aspects as mere Lockean secondary properties that belong not to things themselves, but exist only in the mind of the observer. I will return to these issues in a later chapter. There was also an attempt to overcome a kind of alienation of human self-consciousness that was held to be implicit in the ascendancy of instrumental reason. As Marshall points out, something of the essential character of this alienation was expressed in Hegel's master-slave analysis: self-consciousness has to differentiate itself against the 'other', at which point the other appears as something foreign, therefore hostile, yet desirable (1995, p. 292). To desire it is to want to possess it, the achievement of which is made manifest by transforming it. Full self-realisation of self-conscious human beings, then, involves transforming the world around them as the way of making it their own and of affirming their existence. In short: self-consciousness involves *mastery*. A central aspiration of Romanticism was to bring about two intimately interrelated sentiments that combated or mitigated this motive: to close the gap between observer and observed by re-establishing in experience a sense of oneness with the world, and to redirect human attention to another source of value—the intrinsic value of nature. This led to the re-assertion of a certain organic model of the cosmos.

Thus did that proponent of natural religion in the early eighteenth century, Anthony, Earl of Shaftesbury, see nature as a vast united system of interconnected parts moving according to immutable laws in which 'divine Nature' forms 'the great and general ONE of the world' and claim that what we call evil is simply the result of our ignorance, not truly seeing its place in the greater scheme. Almost two centuries later we find A. N. Whitehead arguing for the organic unity of the cosmos, with individual physical objects conceived of as particular 'events' that are modifications of space-time, internally related to—'interfused' with—all other events in space-time (Whitehead, 1985, pp. 90–91, 128–130).

This conception of nature as an inclusive organic whole, a community of interlocking parts which incorporates all aspects of existence, simultaneously and powerfully re-establishes two things that are frequently incorporated into current ecological thinking: 1) the interdependence of diverse individuals; 2) moral and other value as an intrinsic component of the physical/natural order *in which human imagination plays a seminal constituting role*. These are precisely the qualities that the atomism of classical science destroys. Independently existing entities moved by physical forces are not *inherently* value-bearers or givers—*value is additional to their existence* in a way that it cannot be if they exist *as* parts of the greater whole which constitutes the universe in its entirety. A more detailed examination of current views that attempt to develop this latter perspective into a comprehensive environmental ethic will be offered in a later chapter, but by way of a preliminary it is worth noting here that there are two ways of interpreting this position.

First, it may be saying that value is a constituent of the universe and, as there is a continuity between everything in the universe, then everything partakes of that value. Second, it may be saying that in a thoroughly interdependent universe everything has the value of the unique contribution that it makes. Both positions would seem to hold true if the overriding value is to maintain the *status quo*, since they make everything (equally) valuable by definition as part of it. And even if we did not desire the maintenance of the *status quo*, but rather a process of change, if everything is interdependent (including causally) then every antecedent was necessary for whatever changes occur—so again, in this sense, everything acquires value. Such views raise two problems. First, and *vis-à-vis* the first interpretation, what in an ever-evolving world should we mean by 'the *status quo*' and why should it be valued? Second, on both accounts there can be no *dis*value. And where everything is of equal value simply because it exists as part of a greater whole, does not the term 'value' become emptied of meaning? Has not value become too tightly attached to sheer existence? On the other hand, atomism makes value too contingent, too arbitrary— essentially a matter of what could appear as human caprice. The issue is thus raised of the meaning of nature's intrinsic value. We seem to need a conception in which value is not made arbitrary by being posited as undifferentiated. We need an account of the possibility of *discriminating* value.

Yet the organic view of the Romantics differs from the world organism of mediaeval views in that the former tends to see nature more as a law-governed unity of related individuals, rather than as a *being* possessed of sensitivity and will—a 'mother'. And while not necessarily experienced as an abstraction, this unity is more clearly a self-conscious construction—an idea—and is therefore no longer a naïve apprehension of the oneness of value and nature. Rather, this oneness occurs as a *conclusion*.

For Romantics, such as Wordsworth, man and nature enjoy a certain spiritual reciprocity—particularly in the rural situation. Contact with nature renews and sustains the human spirit, and nature is understood as somehow sympathetic to man. That there should be this need for reunion again suggests the underlying alienation from nature of modern man—though the sense in which this is properly to be understood as only a local historical phenomenon (we were not alienated in previous ages) as against an ontological fact (for example, as self-aware beings we are essentially alienated from nature) remains an issue. Clearly, Max Scheler's characterisation of man as the animal that can say 'No' to nature would be an example of the latter view.

But what do we learn of *nature* from the Romantic view?

The point can readily be made that there is a pervasive ambiguity in the Romantic's conception of nature between nature as an authentic voice, where we attend to its own particulars and processes, and nature as emblematic of themes in human consciousness—our experience of it an implicit vehicle for anthropomorphism, reflecting human emotions such as joy and sadness, and life themes such as youth and mortality. Thus we must be alert to the 'pathetic fallacy' of ascribing human emotions to non-humans, and the tendency of poets to 'fill all things with themselves'. Similarly, the notion of nature as something we can learn from can itself harbour strong elements of anthropomorphism. The general sentiment behind Wordsworth's edifying 'impulse from the vernal wood' was, for example, anticipated in a perhaps less subtle way in Baron d'Holbach's Enlightenment belief that nature bids 'man to be sociable, to love his fellows, to be just, peaceful, indulgent, beneficent, to make or leave his associates happy', also to develop self-reliance and to overcome removable evils through a grasp of natural laws (*Système de la nature*, 1780). In this we have a precursor for an environmental education that is not simply a matter of learning about the environment, but learning *from* it, receiving incipient moral messages and models for how we should live. Clearly, such reading 'from' nature requires any focus on industrious bees and persistent spiders to be balanced by cannibalistic crocodiles. Yet, as Garrard points out, we should beware qualifying the Romantic offering out of existence in a situation where indigenous sources of hope in the West are fast depleting (Garrard, 1998, p. 129). In a period dominated by instrumental rationality, Romanticism's attempt at establishing a positive, open, receptive relationship with the natural world—a world that can be stern, even harsh, but not simply alien—a world that rewards sensitive engagement through the exercise of the full range of our faculties and can provide fresh perspectives on our lives as a whole—may be of the highest significance in shaping a response to current problems.

This brings us to a central theme in Romanticism: the elevation of the imagination as the faculty through which real understanding and truth are achieved. Imagination is conceived as the bridge to nature, its operation bringing humanity and nature into a unity in which both are (re-)created. This contrasts with abstract discursive reason, which reveals the mechanical, atomistic universe of science. Thus in *The Statesman's Manual* Coleridge criticised Enlightenment reason as 'the mere organ of science . . . flattered and dazzled by the real or supposed discoveries that it had made' purchased, most assuredly 'at the loss of all communion with life and the spirit of nature' (Coleridge, in Lively, 1966, pp. 86–88). He put the central problem thus:

> Of the discursive understanding, which forms for itself general notions and terms of classification for the purpose of comparing and arranging phenomena, the characteristic is clearness without depth. It contemplates the unity of things in their limits only, and is consequently a knowledge of superfices without substance (p. 86).

This notion of understanding things 'in their limits only' is very important. It refers to seeing things in terms of the abstracted properties that bind them as members of a certain category. The understanding is shallow because we see them only as *instances* rather than in their particularity, their here-and-now presencing, standing forth from what is hidden and towards an open future. For the Romantics full knowledge of one's natural environment required the intuition, sensibility and feeling of an imaginative entry into that environment:

> The completing power which unites clearness with depth, the plenitude of the sense with the comprehensibility of the understanding, is the imagination, impregnated with which the understanding itself becomes intuitive and a living power . . . the integral spirit of the regenerated man [is] reason substantiated and vital (Coleridge, in Lively, 1966, p. 86).

It is not, then, that the Romantics simply dismissed reason, but what they thought of as false, inert reason. Ultimately they saw the opposition of the mind and the heart, reason and passion, as mistaken—hence Blake's 'a Tear is an Intellectual Thing'. For Coleridge, the imagination itself, distinct from mere fancy (which merely recombines ready made materials (Coleridge, 1973, p. 202)), was truly creative, but in a way that revealed what was deeply interfused in nature and reflected an inherent accord between the creative mind and the external world of nature. As he put it in *Dejection: An Ode*:

> . . . we receive but what we give,
> And in our life alone does nature live . . .
> Ah! From the soul itself must issue forth

A light, a Glory, and a luminous Cloud
Enveloping the Earth!

It is important to note that this speaks not of an extreme idealism, but of an approach to nature; it is not that the mind is conceived as simply creating nature but that the imagination is taken to create a union between two realms of being, the empathic and quickening power of the imagination enabling a dialogical relation to occur. For Coleridge, nature reveals itself if the soul rather than the disengaged intellect takes the initiative. Otherwise it appears as an inanimate, cold world—the world of science, the purely material machine. What we see depends upon how we look and why should the look of cold intellect be privileged? This question as to how to *look* at nature surely remains a seminal one for environmental education. As, of course, is the issue of the privileging of the gaze in Western culture: the early parts of Wordsworth's *Prelude* (especially the 1799 short version), focusing as they do on the young child *acting within* rather than *looking at* nature, are an early intimation of the significance of this.

In some ways this posture of mutual receptivity is better illustrated by the poetry of John Clare than by that of, say, Wordsworth. Clare attempts to use the imagination to identify with nature not by projecting his personal feelings of joy and sadness, etc., onto natural entities, but rather by trying to give voice to how *they* might feel, particularly in reaction to the land enclosures of his time. Consider, for example, his portrayal of an old stone quarry as feeling a loss of freedom and independence. Taken 'literally', while it avoids outright anthropocentrism, such a description clearly involves a high degree of anthropomorphism. But if interpreted not as a projective empathy, but as an expression of sympathy, its posture becomes one of seeing nature neither as a vehicle for human emotion nor as a reflection of human emotion. Rather it can be seen to evince a certain *solidarity* with nature as a realm recognised as other. This may express an important truth about the possibilities of our relationship to the things themselves of nature and therefore represents an important consideration for environmental education, upon which the twin but distinct influences of anthropocentrism and anthropomorphism are so readily attendant. The poetry of Manley-Hopkins is often in similar vein.

Nonetheless, a certain self-consciousness pervades the Romantic apprehension of nature and man's part in revealing it, a self-consciousness that is absent from the mediaeval view. Yet if its awareness of its own participation in revealing nature is apparent, there remain critical differences from the rationalistic humanism of Kant, expressed in his claim that we understand the natural world not by allowing ourselves to be 'kept . . . in nature's leading-strings' but through the application of principles formulated by reason, 'after a plan of its own' and 'based upon fixed laws'. Reason 'must adopt as its guide . . . that which it has itself put into nature', approaching it not as a pupil but as a judge who compels a witness to answer the questions put to them (Kant, 1970, p. 20).

Thus in their different ways Romantic and Rationalist perspectives can be seen as raising the question of the underlying reality of nature in the sense of the extent to which it is a human projection—and whether, if so, it is essentially 'poem' or 'theory'. In turn, this issue of nature's reality has been both a source of confusion and a source of the criticism of naïveté that has been levelled at a belief in nature as some epistemologically founding autonomous realm. Because of their centrality to the thesis of nature as a primordial reality, these issues will be pursued in the following chapter. For the present, I wish to move the focus to another set of distinctions relevant to understanding nature.

KEY SENSES OF 'NATURE'

The purpose of the above section was to outline certain fundamental ways of relating to nature that form part of the indigenous resource of Western culture. In what follows I wish to make explicit some distinctions within our current idea of 'nature' that will have a bearing on subsequent discussion of how this resource might be drawn on to inform environmental education.

There are many ways of coming at the concept of nature as currently experienced, e.g., by drawing a contrast between the 'natural' and the 'supernatural', or the 'natural' and the 'sociocultural', or examining such notions as 'natural law' and 'natural rights'. And there have been numerous attempts at identifying important senses of the term. For example, Kate Soper distinguishes three senses: the 'metaphysical' (nature as independent of human activity); 'causal' or 'realist' (nature as the underlying causal material world); and 'surface', 'lay' or 'empirical' (nature as experienced sensually and emotionally, the nature that 'we want to love and conserve') (Soper, 1995, pp. 155–156). While these distinctions can be useful, it seems to me that, in the context of the thesis that I wish to develop, they are unhelpful to the extent that they suggest a hierarchy that underplays the ways in which the 'metaphysical' and 'causal' senses can be directly experienced at the 'empirical' level, and also that they ignore a distinction between this latter and nature as some abstracted objective theoretical construct. For present purposes I am going to set out four central and interrelated notions that I take to be at work in our ideas of nature and that run across Soper's schema. They are nature as cosmic order, nature as wilderness, nature as innate essence and nature as the 'hale', arbiter of rightness. Each of them has implications both for how we view the world and for how we view ourselves.

First, then: 'nature' thought of as the great scheme of things—the 'cosmic order'—of which everything is in some sense a part or is constituted. This itself may be interpreted in a variety of ways—for example, scientifically in terms of natural or physical laws, patterns of causality, etc., religiously in terms of divine purposes and revelations, perhaps economically in terms of the 'natural laws' of supply and demand in free markets, and so forth. While today there is sometimes a strong tendency to assume that nature in this general sense is basically physical or material, clearly the religious and economic understandings of it introduce other more abstract dimensions. Indeed, the preceding three 'ideal types' represent past articulations of this natural order sense of nature. Moreover, that our views within this general sense of nature shape our conceptions of the real and our sense of identity, seems self-evident. Where we placed ourselves in the 'Great Chain of Being' is an explicit illustration of this, as, of course, is our location within Darwinian phylogeny and models of ecological interdependence today.

Second, there is 'nature' as wilderness, as wild, elemental and quintessentially beyond human control: the powers that create and regulate the material world, the phenomena of growth, decay and death, the existence of mountain crags and ocean deeps, supernova and black holes. Here nature is understood as something non-human, that is, essentially independent of human purposes and culture. Historically, on the one hand, it has been feared as an alien adversary, red in tooth and claw, while, on the other, its 'otherness' has been enjoyed as a refuge from everyday life and as a source of spiritual renewal or inspiration—as celebrated by Romantic poets and, in a perhaps more measured way, by early American environmentalists such as Thoreaux and Emerson. In extreme form it was the subject of Bill McKibben's previously mentioned lament in *The End of Nature*.

Third, there is 'nature' as innate essence—that which is inherent, which constitutes the essential being of a thing, unaffected by compromise or artifice. In the case of humans, it refers us to what we most truly are in ourselves (or take ourselves to be), lying beneath the surface of façades and pretensions in which we may participate in everyday life. It has variously been exhorted as the goal of self-realisation by the Romantics, as something to be transcended or even rigorously suppressed by the Ascetics and as non-existent by Sartrean existentialism, which claims that we have no predetermined essence and exhorts us to rise above the merely 'thing-like' (*en soi*) by constant self-recreation and self-definition through the exercise of choice. (There is, however, a sense in which this capacity for choice can therefore be taken as our natural—that is, given—essence.) If we now hark back to the discussion of Romanticism, the notion of things in nature having their own essence, which deserves to be respected, reflects an enduring intuition of nature as in some sense having its own *telos*. It reflects the idea that we in some sense have a natural sympathy with this—indeed are a part of it—and find it satisfying and right. It is part of *our* nature. The capricious squashing of beetles is wrong not only because of the pain inflicted on them, but because it offends against some sense of all forms of life (and maybe of the inanimate too) *prima facie* as having a being to fulfil. (Of course, this sense can rapidly evaporate in cases where human welfare is seriously jeopardised by other life forms, as with the malaria bacillus.)

Fourth, and particularly related to some sentiments present in the third sense above, there is the previously alluded to idea of nature as what is 'natural', where this connotes the hale, or what is wholesome and as it should be, that is, what is morally—or perhaps more accurately, pre-morally—fitting or *good*. Again, this may have a variety of interpretations ranging through what is taken to be biologically or psychologically healthy, generally socially accepted or approved, morally desirable or religiously true. For example, debates concerning sexual orientation can touch upon all of these aspects. It is clearly present in ideas of the state of nature as a state of innocence and health, to be contrasted with corrupting society, that found eloquent expression in Diderot's primitive paradises and Rousseau's 'noble savage'. But it is equally present in the previously mentioned role played by social conventions to condition what appears 'natural' in almost any situation we may encounter.

Now, it seems to me that, in terms of the ambition to explicate a foundational sense of nature, two important features arise from the above analysis.

First, between them the senses of nature identified present a rich terrain, but they are subject to a serious problem identified in Chapter 1: in their varying specific instantiations they may serve an array of ideological positions. This is obvious in the case of nature as arbiter of rightness, but just as true for nature as innate essence (for example, in gender terms), for this may be held to function as governing our understanding of ourselves, and therefore of right action in an ultimately arbitrary way. Similarly, the very notion of a cosmic order implies one true order that is the ultimate basis of all other understanding and that will necessarily privilege some understandings and motives over others. To know one's place in the overall order of things is to know what is virtuous and how to act, with its potential fascist corollary of individual divergence from this order being perceived as deviant. Thus uncritical acceptance of the concept of nature in these senses invites the charge of being complicit in mechanisms of arbitrary evaluation and policing of behaviour.

However, it is one thing to point out the potential for fascism in particular instantiations of these senses; it is quite another to infer that all instantiations realise this potential or that we should endeavour to do without nature in these senses altogether. Not all evaluation is arbitrary and repressive in this ideological sense (as we shall see, it may be in other senses), and the advocacy of a spirit of critical evaluation itself presupposes some foothold in a framework of understanding that is taken to be non-distorting—in some sense a privileged vantage point from which to weigh arguments and intuitions, and to discern truth.

Second, implicit in each of the four senses of nature outlined above is an intuition of original independence that gives a certain integrity and, therefore, *authority* to phenomena regarded as natural. This may be true not only genetically in terms of an assumed non-human causal history, but phenomenologically in the experience of the self-standing of natural things such as a tree, a mountain or the play of sunlight on water. Thus, it seems to me that underlying and informing our central senses of nature is an important and ancient unifying idea, one to which Martin Heidegger in his retrieval of the Greek experience of nature has alluded: the notion of *physis* as the arising of something from out of itself (Heidegger, 1975,

p. 42; 1977, p.10). Nature thus conceived as the '*self-arising*' is most explicit in the wilderness sense of nature, but it is just as powerful in the other three senses. The force of referring to something as the *natural* order is to convey that it is not simply a human artefact, even though our descriptions of it necessarily bear the imprint of our own perspective. As the natural order, it ever precedes us and lies ever beyond us. To refer to what is inherent or innate has the same connotation, and the point of describing something properly as natural in the sense of arbiter of rightness is to express an intuition that its authority is not up for question because it is rooted in some independently pre-ordained realm—raising again the question as to how ideologically free any apprehension or articulation of this can be.

As it is an ambition of this volume to show that there is an important sense in which nature as the self-arising does constitute our primordial reality, the issue of the truth and reality of nature needs to be pressed. Constructivist and postmodernist critiques of the reality of nature are the subject of the next chapter. Here let me indicate how even the preliminary analysis of the notion of nature provided above starts to bear on our understanding of environmental education.

To begin with, it becomes clear that 'nature' and 'the environment' are not synonymous and that reference to the former can serve a normative function with regard to our understanding of the latter and how we treat it. As the 'self-arising', nature stands as something whose origins are independent of us and as a domain that we need properly to apprehend if we are to understand our environment and our place in it. It is, therefore, an important object of study in environmental education. How can we make progress in understanding our environment if we have an inadequate comprehension of either nature's meaning, or the laws, motives, and inherent processes that govern that greater scheme of things of which we are such a small, but perhaps very significant, part? For example, if something akin to Darwinian evolution is operative in biophysical nature, this makes a huge difference to our viewpoint—our understanding of our connection with the rest of nature and, say, our valuing of biodiversity. And even if we were to accept the view that no truly wild nature survives because of the pervasive effects of human activity, it remains the case that there is still an important sense in which nature remains independent of us. To show that we affect all aspects of nature is far from showing that we are its author. This suggests that a degree of humility and respect is therefore in order, a stance that accepts the desirability of working in harmony with nature.

The encouragement of such an attitude will therefore be an important aspect of environmental education, and again this is an attitude whose influence is not likely to be confined—or confinable—to this area of education only. Truly, it is a world- orientating attitude that, for example, has significant epistemological implications. Furthermore, in the light of our discussion of Romanticism, it raises the important question of the place and nature of the faculty of imagination in environmental education. In this respect, for example, through highlighting a need for a proper appreciation of 'otherness', the wilderness sense of nature raises important questions about what this would mean and the proper role of the imagination in its achievement. It also invites consideration of the significance of the realms of the aesthetic and the spiritual in our dealings with the environment. Clearly such considerations may have extensive implications for the scope and richness of a curriculum adequate to the needs of environmental education.

Then there is the issue of the ambiguity between nature as 'non-human' and nature as what is natural to us—our own essence—the definition of who we really are, what we fundamentally appeal to in identifying ourselves. This latter appears as the reverse of what is other to us. Even if (as we shall see) on postmodernist accounts belief in any such natural essence is a fatal delusion, this part of us that we perceive as *not* having been constructed we can feel to be at the very heart of ourselves. This brings the issue of our own nature into the gamut of environmental education and with it the question of what counts as human flourishing or well-being in relation to the natural order.

Finally, as has been previously noted, the preceding examination of the various conceptions and senses of nature taken to influence our thinking highlights the need to clarify the values that we tacitly assume or actively invoke when we use the language of 'nature' and what is 'natural'. We need to acknowledge the existence and source of these values and to confirm or disconfirm the weight or power that they should wield. Here we have a further set of considerations highly relevant to both environmental education and education in general.

Chapter 4. Retreat from Reality

What counts as nature – a source of insight and promise of innocence is undermined, probably fatally [by postmodernist strategies] (Donna Haraway, 1991, pp. 152–153).

Anyone who continues to speak of nature as non-society is speaking in terms from a different century, which no longer capture our reality (Ulrich Beck, 1992, p. 81).

In the places where the chokeweed lay dark as fungus on the stream bed because the springs had not risen to sweep it away and in the piled-high silts that covered the margins for the same reason and in the new, still places that had decaying weed and the dead eggs of the Baetis flies and the caddis flies and the lank fish in them, silver bubbles wobbled up and burst with a foul smell and the soft-bodied things rejoiced (*The Stream*, Brian Clarke, 2002, p. 199).

THE NON-REALITY OF NATURE AND OUR EVERYDAY FRAME OF MIND

In many ways nature is a taken-for-granted idea that occurs easily and frequently in our everyday observation and dealings with the world. In this everyday frame of mind a suggestion that 'nature no longer exists' likely would be met with outright mystification, if not downright ridicule. What of trees and birds, mosquitoes and midges, birth and ageing—are these not all parts of nature and are they not quintessentially real? At this level, the popularity of natural history, gardening and astronomy programmes on television testifies to our continuing fascination with nature. And does not the box-office success of films about actual and imagined natural disasters attest to an underlying recognition of the power and threat of elemental nature? My point is that it is worth stressing just how counter-intuitive it is to question the reality of nature at the level of everyday experience. Yet the precepts of everyday experience are not sacrosanct and the reality of nature is challenged by various commentators. Such challenges take a number of forms, but all at base portray any straightforward belief in the reality of nature as nostalgic, naïve and/or self-deceptive.

Since this issue is necessarily central to any notion of having a relationship with nature—and the quality of any such relationship—it must be addressed. And clearly, any argument of the kind proposed in the previous chapter that nature experienced as the 'self-arising' sets the standard of our primordial reality falls if the notion of nature in which it is held to be implicit turns out to be a chimera. Furthermore, an education that had truly apprehended the 'end' of nature would be transformed both epistemologically and ethically, if, as previously argued, education is necessarily involved in initiating pupils into views of reality and if our current views of reality are heavily informed, explicitly or implicitly, by the idea of nature. So, the challenge is an important one in several respects.

Though they are often interwoven in argument, I suggest that it is possible to distinguish a number of strands in the challenge to our everyday assumptions of nature's reality, and that each in its own way can illuminate aspects of the meaning of nature.

The first of these strands may be dealt with relatively quickly. It begins with the empirical claim that such is the extent of the influence of human physical activity that there is no part of the planet that is not affected by it in some way. Such a view points out that much of what we take as natural landscape bears the imprint of the human hand, that the effects of substances that we have manufactured and released into the biosphere are showing up in pervasive (and often unexpected) ways, that even 'wilderness' areas now depend on human management for their survival. And if it is true that human activity is affecting the global climate, this would be a conclusive illustration of the view—the only life *as yet* unaffected might be bacteria living well below Earth's surface. Now for writers such as Bill McKibben (1989), this state of affairs represents the 'end' of nature because they see the idea of its independence as central to the very meaning of nature. They hold that, if no part of the natural world now remains untainted by the effects of human activity, this independence is destroyed; we have finally and irredeemably corrupted nature and ultimately there is 'nothing but us'.

Undoubtedly, an important point is being made here. There is something alerting and uncomfortable about the situation so described—it is interesting to ponder precisely why—and the centrality of its independence (its genetic non-humanness) to our understanding of and regard for nature is compelling. Nature as possessing aspects that we can discover, learn from and be inspired by, natural things as having their own existence and even 'inscape', the notion of a natural world that existed before humankind, that exists beyond it and will exist after it, these become hollow if not nonsensical without such independence.

Yet may we not both grant this centrality of the idea of independence to the concept and accept the extent of human influence on the physical environment that is claimed, without consigning 'nature' to some dead history? For is there not an important distinction to be drawn between human actions *affecting* nature and such actions destroying its essential independence? It is clear—and in many respects we may have reason to celebrate—that the long-evolving and changing balance of power in our relationship to some aspects of nature has placed us in the position of instigator (intentionally or otherwise) rather than passive recipient. In this sense both our intentional and unintentional effects on nature grow ever more extensive. But it seems to me that this says nothing about the essential independence of that with which we interact. In planting seeds in the ground, however much they are engineered and howsoever we cultivate and fertilise the soil, we continue to interact with properties and forces of which we are not the author. It is true that our attitude towards these forces may be more manipulative and challenging than was once the case; it is also true that the balance of power may have appeared to have swung further in our direction in that we can modify more of the conditions relevant to the enterprise; but in the last analysis we have to come to terms with a world that is essentially independent of human will and with which some kind of harmony (or at least accommodation) has to be found. Similarly, in the case of our own physical health, in which we continuously intervene, we still have to work ultimately *with* processes which we did not design and whose essence and 'good' are its own. While some aspects of the idea of 'good health' are socially constructed, their achievement is never something of which we are the sole determinants, either physiologically or *conceptually*. Heart failure could never be a criterion of good health. There are parameters for what could *count* as healthy as well as what is involved in *being* healthy that are not human-authored. That is, part of the meaning of healthy is the idea of an organism's own natural processes operating according to its *own*—that is, natural—internal 'ways'.

All this illustrates that there is an important sense in which nature remains always beyond us. Our manipulations create new frontiers with nature, but there is no sign that we are coming to the 'end' of nature; indeed, its depth appears infinite. Another way of making this point is to turn the argument on its head and foreground the many ways in which nature affects *us*—from the flow of natural processes on which our bodily health depends to recalcitrant cancers, from moonlight on water and the recycling of the Earth's atmosphere by innumerable microflora to earthquakes and volcanic eruptions. We are constantly dependent upon, and subject to, natural processes at both micro and macro levels.

Nature, then, remains essentially independent of the human will, if in many ways affected by it. And of course the magnitude of this affectedness in physical terms approaches the insignificant when nature is equated not with the thin and fragile film that constitutes our biosphere, but with the cosmos. While drawing attention to important considerations, the destruction of nature thesis overstates the case by perhaps conflating the idea of (planetary local) 'nature' with the idea of 'wilderness'. But it can be seen as a prelude to more radical strands of argument.

These develop the claim that nature is a *human construction*, not simply in physical terms as with the implication of human agency in much of our 'natural' landscape, but in *psychological* terms. That is to say, they emphasise the point that our very perceptions of nature are socially and culturally conditioned from the start. A relatively mild—but highly significant—example of this is noted by Charles Taylor (1991) in his description of nineteenth-century Romantic poetry in which, as he puts it: 'the poet makes us aware of something in nature for which there are as yet no adequate words. The poems are finding the words for us. In this "subtler language" – the term is borrowed from Shelley – something is created and defined as well as manifested' (Taylor, 1991, p. 85).

It is clearly important to recognise that we are neither passive nor dumb in our relationship with nature. In coming to describe and understand nature we *articulate* it—in a certain sense, give it significant form. But there are influential views—that we might loosely term 'postmodern'— that appear to go beyond this observation to the claim that *there is nothing more to nature* than its human construction; it is *simply* a cultural artefact. As we saw in the previous chapter, if there is a sense in which the Romantic imagination brought things into being, the Romantics none-theless saw themselves as responding to something beyond themselves. They sought to reveal a pre-existing nature in its many nuances, even if in so doing they projected a considerable amount of themselves into nature. The view that I will examine shortly essentially sees nature as a human *invention*, and therefore something that can be humanly re-invented and disposed of.

But before filling out such arguments, let me set out what might be taken to be some of the general consequences of such a view for thinking about the environment and environmental education.

First, it makes 'nature' relative to its human authors—in this case probably most plausibly thought of as a particular culture. What counts as 'nature', part of nature, 'natural', what counts as a right relationship to nature, and therefore what counts as a *problem* in this area—that is an *environmental* problem—depends on one's cultural perspective and may vary significantly from culture to culture. On this view, therefore, there are no universal, genuinely global, conceptions of nature and environmental problems. The dominant cultures project their versions as universal, but these simply reflect *their* (largely economic) interests. In relation to what are identified as environmental problems, this relativism is amply illustrated by the fact that, while the prospect of global warming may appear as a serious problem for some, it may appear as a solution for others. In terms of differing conceptions of a proper relationship with nature, the prospect of the depletion of oil reserves (if not the pollution involved in using them up) may appear as a good to a culture that deplores the exploitative relationship to nature their abundance has supported.

Such a perspective must affect fundamentally the aspirations of environmental education. For example, it calls into question the possibility of a truly global ethic, and it turns notions of environmental education and sustainability into highly parochial affairs, emptying globally orientated discourse of any real intellectual or moral gravitas. The extension of an environmental view beyond the culture in which it arises must be seen as merely a form of cultural colonisation masquerading as moral concern. One educational consequence of this might be that pupils would be encouraged to be sensitive to the issue of whose voice is being heard when appeals to nature are made and environmental problems are identified. On the other hand, without some non-relative standard available as reference, equally it would be compatible with the view that they simply acquiesce in whatever self-serving conceptions happen to be current—since at this level no view can be judged to be objectively superior to any other. In other words the familiar gamut of objections to cultural relativism comes into play.

But another set of issues is also thrown up. What are the epistemological and ontological implications of viewing something as metaphysically significant as the idea of nature as socially or culturally constructed? In order to begin to address these issues we need to examine some key elements of the thesis in more detail. I should say perhaps at this point that while for convenience I shall draw quite heavily upon two or three representatives of the thesis, my overall intention in what follows is not to provide a systematic exegesis of the individual views chosen: rather I intend to use them as a vehicle for both raising some important general issues concerning the intuition of nature as an underlying reality and responding to a range of criticisms of this idea that have gained a certain currency as part of a broader mood or climate of opinion that is frequently, if not always felicitously, referred to as 'postmodern'. Similarly, while I make passing references to some thinkers associated with 'poststructuralism' (principally, Jacques Derrida and Jean Baudrillard), my concern is not with giving an exegesis of such ways of thought. My concern remains that of identifying a set of views that can be seen as challenging a foundational sense of nature and that (rightly or wrongly) have been lent impetus by *some* of the things said by some poststructuralist thinkers. As will be seen, insofar as I offer a criticism of any philosophical movement, the target is certain strands of neo-pragmatism.

THE 'POSTMODERN' ASSAULT ON REALITY

One particularly influential articulation of the social constructivist thesis is given by Richard Rorty, who develops the notion that man invents (that is, constantly re-invents) nature through descriptions whose point of reference is other descriptions rather than some externally existing world. Thus, in *Philosophy and the Mirror of Nature*, he refutes the idea that language in some way represents reality and that truth is therefore a matter of correspondence with that reality. Rather, we just have descriptions that reflect the norms of the day. Truth about reality is always truth about 'reality-under-a-certain-description' and these descriptions are optional— we could always choose others (Rorty, 1994, p. 379). Thus re-describing ourselves and our world is the most important thing we can do—finding 'more interesting', 'more fruitful' ways of speaking—and self-formation rather than knowledge is the goal of thinking. For Rorty, such 'edification' aims at continuing a conversation rather than discovering truth, for there are no essences and indeed truth itself 'is a way of allowing a description of reality to be *imposed* on us, rather than taking responsibility for choice among competing ideas and words, theories and vocabularies'. Sentences are 'connected with other sentences rather than the world' (p. 372).

There are clear resonances here with Derrida's views about the primacy of the text—'there is no extra-text (''il n'y a pas de hors-texte'') . . . There is nothing before the text; there is no pretext that is not already text'

(Derrida, 1981(a), p. 328)—and his view that what appears to be given and self-evident is generated by and dependent upon language and other sign systems. For Derrida, signs have meaning only through their relations with other absent signs—the play of difference. Nothing refers only to itself—and certainly not to some extratextual reality. Meaning is achieved only through the interweaving of significances that is the text, and everything is constituted on the basis of a trace within it of other elements of the 'chain', this 'textile' that is the text (Derrida, 1981(b), p. 26). Hence his critiques of logocentric metaphysics (the quest for an origin or foundation in truth) and the 'metaphysics of presence', which takes what is claimed to be immediately present as such as an origin or foundation. For Derrida, even Heidegger is guilty of striving for a foundation in what is immediately and self-evidently present. Likewise for Rorty, the fact that we rub up against physical reality is heavily discounted as a source of knowledge or understanding: 'we are shoved around by physical reality . . . Yet what does being shoved around have to do with objectivity, accurate representation, or correspondence? Nothing, I think, unless we confuse *contact* with reality . . . with *dealing* with reality' (Rorty, 1994, p. 375). Here, then, we have a pretty thorough rejection of the *significance* of any independent reality—and thus nature—though there is an acknowledgement of a reality with which we have 'contact'. But this latter is strange. *What does contact mean here?* Is it *significant* contact, that is, part of conscious experience—in which case does it not have to be linguistically mediated on this view. And would it not therefore fall into the same category as that with which we 'deal'? If not, is there some sort of pre-linguistic experience after all? Also, does not 'being shoved around' have *everything* to do with objectivity, accurate representation and correspondence? Cannot this be interpreted as the world's resistance and correction to our linguistically structured (and other) intentions, a resistance and correction that provide us with a sense of what is 'other' and its properties—and thus define such intentional activity in 'real' terms?

In *Contingency, Irony, and Solidarity* Rorty refers to Donald Davidson's view of language as a tool, a means of coping (pp. 13–15). From which it again seems to follow that truth is not out there: it is sentences that are true or false and these are human constructions. Thus Rorty writes:

> We need to make a distinction between the claim that the world is out there and the claim that the truth is out there. To say that the world is out there, that it is not our creation, is to say, with common sense, that most things in space and time are the effects of causes that do not include human mental states. To say that truth is not out there is simply to say that where there are no sentences there is no truth, that sentences are elements of human languages, and that human languages are human creations.

> Truth cannot be out there – cannot exist independently of the human mind – because sentences cannot so exist, or be out there. The world is out there, but descriptions of the world are not. Only descriptions of the world

can be true or false. The world on its own – unaided by the describing
abilities of human beings – cannot (1989, pp. 4–5).

And although 'with common sense' he clearly seems to accept the
existence of some non-human world, this cannot validate our descriptions:
Rorty reaffirms the claim that 'the world does not provide us with any
criterion of choice between alternative metaphors, that we can only
compare languages or metaphors with one another, not with something
beyond languages called "fact"' (p. 20). Yet, we learn:

> [W]e often let the world decide the competition between alternative
> sentences . . . In such cases, it is easy to run together the fact that the
> *world contains the causes of our being justified in holding a belief* with
> the claim that some nonlinguistic state of the world itself is an example of
> truth, or that some such state 'makes a belief true' by 'corresponding' to
> it. *But it is not so easy when we turn from individual sentences to
> vocabularies as wholes.* When we consider the examples of alternative
> language games . . . it is difficult to think of the world as making one of
> these better than another, of the world as deciding between them. When
> the notion of 'description of the world' is moved from the level of
> criterion-governed sentences within language games to language games as
> wholes, games which we do not choose between by reference to criteria
> [e.g. Kuhn's paradigm shifts], the idea that the world decides which
> descriptions are true can no longer be given a clear sense (p. 5, emphasis
> added).

So once we have a language game, can the world, or can it not, validate
our beliefs?

> The world does not speak. Only we do. The world can, once we have
> programmed ourselves with a language, *cause us to hold beliefs.* But it
> cannot propose a language for us to speak. Only other human beings can
> do that . . . the notions of criteria and choice (including that of 'arbitrary'
> choice) are no longer in point when it comes to changes from one
> language game to another (p. 6, emphasis added).

Now while we may accept that there is an important sense in which truth
does not exist of itself out in the world, certain critical elements in this
account remain both highly ambiguous and mysterious. For example, what
does it mean to speak of the world containing the 'causes' of our being
justified in holding a belief, of deciding the competition between
alternative sentences, but having no part in validating such beliefs? And
is it language games or sentences that transcend such 'causation'?
Whatever the resolution of these unclarities, it seems evident that the
underlying thesis is one that displaces any role for reality in validating our
descriptions, and this is because, for Rorty, fundamentally all language is
regarded as metaphorical in character; 'literal' meaning is simply the
metaphor that has become accepted as a way of talking within a language
game. It has become dead metaphor: 'old metaphors are constantly dying

off into literalness' (p. 16). And: 'The very idea that the world or the self has an intrinsic nature – one which the physicist or the poet may have glimpsed – is a remnant of the idea that the world is a divine creation, the work of someone who had something in mind' (p. 21). So finally, and very importantly for the position being developed in this volume:

> On the view I am suggesting, the claim that an 'adequate' philosophical doctrine must make room for our intuitions is a reactionary slogan, one which begs the question at hand. For it is essential to my view that we have no prelinguistic consciousness to which language needs to be adequate, no deep sense of how things are which it is the duty of philosophers to spell out in language. What is described as such consciousness is simply a disposition to use the language of our ancestors, to worship the corpses of their metaphors. Unless we suffer from what Derrida calls 'Heideggerian nostalgia', we shall not think of our 'intuitions' as more than platitudes, more than the habitual use of a certain repertoire of terms, more than old tools which as yet have no replacements (pp. 21–22).

Here again, the resonance with Derrida's programme of deconstruction, and its broader political implications, is clear. Through deconstructing the 'transcendental essences' that have been taken as 'natural' or absolute points of reference—and through showing that they are arbitrary signifiers arrested from the chain of signifiers, and privileged or made to seem 'natural' by the power of a group, thereby freezing the play of differences and imposing a fixed structure and hierarchy on society—the political dimension of meaning is revealed. And by subverting this fixation of meaning that legitimises exclusive groups, those who have been suppressed and marginalised by Western civilisation (for example, the colonised, women) can be heard and empowered.

Insofar as this line of argument becomes applied to our understanding of nature, a general rejoinder might be that the persistence of an 'independent reality language' has less to do with the hegemony of powerful groups than its accuracy in representing how things actually are. But if this is seen as begging the question, clearly a crucial question for the Rortian position becomes what on his account constitutes a language game and its boundaries. Many beliefs concerning nature seem to transcend what we might intuitively consider to be different language games, if we were to mean by this something like different cultural perspectives—for example, the belief that day will follow night. On the other hand, if we do not equate 'language game' with something as broad as cultural perspective, we are entitled to ask how it is that certain language games, such as everyday talk of an independent physical world, transcend radically different cultural perspectives. Furthermore, if, say, all talk of the physical world is designated as one language game, then there are no alternatives to it in this context, and, given our ceaseless interaction with the physical world, it is hardly 'optional'. If, on the other hand, there can be different language games describing the physical world, it is far from obvious that, allowing that the world does not 'propose a language for us to speak', it does not in some sense support some ways of speaking about it rather than others. For example, language games that posit that the human body is immune to the effects of gravity, or that the natural world is essentially composed of Earth, Air, Fire, and Water, or that it is ordered by spirits, or that the cosmos is composed of perfect spheres, enjoy very low levels of currency. Obversely, it becomes a great curiosity that, for example, of the 174 kinds of vertebrates recognised by the Kalam of New Guinea, all except four correspond with species, genera and subspecies recognised by Western systematists today, and that there are similar parallels with aboriginal peoples (Rolston III, 1997).

If the rejoinder to a claimed superiority of certain ways of speaking about the world at *this* level is that this is simply to apply the norms of one language game to judge the descriptions of others that are perfectly coherent within their own self-referential systems of sentences, the response may be that from within our form of sensibility we can make no other judgement. That is to say that there is a world of difference between showing that varying descriptions are theoretically possible and demonstrating that even as possibilities they are real options for us or that they can be sustained, or be sustaining, in the world as we live it. This is a point to which I shall return.

Let me now complete this short survey of ontological attacks on our intuitive sense of nature as some innocent non-human realm by referring to one further thinker. Anthony Giddens' denial of the 'traditional' reality of nature can be seen as an amalgam of the above views. For Giddens, 'nature no longer exists' because of the dissolution of the natural order through the combination of extended human intervention in natural processes and a reflexive modernisation that has undermined the authority of tradition—such that we now live in a 'post-traditional' society: 'We live today in a remoulded nature devoid of nature' (Giddens, 1994, p. 206). (It is tempting to ask here: Who is the 'we'?)

This connection between nature and traditional authority is important, for in a sense Giddens is quite right to point out that nature is its epitome. We do (or, for Giddens, we *used* to) experience nature as a final authority that lies ever before and beyond us, and that has to be accepted at some level. We can affect it, but we cannot change it. We can ameliorate its effects on us, but, ultimately, we cannot escape it. It is a constant, if for the most part very implicit, reference point. However, the strong echoes of Nietzsche's 'God is dead' in Giddens' claim that we now live in a 'detraditionalizing society' (p. 6)—including a self-deception over this itself, because we are reluctant to take on the responsibility that goes with the need for choice that emerges when traditional authority falters—are very evident and should alert us to the possible play of parallel underlying motives to Nietzsche's 'Will to will'. (This is a point to which I will return.) Giddens argues that:

> Detraditionalization not only affects the social world, but influences, as it is influenced by, the transformation of nature. Tradition, like nature, used to be an 'external' context of social life, something that was given and

largely unchallengeable. The end of nature – as the natural – coincides with the end of tradition – as the traditional' (pp. 85–86).

The central point about traditions is that 'you don't really have to justify them' (p. 6), they delineate the framework and define the context *within* which justification occurs. But today, according to Giddens, this is precisely what we are often trying to do with regard to our conception of nature—to re-invent it and justify our re-invention. And at the same time, somehow to persuade ourselves that our invention is a given. Giddens provides many examples of the way in which traditional conceptions of the world and of nature, conceptions that hitherto have framed the outlook of grown communities, have become hollow. One of the chief of these is globalisation with its tendency to 'evacuate out local contexts of action, which have to be reflexively reordered by those affected' (p. 81).

On a more personal level, also, we have to choose our individual identities and bodies: 'The self becomes a reflexive project and, increasingly, the body also' (p. 82). For Giddens, identity now has to be constructed and actively sustained, the body is no longer accepted as 'fate'—we have to decide how to look to the outside world. For example, we are all (in the West) on a diet in the sense of actively making decisions about what to eat from a vast range of globally sourced food available all the year round—thus 'deciding how to be in respect of the body'. Thus 'Anatomy is no longer destiny' (p. 214). Increasingly, we can design our physical bodies, and maybe our psychological make-up through surgery and gene manipulation, though presumably we each still—and always—have to work with some givens such as the material we start with and the limits of technology at any particular time.

So, how are we to respond to such assaults on 'nature' and the 'natural'? Undoubtedly they help to highlight some important aspects of nature and our conception of it. For example, they bring out that:

i) The notion of ontological independence from human activity is central to our traditional understanding of nature.

ii) As an idea, concept, conception, there is an important sense in which 'nature' is a human—that is, cultural—product. Thus our ideas of nature are not always politically innocent and there will be occasions when it is right to raise the issue as to *whose voice* is being heard when nature is being described or what is natural is being asserted. Alertness in this respect will be particularly pertinent when nature is being used in its previously identified senses of innate essence and moral arbiter.

iii) Ecological problems are not purely, nor indeed primarily, natural problems, but social problems, and that to naturalise them will prevent us from ever adequately understanding them and addressing them. (In this respect we might recall the notion that 'nature has no problems'.)

iv) In certain very significant ways our relationship with nature has changed, and its *overt* power and authority in our lives has diminished. Nature is increasingly becoming invisible in everyday living.

v) With detraditionalization, in certain respects our ideas of nature are having to be reflexively defended and re-built—which would seem to be in conflict with its force as a given, a primordial reality.

So much may be granted. But none of these important points, requires the withdrawal from the concept of nature as in some sense self-arising that is so strongly implied in much of this criticism. I will argue that nature is not something to be conjured up or dispensed with in quite so cavalier a fashion as the above views seem to imply. Indeed, in my view, a certain arrogant meta(physical)-magicianry inherent in these views needs to be recognised and repudiated, not least because these meta-magicians share a self-absorbed cast of mind that is preoccupied with the active rather than the responsive—itself, a reflection of the modern metaphysics of mastery.

For example, it is interesting the way that these authors speak of the idea of nature as 'constructed', which has connotations of some focused (if tacit) agency at work, thus portraying it as the result of some deliberate or quasi-intentional activity—in a certain sense, an invention. While such agency may lie behind the production of many concepts, it hardly seems to describe the genesis of the majority, and, when applied to what hitherto have been taken as overarching or grounding notions, suggests a kind of arbitrariness and human authorship that would evacuate them of authority. In the case of writers such as Rorty and Giddens this, of course, is precisely the desired effect. On Rorty's account, at the end of the day we have to realise that we are simply involved in an ongoing process of re-describing ourselves and our situations in ways that are more interesting— for example, by helping us to cope better—than their predecessors. There is no such thing as a *true* description, only more or less interesting ones. Indeed, the pursuit of truth is no longer regarded as a proper goal of thought, for what does the issue of truth add to our understanding of whether or not something helps us to cope? Such a view does indeed turn nature (and everything else that is foundational) into a chimera.

But why should we be seduced by this account? A terminal cancer sufferer is likely to receive little comfort from the suggestion that this is just an optional—and perhaps not the most interesting—description of his condition. Does Rorty's account not trade on the authority of the term 'description', while simultaneously undermining it? What are descriptions descriptions *of*? On what basis are some descriptions properly to be held as inappropriate or inaccurate? Such questions cannot be adequately answered exclusively in terms of sets of (optional) local norms. Shared descriptions require shared criteria, but the logic of the notion 'describe' requires also something external that is *being described*. Lest it seem otherwise, I am not here resurrecting some curious ontological argument for the existence of independent things, I simply make the point that the use of the term 'describe' implies that there is something beyond the description.

Rorty, Giddens and others of their persuasion are undoubtedly right to observe that at some levels nature has fallen out of our thinking, but the corollary of this may not be a reflexive, optional, reconstruction, but a *retrieval*—thus the title of this volume. That is to say, the issue is raised as to whether we can retrieve nature in a sense reflexively—for at one level we can no longer pretend innocence of our part in the production of the concept of nature—but in a way that allows it to remain genuinely foundational. Do we have to accept as inevitable Baudrillard's notion of coming to inhabit a burgeoning hyperreality of simulacra, or are there ways of disposing ourselves that enable us to re-engage with nature in a different manner that allows it to be founding again, that is, to come to know nature afresh, in a way that allows it to speak to us? Such a possibility will be explored in Chapter 6.

Interestingly, in parallel vein to Rorty, in their discussion of the relevance of what they term 'postfoundationalism' to educational aims, Nigel Blake, Paul Smeyers, Richard Smith and Paul Standish (1998) consider the counter-claim that the critical philosophy that has led up to the scepticism over (extra-linguistic) foundations one day might conclude that some candidate claim for foundational status were right. But then, they claim:

> we would not know it to be right because it were foundational, but only because it had survived critique. It is not that there are no constraints on meaning or knowledge, language or belief. Rather, the constraints are not foundations, ontologically prior to discourse, but the intrinsic constraints of critique itself, internal to discourse and intrinsically social' (Blake *et al.*, 1998, p. 31).

Consistent with this hermetically sealed internalisation of truth to discourse, they conclude that with regard to normative, and, presumably any other, 'truths', 'no appeals to foundations will settle the question. But nor do we assume that anything is possible. We can only wait and see what our language lets us do. But that is all we need to do' (p. 33).

Again, the internal norms of language, critique, dialogue are the only constraint we really have—the source of objectivity. But in a language one can dissemble and fabricate—so we should be wary of running together 'language' and 'critique' as they tend to do. More worryingly, as postmodernists themselves are wont to point out, language itself is ideologically laden and its use can be manipulated by those in power. It is often what language *dis*allows that is significant, and we hardly need to evoke Orwellian 'Newspeak' by way of illustration when we have the imposition of managerial discourse in education so close to hand. (See, for example, Jean-François Lyotard's (1984) seminal account of the pervasive demands, cabining effects and linguistic 'terrorism' of 'performativity', and Ian Frowe's (1992, 2001) discussions of the effects of managerial language in education in the UK.) Why should we be content to allow language thus understood to determine thinking? Furthermore, often one of the norms of critique is a reference to—such as accurate observation of—some reality that is taken to lie beyond what is being said: the thing being described. On the frequent occasions when language allows—indeed, *requests*—us to do this, is it mistaken? And, if so, by what warrant? Either we simply do what language 'lets us do', or we do not. Perhaps, too, echoing Lyotard's sensitivity to the conflict involved in language expressed in his claim that 'to speak is to fight' (1984, p. 10), we might be alerted to the possibility that below the surface of modest expressions of waiting upon language lies an implicit bid for power: what might be seen as an arbitrary move to assert one kind of language or vocabulary ('post-foundationalist') over another (foundationalist) in a context in which language *per se* does not adjudicate the matter.

Essentially, a similar motive can be detected in the attacks on the notion of 'essence'. For example, Rorty claims that to think of human beings as having an essence is to turn them into objects because it is to impose one optional description on them as defining. But many features of the human condition (presumably a term that should make no sense to Rorty) seem to endure over the millennia and facilitate understanding across cultures—e.g. birth, death, loss, desire of power, recognition, love, etc. And without some notion of nature and human nature that is not *simply* culturally produced, and therefore 'optional', there can be no basis for talk of repression, distortion, injustice, for there would be no underlying reality to be violated, *nor to limit alternative descriptions.* If the point were to be that we need to be cautious in our use of the term 'the human condition' lest we universalise very local values—as arguably occurred with the Enlightenment elevation of European bourgeois reason to the status of universal arbiter of thinking, and which Robert Solomon (1980) aptly dubbed the 'transcendental pretence'—the point is well taken. But to set it up as a complete impostor is to assume a level of incommensurability that has yet to be demonstrated by its critics. Furthermore, not all descriptions, essences, are objectifying. Saying that part of the essence of human being is that it has a certain freedom, or that it can question its situation, or that it is capable of feeling loss, is not to 'sum it up' in the way that saying that someone is unintelligent is. The former points to an infinity of open possibilities whereas the latter can be seen as closing possibilities down. That a metaphysics of definable 'objects' rather than indefinable 'things' surreptitiously pervades certain assaults on the idea of 'essence' will be developed in the next chapter.

But the fundamental criticism of all the views that I have been alluding to is this. There is, literally, a world of difference between saying that there is some underlying reality (nature) of which we only ever see limited aspects or different profiles according to *how* we look at it (under what aspect or description) and saying that it is *only* the ways we look—that is, the descriptions and the norms that inform them—that give meaning and reality to things. Those who claim the latter trade on, can only express their view in terms of, a vocabulary that presupposes some independently existing reality—something that is capable of being *described*. To make their case, those of a Rortian persuasion need to produce a vocabulary that does not do this and to persuade others to use it. This they have singularly failed to do (on both counts). Certainly, that wonderfully incoherent confection, the 'pure simulacrum'—sign without referent, introduced by Jean Baudrillard to denote the postmodern phenomenon of a 'hyperreality' of self-referential images that 'bear no relation to any reality whatever' (1988, pp. 170–171), and which might be seen to meet the former problem—fails to seduce in this role. For, again, such a notion only makes sense against a remembrance of the reality it replaces.

As it stands, nature can be described as mysterious, infinite, pre-existing and so forth. What are the grounds for saying that this kind of vocabulary is no longer legitimate? To claim, as Rorty does, that it has outlived its usefulness reveals the instrumental metaphysics that he expresses—and the poverty of the pragmatism that informs his view. And even in terms of usefulness, experience suggests that effective thought and action is less a matter of, as William James put it, 'breaking the flux of sensible reality at our will', and more a matter of carving nature at the joints.

I will conclude this section by briefly noting some further considerations relevant to environmental education invited by my sketch of what I am loosely calling 'postmodernist' attacks on nature.

A. *Conflation of senses of nature*

Giddens constantly slides between nature as a conception and what may be empirically going on in nature. For example, he criticises ecological thinkers' attitudes to modern science as something that they rely on to inform them as to what nature is and yet criticise as an enterprise (p. 208). But it was not the interventionist approach of modern science that discovered that nature speaks a reality characterised, for example, by wholeness and interdependence, etc. As noted in Chapter 3, these ancient intuitions were already part of our understanding of nature as underlying reality. They are part of the form of sensibility within which science once made its start, and when its models contradict this—as maybe with quantum theory, or a notion of separate parallel universes—whatever sense can be made of them is parasitic on our more primordial horizons of significance in which nature is a founding notion. Furthermore, if at the 'extremities' of reality we need to entertain 'foreign' notions, this hardly vitiates the conceptions we bring to bear in nature expressed in our normal life-world, which is the home of environmental issues. For example, at present it is hard to see how events at the quantum level have discernible relevance to environmental (including social) issues.

B. *Gratuitousness*

Giddens' identification of a generous set of values that (should) guide us, such as the 'universal right to happiness and to universal self-actualisation—coupled with the obligation to promote cosmopolitan solidarity and an attitude of respect towards non-human agencies and beings, present and future' (p. 253), rests upon what he thinks can be read off as emerging values in a globalising post-traditional society. He makes little attempt to justify them or morally evaluate them; the issue of why, if at all, we *ought* to follow such values is barely addressed. This finds parallels in Rorty and is entirely characteristic of a perspective whose premises ultimately undermine the enterprise of justification. This clearly raises issues for the enterprise of developing an environmental ethic.

C. Dilution of understanding

Rorty's pragmatism poses the question: What purpose does asking about the truth of something serve? Whether or not a sentence accurately reflects some underlying reality is both otiose and unknowable. What is central is the question of whether a sentence (description) enables us to cope better, enables us to meet our desires better? Asking about the truth does nothing to further us: it is unnecessary—a disengaged cog.

But questions of truth and reality arise in many contexts and may serve varying purposes. Does not the notion of truth as something in which an underlying reality is expressed or revealed do important work in our understanding of the world at large—a place where explanations have a point because they are taken to connect with such reality, even if, as we shall see, it is a reality that is neither some preformed fixture nor one that presents itself to us unambiguously and univocally, but rather as a reality of endless (though not random) possibilities? Believing that we can reveal some of this reality and that we are embedded in it is a—*the*—central condition of having an understanding of ourselves, of others, indeed of *anything*. This applies with particular cogency to environmental concerns. An entirely free-floating explanation or understanding is *no* explanation or understanding. As Baudrillard noted in his essay 'Symbolic exchange and death':

> Theoretical production, like material production, is . . . losing its determination and is beginning to spin on its own, disconnectedly . . . towards an unknown reality. Today we are already at that point: in the realm of undecidability, in the era of *floating theories*, like floating currencies . . . their only purpose is to signal one another (Baudrillard, 1988, p. 99).

For him, this may be purely descriptive of a developing state of affairs, but for the view expressed above it is the end of understanding. In contrast to postmodernism as 'the philosophy of inverted commas' (Scruton, 1994, p. 504) in which only the unsophisticated can hold beliefs and values, I would argue that truth sets the standard of what *really* works as against what has only the appearance of coping, that is, it alerts us to the possibility of dissembling. It sets the standard for what *ought* to satisfy us and what we ought to know regardless of our dominant desires—for example, regarding the effects of satisfying those desires on other aspects of reality.

D. Hubris

Since for Rorty (and, in a parallel sense, Giddens, with his 'remoulded nature') descriptions, vocabularies, are 'optional'—matters of choice and local norms and not validated by any external reality—it would seem to follow that we can be regarded as 'authoring' nature in choosing the descriptions and vocabularies that we use to articulate it. It is interesting to ask what motives are expressed in the choice of this kind of postmodern account. Is not a form of mastery again in play here? Yet, arguably, its arrogant supposition that ultimately we are nature's author is ultimately degrading. Under the illusion of becoming the lord of beings we become merely orderers of the ordered, and so positioned, undermine the possibility of a genuine receptiveness, a listening to what is other. Set up as authors of all we survey, we are in danger of seeing only ourselves beyond ourselves.

THE REALITY OF NATURE AND THE NATURE OF REALITY

I have been examining a set of views that suggest that there is a radical sense in which nature and humankind are far from being independent, not simply in the sense of ecological interdependence, but in the profound sense that at bottom 'nature' is a human construction. And again, here, not simply in the sense that much of what we take as natural has been shaped by the human hand, but in the deeper sense that the ways nature exists for us at all are products of the human mind.

So, in sum, what are we to make of the general claim that nature is (merely) a social construction and that therefore it is a mistake to attempt to identify some enduring underlying reality in its name? There are a number of responses that can be made to such an objection.

I think the first thing to do is to recognise certain senses in which there is *some* truth in this, but that it needs to be understood in terms of certain distinctions. We must distinguish between: (i) 'nature' as a concept; (ii) 'nature' as a realm of experience that people have under that concept. As a *concept*, certainly nature is socially produced (rather than 'constructed' with its connotations of deliberateness), but this hardly turns it into a chimera. Indeed, it is to say nothing very much at all—for by definition *all* our shared concepts and ways of understanding the world are socially produced. This makes them neither purely arbitrary nor *shallowly* ephemeral (though some may be). They, along with the literacies and practices in which they are embedded (all socially produced), constitute the chief—some would argue the only—means by which we understand the world at any particular time.

As a concept, 'nature' is produced in the sense in which any idea is a human artefact: it has arisen in human consciousness in its interaction within a world, an interaction through which it understands aspects of that world. There are good reasons for supposing that there is a significant amount of transcultural common ground here: that human beings across a range of cultures need to carry out common functions and that different 'world views' seem to be translatable from one language into another suggest *inter alia* a common reality. But also there is a sense in which 'nature' is dependent upon and relative to particular communities of humankind, and this will be nuanced in different ways in different cultures. Indeed, it has been argued that, for some indigenous cultures, the complete sense of oneness with their environment leaves no space for an explicit sense of nature at all (Milton, 1998, p. 89). And so it has always been; each culture lives with and through its own *ideas* of nature. But none of this need affect what *we*, as a culture, mean by nature. However we came by the concept and however many versions there are of it across different cultures, we may still mean by it—that is, wish to convey the idea of—say, an independent order of things, and we may seek to devise ways of testing and exploring this idea in terms of its fit with experience. That others see the matter differently, have different conceptions or none at all, is irrelevant to the fact that this (whatever it is) is part of *our* concept of nature and that it fundamentally orientates our experience of the world.

It is relevant to note the parallel here with the closely related debate over the relativity of truth. With regard to different things, different people will no doubt have different versions of what is true and how to test for it, and different cultures may have different versions of what truth itself is, but none of this detracts from a meaning of truth that involves that what is true is actually the case and not simply—i.e. simply and no more—some culture's 'take' on a situation. To show that truth—that is *particular truth claims* (this is a crucial ambiguity in the use of the word 'truth')—may be historically and culturally local is to say nothing about the validity of the idea of truth itself. From within a situation that is always relative in the sense of being a particular context, we can still *project* an idea of objectivity and use it as a standard of evaluation. Truth is an aspiration. To find that other intelligent beings have beliefs that differ from ours requires neither that we simply give up our own beliefs nor that we simply reject theirs, but that we attempt to check out their validity in terms of their relationship to reality as given to us in our experience. And if our conclusions are provisional—for example, through want of sufficient understanding or evidence, etc.—this refusal to ascribe 'final' truth, far from supporting the relativity of truth, only confirms the power of the sense of objectivity inherent in our notion of it. Our withholding and our sense of provisionality are a measure of our commitment to an ideal of truth. What we may at times *take to be true* may be relative, but not truth itself.

To return, now, to the argument in relation to nature. Some senses of nature certainly imply a physical order that exists totally independently of human beings and that therefore has its own properties and maybe value. But, it might be argued, whatever these are we can never know them as they are in themselves because they are mediated by our sensory apparatus and conceptual schemes. Thus, again, nature is merely a human construction—with the implication that this represents some sort of inadequacy. But this is perverse. Everything we can feel, think, understand occurs within a world of human significances, including any postulations of a world that might exist in *one* sense outside it. It is perverse to see the limits of this (constantly expanding) world of significances as a *limitation*, for it is precisely this that enables experience and understanding in the first place, and *by means of* its limits. All understanding involves a perspective—some 'meaning-giving framework' or 'horizon of intelligibility'—that operates by making some meanings and experiences possible by denying others. This is inherent in any form of sensibility. In this context the claim that nature is (merely) a human construction loses its sting, for it no longer carries with it the implication that it is thereby purely arbitrary and bearing no special relationship with reality—as if we could simply choose it to be otherwise, reconstruct it at will, provide for ourselves some other reality. It is the only reality available to us and as objective as any reality can be.

TO SUMMARISE

The examination of certain postmodernist and other critiques of the reality of nature undertaken in this chapter, as well as clearing a way for further development of the notion of nature as primordial reality, has contributed to the basis upon which it is to be undertaken. It has led to the conclusion that nature as both a concept and an aspect of experience is a deeply constitutive element in our form of sensibility—meaning by this latter, that through which our awareness, cognitive and emotional, occurs and is made possible. We take our form of sensibility to be a product partly of our physiology, relating to our biological needs and capacities, and partly of our culture, relating to our languages and conceptual schemes, which mediate whatever is physiologically given—and which in turn are taken to be the product of a history of interaction with a world whose features, such as the existence of solid bodies, are not all determined by our will and therefore require our accommodation. There are clear parallels here with Wittgenstein's notion of a 'form of life', and indeed I am perfectly happy for it to be so assimilated, provided that its Wittgensteinian employment to indicate the roots of language (and any surrounding exegetical issues) does not then jeopardise the above characterisation.

The argument, then, is that nature in the underlying sense of the self-arising identified in the previous chapter can be construed as a primordial reality in the sense of being deeply embedded in our historically grown form of sensibility. To exorcise it would be to bring about a change so fundamental as to lie beyond our comprehension, if indeed it were even possible. Thus, if the postmodernist critique of nature is directed at our inability to know a reality that lies outside our form of sensibility, then it is correct, but otiose. We can only know—or imagine—*anything* from within our form of sensibility. This does not prevent us from, say, imagining the possibility of beings differently constituted from ourselves for whom what for us are given as solid objects are not such, but we cannot live in any such world—our everyday experience of the world we inhabit makes it clear that it is not an option. The significant point is that our experience which is necessarily undergone within our form of sensibility is conditioned by a concept of nature that is constitutive of that sensibility—a form of sensibility that we can properly regard as neither optional nor arbitrary in any real sense. Henceforth, when I refer to 'nature' it will be nature so located. And therefore *as experienced*, nature is not culturally produced, but *given*.

Thus the issue now becomes a matter not simply of whether there is 'empirically' an independent natural order that has its own properties—for us there manifestly is, this is simply and *unavoidably* how we experience many aspects of the world—but of what the meaning of this order, the quality of the space in which it presences (and thus the way it is interpreted), the value and the implications for thought and action that we attach to it, are. This being so, I will now move on to exploring the features of the understanding of nature that we have, or that can be retrieved, and that may be relevant to addressing environmental issues. Lest, as we expend ourselves in a clamour of interesting re-descriptions, the 'soft-bodied things' inhabiting Brian Clarke's stream come to 'rejoice'.

. . . But then, again, why should we not rejoice with the soft-bodied things and the foul smells? Why, for example, privilege the plight of a parasite-ridden trout, whose now dull eye was once—before the insidious effects of water extraction—as quick and as clear as was the stream itself?

Chapter 5. Nature as our Primordial Reality

'nature' has become the fundamental word that designates essential
. . . relations that Western historical humanity has to beings, both to
itself and to beings other than itself (Heidegger, 1998, p. 183).

THE POSITION SO FAR

In the two preceding chapters I have attempted to sketch some basic
perspectives on the meaning of 'nature' and to indicate some of the issues
that arise for environmental education. Thus in Chapter 3 I outlined three
influential ways (in the form of ideal types) in which nature has been
experienced in the West and four central current senses of the terms
'nature' and 'natural' which both draw upon these modes of experience
and draw out distinguishable strands that run through them. Within these
senses it was argued that an underlying unifying intuition of nature as the
'self-arising' could be discerned. Chapter 4 addressed a set of fundamental
questions raised by reflexive philosophy concerning the reality of nature:
Is it (merely) a social construction? Is it an arbitrary construction? Is it
now an anachronism miring thought in nostalgia and suspect ideology? On
the postmodernist accounts discussed, an 'ultimate' reality such as nature
is not some original source of meaning, something, as it were, pre-
existing, which may be more or less adequately represented by our
languages, signs and images, but the *product* of these. As Robin Usher
and Richard Edwards put it: 'the referent becomes an effect rather than
the source of the sign' (Usher and Edwards, 1994, p. 14). So conceived,
we are invited to view 'nature' as a highly derivative, politically
compromised and potentially ephemeral notion, hardly fitted to any
founding role. If, as was argued in Chapters 1 and 2, our notions of nature
constitute an important part of the metaphysical underpinning of both
environmental education and education as a whole, it is clear that answers
to the above questions and challenges are essential to sound, as against
cosmetic, progress in understanding what ought to be the stance of
education towards the environmental problems that now confront us.

My response was to argue that these postmodernist challenges to the
reality of nature disturb, but do not dislodge, a founding sense of nature as
the self-arising. They properly alert us to certain dangers in taking nature
as founding, but they are not fatal to the argument, for to achieve this they
would have, amongst other things, to assume just such a founding position
as postmodernism itself rejects. Furthermore, they overlook the distinction
between a socially produced concept that is deeply embedded in an (*our*)
historically grown overarching form of sensibility and the experience had

within that form of sensibility. Thus located, and at a *meta* level of analysis, we may understand that such a concept is socially produced, but *not* thereby in any substantive way arbitrary or 'optional'. And certainly in terms of the experience had under that concept, nature is precisely *not* socially produced. Therefore, my analysis does no more—*and no less*—than claim to reveal certain fundamental aspects of how we understand/experience the world in our time, in this case namely that implicitly we understand/experience nature as the self-arising. In addition, while it is clear that particular instantiations of nature in its senses of arbiter of rightness, innate essence and cosmic order may inherently reflect ideological purposes, it is far less obvious that this need apply to the underlying notion of nature as self-arising. It is important to note that this is not simply, or primarily, because it refers to 'purely empirical' aspects of nature, but because the significance of, say, a germinating seed or a leaping salmon as symbolising such themes as hope, rebirth, determination, etc., both possesses a certain non-arbitrariness—the leaping salmon could hardly be taken to symbolise indolence—and can be perfectly well understood in ways innocent of distorting political motives. Though, of course, *any* understanding can become subverted by ideology.

The task for this chapter is to elaborate this conception of nature as the self-arising by identifying some key features of our experience of nature so understood, that is, the reality that it displays. I will then address some objections to which this display of reality may be felt to be susceptible.

THE REALITY OF NATURE AS THE SELF-ARISING

What, then, in these more detailed terms, and at the level of our experience of nature, are we to make of the claim that, despite the diversity of interpretation, there is an underlying unifying idea implicit in certain central ways in which we use the term nature: the notion of what is essentially non-human and self-arising? On this view, we might recall that, for example, even when we attempt to shape nature's course, as, say, in the case of nurturing crops or our own health, we recognise that we are working with something of which essentially we are not the author and with which we therefore have to seek a certain harmony. There are a number of interrelated features to nature so experienced.

First, ontologically, 'nature' refers to a certain 'otherness', that for which we are not *ultimately* responsible and which therefore has its own movement and spontaneity. It is therefore *epistemologically mysterious* in the sense that it has aspects that lie always beyond us, withdrawn—still (and perhaps, never) to be revealed or discovered. As self-arising, natural things possess a certain inscrutability, no matter how developed, say, our scientific understanding of them becomes. Generalised causal explanations say nothing about their sheer existence, give no insight into the experience of their individual standing forth in their suchness. *Par excellence*, natural things each have their own unique history, potentialities and, to a significant degree, unknowable future. They have profiles and countenances we shall never witness; they possess the ability to affect us through invitations to participate in their being in unique and never wholly predictable ways as attested, for example, by Romantic poetry. But not only this—though Manley Hopkins' notion of the 'inscape' of natural things is a particularly powerful articulation. It will be argued, presently, that experiencing things thus as open and infinitely faceted illustrates a metaphysical contrast with the defined *objects* produced by rational inspection, objects whose being is ultimately exhausted by the characteristics of category membership. That is to say, aspects of nature can be apprehended when their appearing is arrested as an object, but they are more fully apprehended through a non-objectifying kind of perception.

Second, this brings with it another formative feature of this underlying intuition: *nature's integrity.* Central to our experience is the idea of some underlying coherence or logic at work in nature that pervades it as an interrelated, interdependent, spatially and temporally continuous whole. There are no lacunae in natural space, everything is interrelated and all relationships are reciprocal. Everything arises out of, and in distinction from, everything else and is therefore ultimately affected by everything else. The space something occupies is implicitly understood as being conditioned by all that went before it, by all that coexists and by all that we conceive might be. This is true of nature whether it be otherwise conceived in material or spiritual terms; whether it be the teleological system of the Greeks, the mother organism of the Renaissance, the great clockwork of the Enlightenment, the overarching ecosystem of late modernity, or the Gaia of latter-day quasi-romantics. *And we humans understand ourselves as a part of this integrity: in certain respects we both express it and it is expressed in us.* Importantly, we understand there to be certain basic general human needs, sentiments and capacities—and also aspects of ourselves as individuals—that constitute part of our own flourishing, that we did not choose and of which we are not the author. These constitute our own nature and sustain us in our own being. We need to acknowledge them, in order truly to develop, that is, to develop *organically.*

Third, the continuity of natural space means that ultimately it is inescapable and unrepeatable. To really escape from natural space would be to negate nature as an intuition, and thus to massively change our understanding of ourselves and the world. Central to any notion of the human condition is a sense of the contingency of life, that every event is unique in time and space, and, as it were, cannot be wound back and replayed. The whole edifice of human freedom, choice, responsibility, purpose and planning presupposes this.

Fourth, nature as self-arising has intrinsic value—which, though human-related in that only human beings can discern it and thus bring it into being, is not anthropocentric in the sense that it has therefore to provide human satisfaction (for example, aesthetic satisfaction). Connelly and Smith have used the term 'anthropogenic' to denote a value that in some sense originates from, but is not necessarily beneficial to, human beings (Connelly and Smith, 1999, p. 20). This issue of the sense in which nature has intrinsic value is clearly decisive for any notion of an environmental ethic, and I will return to it presently.

To return to the current strand of argument, these features of nature as the self-arising indicate that it is both what we have simply to accept and that from which we may genuinely learn and be inspired. This is its essential character in relationship to the human spirit. Thomas Berry suggests that nature is the primary educator, healer, commercial establishment and lawgiver 'for all that exists within this life community' (T. Berry, 1988, p. 120). It is in terms of this 'other' that we necessarily define ourselves—an 'other' that has certain parallel key qualities and whose presence affirms that 'man' is *not* the measure of all things, with its consequent nihilism. *Other things matter.* As Ralph Waldo Emerson once put it: 'The whole of nature addresses itself to the whole of man [sic]. We are reassured. It is more than medicine. It is health' (Geldard, 1995, p. 13). Such a view implies that some significant sensuous and spiritual contact with elemental nature is important for our ultimate well-being.

Something of its ability to restore a proper perspective in our experience is reflected in the following observation from Iris Murdoch: 'I am looking out of my window in an anxious and resentful state of mind, brooding perhaps on some damage done to my prestige. Then suddenly I observe a hovering kestrel. In a moment everything is altered. The brooding self with its hurt vanity has disappeared. There is nothing but kestrel. And when I return to thinking of the other matter it seems less important' (Murdoch, 1997, p. 369). This is not simply or primarily a therapeutic remedy, where nature as it were is sought out to provide a balm, but an essentially non-instrumental experience in which the other *befalls* us and is attended to in itself and for itself, making no reference to our immediate concerns. Thus Murdoch goes on: 'More naturally, as well as more properly, we take a self-forgetful pleasure in the sheer, alien pointless independent existence of animals, birds, stones, and trees' (pp. 369–370).

It is important to note that on the view that I am now developing, we are able at a more reflexive level to discern a sense of nature as essentially a *dimension (aspect) of experience* rather than a realm in the sense of a set of entities. Nature as a dimension is everywhere *to some degree*, that is, it is not *everything*. A plastic flower partakes of nature to a degree: its significance, at least in part, derives from its natural counterpart—it is a (perhaps faint) reflection of it. Wilderness partakes in nature to a very high degree; a piece of computer code, perhaps not at all—or at least only at several removes. Such a view overcomes any absolute dualism of nature and culture, nature and artefacts, nature and humanity—but not in a way that obliterates important distinctions. It recognises self-arising *and* artefactual aspects of the world while acknowledging their mutual rootedness, and reveals their real character and significance through recognising their interrelationships in experience.

Thus on this view Passmore is wrong to say that we have *either* nature as meaning the 'non-human' *or* an ultimately unifying sense of nature 'as whatever is subject to natural law' that can only be contrasted with the supernatural (Passmore, 1980, p. 5). We need to be able to recognise the 'nature' in human beings and artefacts—for example, that they have aspects that are subject to 'natural law', or that some of them, such as works of art or craft, reveal aspects of nature (as when a cabinetmaker reveals the figuring in a piece of walnut) and are valuable for that reason—*without simply reducing them to nature*. Similarly, the view that I am developing gives the lie to the claim that 'it makes little sense to talk about the interconnectedness of everything, and everything's dependence on everything else, while at the same time disconnecting artefacts [from nature]' (Wissenburg, 1993, pp. 6–7). Nature refers to a certain kind or quality of interconnectedness. *Some aspects* of artefacts partake in this. Also, of course, there is the sense in which we regard physical artefacts as occupants of natural space and, when viewed scientifically, as ultimately composed of natural matter. But as artefacts they do not exist in the world simply as natural things do, for they participate in sets of intentional relations that go beyond nature. Yet nature's interconnectedness (its kind of continuity and integrity) is the founding kind of interconnectedness—the one that most fundamentally characterises our understanding of reality in its fullest sense. Even with regard to ourselves as persons—the very originators of the artefactual—it has been argued by Peter Strawson (1964) and others that our material bodies, as occupants of natural space, are necessary to our individuation.

THE METAPHYSICS OF OBJECTS AND THE METAPHYSICS OF THINGS

> Our everyday experience of things, in the widest sense of the word, is neither objectifying nor a placing-over-against. When, for example, we sit in the garden and take delight in a blossoming rose, we do not make an object of the rose, do not even make it something standing-over-against, i.e. something represented thematically. When in tacit saying we are enthralled by the lucid red of the rose and muse on the redness of the rose, then this redness is neither an object . . . nor a standing-over-against (Heidegger, 1976, p. 26).

It seems to me that an important dimension to this discussion of the reality of nature is reflected in a contrast to be drawn between the metaphysics of *objects* and the metaphysics of *things*. Objects are defined by the abstract categories in which they have been placed, their being consists in (that is, is exhausted by) the characteristics of category membership, and thus stabilised and thoroughly 'known', they can, for example, be stored in a database, tagged and searched for algebraically. They exist as organised, ready for inspection or use. They are the product of the motive to get things 'sorted'—intellectually processed and possessed. Open, infinitely faceted, fluid, epistemologically mysterious *things*, on the other hand, are neither knowable nor taggable in this way. Their own relationship with each other is not 'logical', but organic. This is the reality of nature as the self-arising—a reality that in this regard reflects certain aspects of previously described organismic and Romantic intuitions. When reduced to the reality of objects, things arise in a space from which the dimension of intrinsic and moral value has been stripped, because what is authentically *other*—has its own being, with the spontaneity and mystery that are its concomitant—has fallen away. Becoming habituated to such a milieu reinforces a view of reality—nature—in which holism, the peripheral, fluidity and spontaneity are absent, and contrasts with a nature whose intrinsic integrity and epistemic mystery can refute our initial intuitions and provoke new ones.

Something of the quality of things in this sense is well illustrated by Heidegger's description of Van Gogh's painting of the peasant's shoes in *Origin of the Work of Art*. He suggests that somehow the shoes disclose themselves as they are—in this case as essentially pieces of equipment—through the invocation of the world in which they have their being—the dwelt world of the peasant woman:

> As long as we only imagine a pair of shoes in general, or simply look at the empty, unused shoes as they merely stand there in the picture, we shall never discover what the equipmental being of the equipment in truth is. From Van Gogh's painting we cannot even tell where these shoes stand. There is nothing surrounding this pair of peasant shoes in or to which they might belong – only an undefined space. There are not even clods of soil from the field or the field-path sticking to them, which would at least hint at their use. A pair of peasant shoes and nothing more. And yet –
>
> From the dark opening of the worn insides of the shoes the toilsome tread of the worker stares forth. In the stiffly rugged heaviness of the shoes there is the accumulated tenacity of her slow trudge through the far-spreading and ever-uniform furrows of the field swept by a raw wind. On the leather lie the dampness and richness of the soil. Under the soles slides the loneliness of the field-path as evening falls. In the shoes vibrates the silent call of the earth, its quiet gift of the ripening grain and its unexplained self-refusal in the fallow desolation of the wintry field. This equipment is pervaded by uncomplaining anxiety as to the certainty of bread, the wordless joy of having once more withstood want, the trembling before the impending childbed and shivering at the surrounding menace of death (Heidegger, 1975, pp. 33–34).

Here the shoes, as things, are deeply imbricated in and expressive of elemental powers whose motifs inform authentic human dwelling. Such a characterisation contrasts starkly with the experience of, say, a pair of modern mass-produced fashion shoes as they sit boxed and labelled 'Style X, Brown, Size 6, Leather uppers, Man-made soles'.

Things, in this Heideggerian sense, are located in a 'lay' sense of nature in which the previously identified senses of nature as cosmic order, wilderness, innate essence and arbiter of the hale are in rich and productive interplay. This is the world in which we live emotionally. Things are therefore of human dimensions in that they are experienced as commensurable with the scale of human activity and values—unlike the world of, say, ultimate physical particles whose character as objects is the upshot not of human encounter but of the theoretical speculation that defines them. Excessive engagement with the latter is alienating because it abstracts us from the rich emotionally charged world of the former.

Not that such things, even when themselves human artefacts, necessarily limit perception to *within* the scale and qualities of human activity. Rather they can reveal the true character of authentic human activity by locating it in a larger world. Thus Heidegger claims that for the ancients a temple could make manifest the quality and vastness (scope) of its natural surroundings, bringing them to a stand in their human significance (which is in no way thereby simply human-*centred*). Through such things, which are an expression of their dwelling, people are enabled to become rooted in their world:

> Standing there, the building rests on rocky ground. This resting of the work draws up out of the rock the mystery of that rock's clumsy yet spontaneous support. Standing there, the building holds its ground against the storm raging above it and so makes the storm itself manifest in its violence. The lustre and gleam of the stone, though itself apparently glowing only by the grace of the sun, yet first brings to light the light of the day, the breadth of the sky, and the darkness of the night. The temple's firm towering makes visible the invisible space of the air. The steadfastness of the work contrasts with the surge of the surf, and its own repose brings out the raging of the sea . . . The temple-work, standing there, opens up a world and at the same time sets this world back again on earth, which itself only thus emerges as native ground . . . The temple in its standing there, first gives to things their look and to men their outlook on themselves (1975, pp. 42–43).

The making of such things involves a responsiveness to materials and environment that itself includes a certain incipient fore-knowing or acquaintanceship, the content of whose knowledge is realised through the process of making. It therefore involves a certain co-responsibility with the physical attributes and cultural powers whose creativity gives the work meaning and in which they are revealed and expressed. Thus, unlike the production of objects where, today, an overriding concern is for yield and material is used up in the process of producing, in the making of things the material is not simply 'used up', but comes into its own (as with 'the lustre and gleam' of the temple's stone). Aspects of its erstwhile hidden character are revealed as it plays its part in revealing its environment. Engagement with things has the character of an ongoing receptive-responding rather than the challenging-imposing that characterises the process of producing objects, whether physical or intellectual, whether as market commodities or as acts of non-commercial mastery or will.

Thus Heideggerian things inherently express and facilitate authentic dwelling—that is, dwelling that is imbued with a sense of the 'other' in which it participates, a sense of divinity and of finitude, of groundedness and of vulnerability to changing conditions—and in this way they open up a human world. This latter is well illustrated in Heidegger's example of the old stone bridge that 'swings over the stream with ease and power', reflecting the sky's fickle nature in its readiness for quiet flow or storm surge, and which thus 'gathers' the earth as landscape around the stream, causing the banks to emerge *as* banks in granting to mortals their way (Heidegger, 1975, p. 152). Here, the bridge, as a thing, is not inserted into some pre-formed location, but itself creates a neighbourhood, a world of relations. In this sense, in the making of things and in their holding sway, the process and the product are 'poetic' and the integrity of all is preserved.

Such examples of human building illustrate how an artefact can gather and thereby reveal its world by acting as a locus of relationships in which, amongst other things, the dimension of nature as the self-arising is made manifest. In a parallel way, 'natural' things themselves—if allowed to remain things—gather and reveal the world of nature, expressing such qualities as I have previously listed. Take a small flower, inconspicuous in the grass beside some footpath or lodged in some brickwork crevice of a wall bounding a city pavement. If attended to in its simple standing there, it arises in its sheer inscrutability—its self-authored otherness and its epistemological mystery—as it stands forth from what is not, yet speaks of the holism and mystery of everything that is. What is so manifested far outruns the confines of any category membership and is immediately destroyed by any attempt so to assimilate it—witness the loss involved if we attempt to turn this flower into an object by defining it in terms of objective properties that might be entered into some database. As its specification is drawn up, it is turned into a mere instance of some broader classification. So installed, it can, of course, be called up at will and manipulated by thought, but equally the thing itself—the flower in its presencing—has been left far behind and returns to invisibility. Our fleeting contact with nature has been ruptured and we return to live life at a remove from that which sustains it.

There is a strong sense in which in such perception things are not fixed—cut off from the process by which they come into view, from their occurring—but, again, *befall* us. Through our viewing and listening we come upon things that present themselves *as* having been come upon; thus their ability to surprise and to fascinate in ways unknown to objectifying thinking. Not, as I hope has been made abundantly clear, that the human world and the natural world are to be regarded as mutually exclusive. Quite the reverse. Authentic dwelling gathers them both—as distinct yet interfused. And authentic human activity, as the temple example shows, brings aspects of the natural world into appearance and vice versa.

Some of the issues raised by such a view are nicely illustrated by turning to a discussion by Giddens of the view of Robert Goodin (1992) that 'What is especially valuable about the products of natural processes is that they are the products of something larger than ourselves' (see Giddens, 1994, pp. 204–206). Goodin argues that the natural landscape, as part of the wider natural world, is valuable because it thus provides a context in which people are able to see 'some sense and pattern to their lives'. Environments and ways of living that obliterate this deny us contact with this source of sense and satisfaction. Yet, Giddens supposes, in comparing a traditional English village 'with its church, houses and hedgerows that adapt to nature' with a city such as Los Angeles 'which imposes its own artificial order on nature' one cannot say that the first is any more natural than the second (p. 205). For Goodin: 'What is at issue is not the naturalness of its creation . . . it is rather that, in the one case, humanity does not ride roughshod over other parts of nature. And that allows humanity to derive satisfaction from reflection upon its larger setting, in a way that it cannot where that larger setting is more exclusively of its own creation' (in Giddens, 1994, p. 205). But for Giddens, any such comparison leads to 'the impossible task of having to say that Los Angeles is in some way less natural than an English village' for we live now only in a 'remoulded' socially reconstructed nature that is devoid of nature. Thus appeals to nature are irrelevant, ecological debate needs to focus on the environment as a whole, and 'Los Angeles is as much part of the environment as a country village' (p. 210).

Now it seems to me that this discussion is instructive in provoking reflection on a number of seminal points concerning the ways in which nature comes into play in our understanding of environments. I set them out below in order of ascending importance.

First, it can illustrate how Giddens' claim that we now have only a 'remoulded nature devoid of nature' has little purchase on the wilderness sense of nature and nature as the self-arising in a context like this. For a response to the above 'difficulty' is to make the fairly obvious point that there is a perfectly good sense in which the traditional English village can be thought to be more natural than Los Angeles: it is *older* than Los Angeles and nature has had more time to 'reclaim' it in certain respects. Its features will have been softened by the weather and decay; lichen, moss and other flora inhabit it and modify its texture. In such ways the dimension of the self-arising has had the opportunity to reassert itself and insinuate itself into the fabric and demeanour of the village.

Second, Goodin, as portrayed here by Giddens, is too timid concerning the naturalness of the creation of the village. For example, we may imagine that its location and original building will have reflected an intimate harmonious working relationship with relevant aspects of local nature and that the materials out of which its buildings are constructed are themselves more natural and (partly because of lesser technological power) have been worked with more responsively so as to acknowledge and thus reveal their inherent virtues. In comparison materials such as concrete and plastic, with which modern building treats, are engineered to a blueprint and the dimension of the self-arising is again subdued.

Third, and perhaps most important, the village is built in a spirit of dwelling that is closer to elemental nature than the skyscraper—even though, for example, physically the skyscraper reaches into the heavens to a degree that the village church spire cannot match. For the occupants of the skyscraper, insulated from the world by double glazing and air-conditioning and distracted from the fall of dusk by the creation of endless fluorescent and neon day, are neither invited to experience their elevation *as* towards the heavens nor their time as modulated by natural rhythms.

Here then are some significant 'unremoulded' senses in which the English village may rightly be regarded as more natural than Los Angeles, though, to be sure, with the 'death' of English villages as they become dormitories and holiday locations, severing their current life from a once intimate connection with local agricultural work, some elements of their 'naturalness' increasingly consist in remembrance.

Much of what is essential here is captured in Heidegger's description of a Black Forest farmhouse:

> *Only if we are capable of dwelling, only then can we build.* Let us think for a while of a farmhouse in the Black Forest, which was built some two hundred years ago by the dwelling of peasants . . . It placed the farm on the wind-sheltered mountain slope looking south, among the meadows close to the spring. It gave it the wide overhanging shingle roof whose proper slope bears up under the burden of snow, and which, reaching deep down shields the chambers against the storms of the long winter nights. It did not forget the altar corner behind the community table; it made room in its chamber for the hallowed places of childbed and the 'tree of the dead' – for that is what they call a coffin there . . . and in this way it designed for the different generations under one roof the character of their journey through time. A craft which, itself sprung from dwelling, still uses its tools and frames as things, built the farmhouse . . . Our reference to the Black Forest farm in no way means that we should or could go back to building such houses; rather it illustrates by a dwelling that *has been* how *it* was able to build (Heidegger, 1975, p. 160).

By using such an illustration one is not necessarily endorsing the social relations in which this kind of dwelling was implicated; for example, it is not implausible to suppose that houses of this character could have been constructed by people dwelling in a more egalitarian, even communal, society. But certainly a strong contrast can be drawn between such building and, for example, modernist building, which, according to Mordaunt Crook, involves something other than a dialectical relationship with nature:

> It is self-evident that the *tabula rasa* tendency of modernization favours the optimum use of earth-moving equipment . . . The bulldozing of an irregular topography into a flat site is clearly a technocratic gesture which aspires to a condition of absolute placelessness, whereas the terracing of the same site to receive the stepped form of building is an engagement in the act of 'cultivating' the site. It is possible to argue that in this last instance *the specific culture of the region – that is to say, its history in both a geological and agricultural sense – becomes inscribed into the form and realization of the work* (in Abbs, 1996, pp. 58–59).

Modernism, so characterised, rejects the past and the particular and creates an abstract, rational space of 'universal civilisation' in contrast with 'autochthonous culture'. There is much in Peter Abbs' observation that, because of its unremitting functionalism, modernist architecture isolated 'the technical problems from the environment, from the community, from the actual places where the buildings were sited, from the whole web of connections which define the human-cultural-natural continuum of our lives' (Abbs, 1996, p. 66). An example that readily springs to mind here is that of high-rise flats as a solution to the UK housing problem of the 1960s and 1970s, which so singularly failed to reflect and to facilitate the continuum of people's lives.

SOME OBJECTIONS: THE ISSUE OF DWELLING

An account of the above kind that valorises a certain human-nature relationship is subject to a number of objections in terms of the distinctions it attempts to draw. I set out some of the chief of these below, along with my rebuttals.

First, in relation to the distinction drawn between *things* and *objects*, an objection might go along the lines that these are simply correlates of frames of mind rather than independently existing entities. Therefore, to hark back to an example given above, a modern mass-produced shoe could equally well be viewed as a 'thing' with associations that parallel Heidegger's peasant shoes. Furthermore, it remains unclear why the frame of mind whose correlate is things should be privileged over the frame of mind whose correlate is objects. I think there are two points to be made by way of rejoinder.

a) The idea that the frame of mind or aspect under which one is perceiving determines what one perceives requires examination. Clearly there is a degree of truth in it, but stated thus it overlooks the reciprocity that is involved. In reality consciousness (mind) and things are equi-primordial. If things are nothing without consciousness, consciousness is nothing without its things. Both arise in their mutual relationship as a reaching out to each other—i.e. as elements-in-relationship. Thus, as I have argued elsewhere (see Bonnett, 1994, p. 178–179), when we are struck by the character of things such as the brilliance of a colour, the solidity of a building, the magnificence of the heavens, the appeal of a story, the elegance of a proof or theory—all these qualities of things that *make them what they are* are neither simply human projections (there is a clear sense in which we regard them as belonging to the things themselves) nor *simply* independently existing properties (they stand forth, display their particular significance, suchness only in being apprehended by consciousness). That is to say, they are not separately pre-specifiable, but exist as expressions of the relationship in which consciousness and things are rooted.

To hark back to previous discussion, clearly there is, at one level, a sense in which the 'things themselves' of nature are indeed culturally produced—provided that this is not taken as a denial of the senses in which things other than culture play a part. That is to say, aspects of their *significance* are culturally produced. But that we 'produce' nature in this sense does not make it simply a product that we can either comprehensively know or redefine at will. And even from the standpoint of culture, integral to such 'production' of things are the subtleties and nuances of culture and the unique ways in which *this* thing as it stands forth here and now expresses our culture—including its understandings of mystery and 'otherness', including what is inchoate in that culture and yet to be articulated or imagined. From the perspective of significance, these are what make things what they are in themselves, for they are, precisely, 'incarnate' loci of an infinite web of such strands of significance, opening up a particular world for us.

Furthermore, even at this meta-level of analysis there is the sense in which things *disclose* a world and themselves and are therefore there to be dis-(un-)covered. Not only do we accept a brute component to reality, but also at the level of significances no one simply *decides* the lustre of gold, the majesty of a soaring eagle, the fearful symmetry of a tiger, etc., and their human significances. We are struck by them, or we come to realise them—both of which have a passive dimension. Without this they are unrooted.

b) The point about mass-produced shoes—and much else—is that they rarely invite us to see them as things. To the extent that we attend to them, their *thingness* is frequently effaced because of the kind of space that they (and *we*), through a mutual reinforcing, ordinarily inhabit. This quality of space holds dominion not only in the manner in which such shoes were produced (to a blueprint with no receptivity to material during the process of making, etc.), but in an everyday awareness in which everything is essentially levelled off, generalised and preoccupied with consumption. If such shoes do come to be apprehended as things, which is perfectly possible, then they will *reveal* just such features (plus, no doubt other more personal associations) of their world—a world in which the particularity of things and materials is occluded in the overweening interests of efficiency and yield, and the set of needs that has to be met in their service. Thus the richness and depth of the associations that constitute the mass produced shoes are often severely limited, above all lacking a proper rootedness in a sense of dwelling that far exceeds such a highly instrumental attitude in the scope of human sensibility that it expresses.

And what do I mean by dwelling, here? I mean, drawing in part on Heidegger, a sensibility that resonates to a sense of nature's gift and refusal, to a sense of natural rhythms, to a sense of ideals and aspirations that call us from beyond ourselves—especially our preoccupation with material acquisition and consumption. Part of this will be a sense of finitude brought home to us by awareness of our own mortality, which in turn engenders a certain sense of urgency in acknowledging the different demands that different times make, and in so doing provokes us to create our own history—that is, a history that is authentic to us. Perhaps pivotal to such dwelling is the play of cyclical time, which contrasts with a time so linear that in its unreturning moments objects can be at once defined and the past simply be left behind. There is a sense in which in such time we constantly escape the consequences of our living—ever focussed on 'progress', our living through linear time constantly moves us on to the next 'new' thing—giving rise to, as Milan Kundera puts it, an 'unbearable lightness of being'. Of course, there is a sense in which cyclical time, while precipitating a certain releasement to the job in hand because of its inescapable and in a sense eternal consequences, is imprisoning and can be highly repressive—little essentially different to the general *status quo* being conceivable within its circles. Perhaps what is needed is that something of the sense of responsibility enforced in cyclical time, where there is no escape from the returning consequences of actions, be insinuated into life in linear time such that the past may again inform the present and future—a continuity of experience being preserved. Such continuity might better reflect the character of natural space and might be characterised as 'spiral' time.

Second, an oft-voiced criticism of Heidegger's general account of authentic dwelling and 'things' is that it is haunted by an element of rural ideology that, for example, in his re-counting of the picture of the peasant shoes, generates a naïve romanticising of the world of the peasant woman. Theodor Adorno in his *The Jargon of Authenticity* is particularly trenchant on this general point. In his view, the language of authenticity is a fetish language, a jargon that reifies the abstract, the figurative, the culturally pre-formed and ideological imperatives into what is supposedly 'essential' and 'primal', and, thus 'absolutized', puts itself beyond rational inspection. For example, it assumes that some alleged original meaning of words can be retrieved that automatically claims an authority over thought through its ancient rootedness, or that some alleged past agrarian activity or ceremony (often described in highly romanticised terms) is an expression of the 'hale'—its status in this respect guaranteed by some inexpressible absolute, proper reverence for which forecloses on any scrutiny, rather than being recognised simply as a response to a particular set of past historical circumstances. As he puts it:

> the categories of the jargon are gladly brought forward, as though they were not abstracted from generated and transitory situations, but rather belonged to the essence of man, as inalienable possibility . . . Past forms of societalisation, prior to the division of labour, are surreptitiously adopted as if they were eternal (Adorno, 1986, p. 59).

> It was not Man who created the institutions but particular men in a particular constellation with nature and with themselves (p. 62).

Furthermore, the jargon undermines, through tacit vacillation between concrete and abstract, its own key distinction between the 'ontic' (roughly the factual aspects of entities, for example, including those that are studied by science) and the 'ontological' (the being of entities, how they are in their arising) ultimately trading on connotations from both in order to keep its key concepts afloat. Thus, it meets the need to give them enough substance to provide a level of intelligibility, at one and the same time keeping them sufficiently abstract to shelter them from criticism arising from counter-observations that it would be possible to derive from the empirical world. For Adorno, such obfuscation conjures up a spurious neutrality in setting out the ontological framework for understanding the human condition and its relation to 'Being' in such terms as surreptitiously to incorporate perspectives on key issues that are thus constantly put beyond the reach of critical scrutiny. He suggests that the key notion of 'commissioning'—the idea of responses that are fitting to things themselves—provides ample illustration of this:

> The term 'commission' sets itself up with unquestioned authority in the vulgar jargon of authenticity. The fallibility of the term is hushed up by the absolute use of the word. By leaving out of consideration the organizations and people which give commissions, the term establishes itself as a linguistic eyrie of totalitarian orders. It does this without rational examination of the right of those who usurp for themselves the charisma of the leader . . . By eliminating all linguistic traces of the will of the superior, that which is intended is given greater emphasis (p. 88).

Through its service to a simulation in which demands are dressed up as—and given the force of—issuing directly from things themselves, their real authors with their particular pretensions and agendas thus remaining entirely covert, he claims that 'The jargon of authenticity is ideology as language, without any consideration of specific content' (p. 160). As such—and notwithstanding its frequently parading itself as radical investigation—it invariably commits the very thing it purports to indict: the putting forth of a confused, superficial and 'averaged-off' understanding as though it were unquestionable truth. So characterised, the language of authentic dwelling could itself be considered a particularly virulent form of what Heidegger himself terms the 'they-self'.

Clearly, if Adorno's analysis is correct it represents a grievous criticism of the view that I am developing. But it seems to me that throughout he over-states his case and the result is caricature. To show that, for example, our relationship with nature and the Black Forest farmhouse seen as an expression of this are imbricated in a set of historical social relations is not to show that they are *no more than* a set of social relations—or, indeed, that they are *primarily* a set of social relations. For example, our relationship to nature and the artefacts that express this might be seen to be determined as much, if not more, by a set of transgenerational, and to a degree transcultural (even if culturally mediated), human needs that require accommodations to elemental nature and also, where possible, some kind of spiritual and aesthetic harmony with it. These can be experienced as in tension with current social-economic 'determinants'. While by no means wishing to defend some of the excesses of the 'jargon' that Adorno goes on to identify, it remains far from clear that on this point it should be regarded as merely 'ideology as language', if what is meant by ideology is a set of descriptions and understandings that is optional and flawed, a distortion of reality to be contrasted with some truer consciousness of it. Of course, if ideology is intended to denote *any* way of understanding the world as partial, then his assertion becomes formally correct but substantially otiose. Our (and any) form of sensibility necessarily involves partial understandings, but for reasons elaborated in the previous chapter, this hardly constitutes a criticism. Undoubtedly, Adorno's analysis alerts us to certain dangers inherent in reifying some version of human essence, but in many ways it also reveals the poverty of its own perspective.

The issue of Heidegger's 'archaizing' approach is further nuanced by Jay Bernstein. He rightly recognises that Heidegger wishes to refer us to a way of being with things in which things and nature engage one another differently to the way that people, instruments and nature for the most part interact currently. Part of this is to relocate things from an indifferent geometric space where they exist abstractly categorised to a dwelling place where their intrinsic virtue is implicitly accepted, a space in which they *belong*. But for Bernstein:

> Instead of providing access to a 'true' account of equipment (or space) . . . Heidegger can be seen as referring us back to an earlier form of understanding and practice; to be, precisely, valorising a representation of a past possibility; and hence to be proposing a past rural ideology as his critique of the present. Surely, hydroelectric dams or assembly line robots are not instruments in the same essentialist sense that Heidegger proclaims for . . . the peasant woman's shoes; the essence of equipment has changed since then. And if this is so, then the mere presentation of a past conception of equipment must remain critically vacuous, a stroll in a pleasant imaginary world (Bernstein, 1992, p. 133).

Yet is this as otiose and perniciously ideological as Bernstein (and Adorno) supposes? Or can it be seen as a step towards a retrieval of elements that may be suggestive of a fuller and more respectful way of relating to the world than the technologically driven one with its disastrous environmental consequences? Furthermore, by what authority does Bernstein assume that the 'earlier' way of relating to things is an anachronism, that it can only be present to modern consciousness as 'an imaginary world', as against a reawakening of deep intuitions that can still shape our outlook and sense of what is satisfying—and without which we would be denied an important perspective from which critically to evaluate the progress of technology?

If assembly-line robots are not instruments in the essentialist sense identified by Heidegger, might this not be a reason for taking stock rather than for assuming that the latter is simply passé? Perhaps we should criticise the capitalist ideology in which assembly lines are embedded and note that what Bernstein is characterising as anachronistic understandings of what is congenial to authentic human dwelling continue to inform some of our most popular leisure pursuits and aspirations—that is, the activities, situations and kinds of equipment that many aspire to engage with when they have the freedom to choose. It may also be well to remember that such understandings inform the lives of many cultural groups that, as C. A. Bowers has pointed out, though categorised as backward and undeveloped by certain high-status ways of thinking in the West, 'are contemporary in every sense except for the modern technology they have avoided embracing' (Bowers, 2001, p. 11). Perhaps it should be these understandings, rather than what we now have to adopt as the means to pursue them, that should set the underlying agenda for how we should live? Of course, I am not proposing some straightforward translation of motives expressed in leisure and non-Western contexts into life more generally. Nor am I suggesting (anymore than was Heidegger) that it is either possible or desirable to attempt simply to reinstate past ways of relating to nature and the world. Rather, I am arguing that the *issue* of what might count as authentic dwelling in our time needs to be opened up and that we should not simply discount the contribution of sentiments peripheralised or made to look archaic by the motives, attitudes and social relations that dominate late modernity. Indeed, it may be that these sentiments, *properly rethought*, are precisely the kind of resource that is appropriate to a retrieval of a dwelling that is authentic for us. Such rethinking is the present challenge and need.

The implications of the account being defended here for knowledge of nature and therefore for the content of environmental education will be developed in later chapters. The business of the next chapter is to return to a feature of nature as the self-arising identified above that has yet to be elaborated: the problematic notion of nature possessing intrinsic value and the significance of this issue for environmental education.

Chapter 6. Nature's Intrinsic Value

As the Minister opened the scissors with his right hand and offered the ribbon to them with his left and paused and smiled this way and that for the cameras, the tail of the trout in the stream that had flowed as clear as melted time through meadowsweet and hemp agrimony, through burr reed and brooklime, through purple loosestrife and flag iris and cress, trembled and fretted and arranged itself slowly.

The eye of the trout that the kingfisher had scarred tilted forward. The crowd pressed closer anxious to miss nothing.

As the cut ribbon separated and the silken ends fluttered, the eye of the trout that had lived as quick and light as water itself, stared sightlessly as though at something finally arrived, then rolled loosely back.

The dome of the sky looked down on it.

And the applause rang out.

The Stream, pp. 236–237

This is the denouement in Brian Clarke's story of the development of an industrial park in an economically depressed rural area and the cumulative effects of resultant water extraction and release of toxins on a neighbouring valley with a stream running through it. Powerfully, it raises not only issues of priorities and definitions of success in judging human activity in relation to the natural world, but also the question of why and how the latter is to be valued. Undoubtedly, the above description of events is evocative, but *why* is it evocative? Why do we—should we—feel moved by the changed circumstances of the stream and its inhabitants? Why should we value a world in which each preys on each and the weak go to the wall? And why should it matter that this *particular* world has been wiped out? There are other streams. We could make new ones.

Such questions raise issues that lie at the heart of understanding an environmental education that seeks some kind of rapprochement with the self-arising in respect of its mystery, integrity, continuity and intrinsic value. Different answers will produce different conceptions of environmental education, each expressing and conveying a different relationship towards nature.

NATURE'S VALUE AND THE AIMS OF ENVIRONMENTAL EDUCATION

In Chapter 3 I indicated how the Western tradition has encompassed a variety of attitudes towards nature during its history and how these have the capacity to influence strongly how nature is treated and investigated. Is it possible now to make headway on the question: What *ought* to be our attitude to nature? Given the issues raised above and the account of nature developed in the previous chapter, central to this question is the issue of whether—and in what sense—nature has *intrinsic value*, meaning by this phrase one of two things. First, it may mean what we value non-instrumentally, for itself, in the sense of the pleasure or satisfaction it gives of itself. As in this sense its existence is dependent on satisfying a valuer, I will refer to this as nature's *derivative intrinsic value*. Second, it may mean the value that attaches to nature itself for its own sake, that is, *independently* of how it may serve or satisfy human beings—even though its recognition may require such conscious beings. I will refer to this as its *inherent intrinsic value*. Both of these senses stand in contrast to nature having purely instrumental value—a means to ends that makes no reference to human satisfaction or respect in the experience of nature itself.

It is important to appreciate the precise relevance of these senses of nature's intrinsic value to environmental education, for it is easy both to underestimate and to overestimate their implications—and thus overlook the real points on which they have a purchase.

Let us begin with the supposition that nature has no *inherent* intrinsic value—the view attributed by Singer to the dominant Western tradition (discussed in Chapter 2). Given this stance, action that affects the natural environment will be weighed entirely in terms of how its consequences affect human self-interest. This will include any derivative intrinsic value ascribed to nature. On this view, presumably, environmental education will be concerned to elucidate the different ways in which human self-interest can be served (for example, long term or short term), *whose* self-interest (for example, the North's or the South's, producers' or consumers', corporations' or workers', current or future generations'), followed by developing knowledge and understanding of human action and its environmental consequences for such self-interest. This might include preparation for being proactive in terms of actively shaping the environment to suit us, as well as reactive in the sense of trying to minimise potential harm to us caused by previous attempts to exploit it. This, in turn, would seem to lead directly to the underlying issue of what counts as human flourishing, and to pose the question: What sort of environment do we want to live in? We might here note the imperious tone of this question—which is perfectly in keeping with a view that is setting up human welfare as the overriding moral value—and also that, as the question of what we desire in *our* environment becomes explicit, there is no serious questioning of the assumption that humankind constitutes the moral community.

If, however, we begin from the supposition that nature has inherent intrinsic value, the issues of environmental education take on a different complexion, and some are transformed. To begin with, the assumption that the overriding principle in making environmental decisions is what will best serve the interests of human beings will at least be open to challenge, and on occasion it may be compromised. Environmental education will attempt to make clear what will be 'in the interests' of non-human nature, even when this appears to be in conflict with the interests of humankind.

While this of course raises the question of what it is for non-human nature to have interests and how these could be identified, for present purposes we may grant that certain examples of human activity do not respect such interests—such as the slaughter of 307,000 harp seals for their pelts in Canada in 2002, or the bear farms in China where it is alleged that over 7,000 bears are held in vice-like cages and milked for their bile through crude metal catheters attached to their gall bladders (*International Fund for Animal Welfare Newsletter*, January 2002). Not to mention some of the farming techniques used in the UK in the production of eggs, poultry and veal.

Such a re-orientation has the important implication that it would require the marshalling of different sets of knowledge and understandings from those required strictly for the determination of human interests. For example, the complexity and fragility of organisms and ecosystems that are not perceived as directly relevant to human well-being (however that becomes defined) might be studied with as much alacrity as those that are. One result of this might be that a heightened awareness of the extent and subtlety of its organisation will in turn evoke or increase an appreciation of nature's inherent intrinsic value. But of equal or greater significance, membership of the moral community—that is, the community to whom we feel some moral obligation—would be extended to include all those aspects of nature taken to have inherent intrinsic worth. Furthermore, a variety of issues concerning what will *count* as the well-being of nature will need to be explored. For example, will the 'value bearing units' be individuals, populations, local ecosystems or one great organic ecosystem? What state(s) of nature constitute(s) its own 'fulfilment' or essence? How issues such as these are decided will have large implications for how things should be treated and the relative importance that should be attached to the welfare of human beings; and again in what sense—as individuals, in cultural terms, as a species, etc.?

Yet, as suggested earlier, we must be careful not to overstate the practical significance of delineating these two stances. There are two considerations that suggest that there may be some melding of the concerns listed under each. The first consideration is that of how human well-being is defined. A *rich* definition, which extends well beyond exclusively material and economic needs to include those that are aesthetic and spiritual, is likely to lead to a greatly enhanced sense of nature's worth through its capacity to satisfy—or at least contribute to meeting—this broader and deeper spectrum of human need. This may well, for many practical purposes, include many aspects of nature that are of concern to the inherent intrinsic value view—for example an appreciation of the otherness of wilderness, or of an inherent beauty in nature, or the valuing of biodiversity and the like. Second, given the complexity, current unpredictability and interdependence that apparently characterise both local and global ecosystems, longer-term human self-interest would itself require very widespread concern and investigation into the natural world in order that the best picture of what may affect human well-being might be achieved. Such a growing sense of humankind as an integral *part* of the natural community—and thus subject to its developmental nuances—has the potential to produce considerable concordance of interest between 'intrinsic' and 'extrinsic' views. Some have seen the growing perception of an alliance between what is in nature's interest and what is in the interest of human beings pragmatically as the most effective guarantee for nature's welfare in a world where the track record of human beings has been manifestly dominated by their self-interest.

Yet, it would be wrong to imagine that all of the concerns of the inherent intrinsic value view would be met by this enriched and enlightened version of human self-interest. For example, not *all* aspects of nature would be included. And what would happen when there was a perceived conflict of interest, as perhaps in the case of disease carrying animals? Take the case of the alleged transmission of bovine TB to livestock by badgers in the UK. From the inherent intrinsic value perspective, might not the welfare of badgers be too readily sacrificed to that of humans? This issue need not be expressed in extreme terms of *either* badgers *or* the spread of bovine TB. For example, a view that was not exclusively orientated around human self-interest might tolerate a higher degree of economic cost and human inconvenience in terms of changed farming practices, if it avoided the eradication of badger populations. Furthermore, even on the 'enriched' version of human self-interest, priorities, say, in research or the deployment of resources, ultimately would be determined by the perceived needs of humans only.

But perhaps the most serious reservation of all would be that at base an anthropocentric outlook would prevail. For those whose concern is the quality of our relationship with nature, this would remain a very significant drawback. It could even be the case that some (for example, those who do not believe that the end can always justify the means, or who see the quality of our attitude towards nature as an important *constituent* of the end), would prefer to sacrifice a degree of nature's immediate 'purely physical' welfare if at some point this was necessary for the furtherance of a 'right' attitude towards nature. For example, it might be argued that even if they are effective according to the scale of measurement of immediate physical outcome, we should reject highly managerial and/or restorationist policies because of the masterful stance towards nature that they express.

These, then, are some of the issues raised by the two perspectives on value. Having outlined their significance for the stance and content of environmental education, I now turn to the issue of whether it is plausible to maintain that nature possesses inherent intrinsic value.

IN WHAT SENSE DOES NATURE HAVE INHERENT INTRINSIC VALUE?

There are many who feel that nature is somehow imbued with inherent intrinsic value. For some this continues to have a religious foundation, as in the belief that nature is the expression of God, revealing his purpose. Indeed, as previously noted, the natural world is sometimes characterised as his 'body' (see, for example, McFague, 1993). This view clearly implies a value that may be independent of nature's ability to furnish human needs, although on some such accounts nature was created by God to do precisely this.

Yet there are others, such as some of the Romantics, who attribute inherent intrinsic value to nature that is not—or not only—derived in this way. What sense can we make of this claim? The main obstacle to its coherence seems to be the following: value is not something that simply exists 'out there' in nature, as physical properties are taken so to exist. Value, it is said, is not an internal property at all, but a *relational* property: the value something has is dependent on its relationship with some conscious being that values it. Value is thus in a certain sense *conferred* and only entities that function at a certain level of self-consciousness can confer value, see something *as* valuable. Now we currently believe that much, if not all, of non-human nature does not possess this level of consciousness and is thus unable to do this. Therefore any value that such aspects of nature have is not fully intrinsic, i.e., is not inherent within nature itself, but the result of human beings (or their mental 'equivalent') valuing it. If all such self-conscious entities were to disappear, nature would be left, but no valuing would be possible and therefore nature could no longer have value. Thus any intrinsic value ascribed to nature is not truly inherent—belonging to it independently of anything else—but is a product of human sensibility (perhaps even an individual human being's sensibility) and is always relative to it. Nature either does or does not have value, and the particular way it might have it, depends on something else that is external to it.

This view has been taken to have a particularly unfortunate consequence. If a 'valuer' is necessary to the existence of value, won't this always make the value of a thing a function of its meeting the needs of the valuer? Thus the valuer may value a beech tree in spring not for how they can use it (which would be overtly instrumental), but because its very presence gives them aesthetic pleasure. Derivative intrinsic value now appears to be implicitly instrumental—essentially nature is being valued for its use—for what it does for the valuer, rather than what it is in itself. Therefore, if the beech tree ceased to give them pleasure, they might no longer value it. Its 'intrinsic' value would evaporate with their change of disposition. Furthermore, while it might be said that the tree had certain 'value-adding properties' (maybe the aesthetic quality of its bark, its graceful shape, etc.), it is hard to see that there could be any logical or rational compulsion on a particular individual actually to view them as valuable, that is, accept them *as* value-adding. That is, ultimately there may be no compelling reason for rejecting their change of disposition. In which case the tree's intrinsic value appears fragile and potentially ephemeral. Thus the question is raised: do we not need something more solid than this upon which, for example, to base an environmental ethic—which would in turn inform environmental education?

There are a number of possible responses to this kind of objection in its severe dilution of intrinsicality. The first is to deny the subjectivist and relational account of intrinsic value by providing a plausible objectivist non-relational account. For example, could it not be argued that value could be inherently intrinsic in the sense that its production is internal to the thing itself—as we see in the way that a human values herself, has her own purposes? This traditional (that is, Enlightenment) ethic encourages us to see human beings as ends-in-themselves and while we tend to assume that this does not apply to most of non-human nature, some argue that this assumption needs to be reviewed. That human beings can, and on occasion *do*, view aspects of non-human—indeed, non-sentient—nature in this way is illustrated by the following account given by Holmes Rolston III:

> In the 1880s a tunnel was cut through a giant sequoia in what is now Yosemite National Park. Driving through the Wawona tree, formerly in horse and buggy and later by car, amused millions. The tree was perhaps the most photographed in the world. The giant blew over in the snow storms of 1968–69, weakened by the tunnel. Some proposed the Park Service cut another. But the rangers refused, saying that one was enough, and that this is an indignity to a majestic sequoia. It is better to educate visitors about the enormous size and longevity of redwoods, their resistance to fire, diseases, insect pests, better to admire what the stalwart tree is in itself. The comedy of drive-through sequoias perverts the best in persons who ought to be elevated to a nobler experience. But there is a deeper conviction; using trees for serious human needs can be justified; a silly enjoying of prime sequoias cannot. *It perverts the trees* (Rolston, 1999, p. 120, emphasis added).

Here would seem to be a case of valuing an aspect of nature not because it gives the valuer pleasure, but through a direct sense of, and respect for, the integrity of its 'otherness'. Of course, a certain pleasure may be experienced in its otherness, but in such a case it is not the experience of pleasure that lends it value, but recognition of its value that gives the experience of pleasure.

In this vein, Rolston holds that a plant as a living organism should be regarded as an axiological, evaluative system—exemplified by the tree that maintains an independent identity by posting a boundary between it and its environment; it grows, reproduces, spontaneously repairs its wounds and resists death. Using what he terms 'botanical standards', plants *care*. They care 'in the only form of caring available to them' (p. 120)—each plant defends its own life *per se* and objectively certain things are *valuable* to it for its survival. He writes:

> The physical state that the organism seeks, idealized in its programmatic [genetic] form, is a valued state. Every organism has a *good-of-its-kind*; it defends its own kind as a *good kind* . . . When humans encounter such living organisms, they become responsible for their behaviour toward them . . . [they] ought to take account of the consequences for other evaluative systems. We do have a responsibility to protect values, anywhere they are present and at jeopardy by our behaviour (Rolston, 1997, p. 122).

So the interesting question is raised about seeing aspects of non-human nature as objectively having their own ends that need to be respected, and possessing properties whose value may be recognised by humans, though they are not the source (conferrers) of it.

Alternatively, *pace* G. E. Moore, it may be argued that a thing may possess intrinsic value in the form of certain 'non-natural properties' that parallel its possession of natural properties, such as its shape and colour, etc., but that cannot be physically observed by the senses. For Moore, such non-natural properties, discerned by the intellect, reside within the thing itself and are no more dependent for their existence on something external to it than its physical properties are taken to be. Indeed these too, it might be argued, have to be perceived to become actualised: particular colours and shapes only exist for entities so constituted as to perceive them. In this sense, then, such values are also objective, and the warrant for taking account of them in the area of moral debate is as strong as the warrant for taking account of physical properties (such as shape and colour) in debate concerning the material world. If, in formal terms, such an intellectual intuitionist account of values is susceptible to problems concerning its metaphysical underpinning (for example, concerning the problem of giving an account of non-natural properties adequate to explain the character of their dependency on natural properties) and disagreements in intellectual perception, in phenomenological terms, and for reasons to be elaborated presently, it may yet have something to offer.

The second kind of response to the subjectivist-relational objection to objective intrinsic value is to accept both its subjectivist and relational elements, but to show that they are consistent with a non-arbitrary and non-fragile notion of intrinsic worth.

Robert Elliot (1997) attempts to develop an indexical account of intrinsic value that begins to address the charge of arbitrariness by positing a notion of non-moral properties upon which ascriptions of intrinsic value depend, which he terms 'value-adding properties'. These are aspects of a thing that, other things being equal, add to its overall value (and, indeed, the overall value of the universe). If these outweigh any value-subtracting qualities, the thing has (net) intrinsic value. Value-adding properties in the case of an ecosystem might be qualities like the richness and diversity of the life it supports, or the degree of its 'naturalness'. Elliot suggests that we can support a claim for the intrinsic value of something by specifying its value-adding properties and that the validity of the claim will be determined by reflecting upon the properties identified. But while this has the virtue of inviting deeper, more refined and focused reflection on nature's value, as it stands it hardly avoids the charge of arbitrariness and potential fragility; it simply moves the need for commitment and criteria for valuing further down the line of argument. We may still ask: why is X value-adding? How is it to be defended against those who might disagree that it is? It would appear that whether a property is value-adding remains a subjective/intuitive matter, or perhaps a matter of obtaining (by whatever means, including non-rational?) a level of inter-subjective agreement.

At one level, this kind of consequence is fully acceptable to Elliot who goes on to answer the question of what makes a property value-adding by connecting it to an attitudinal framework. In his 'indexical theory of intrinsic value' 'the property of being value-adding is identical with the property of standing in the approval relation to an attitudinal framework' (Elliot, 1997, p. 16). Intrinsic value is relativist in the sense of being naturalist (that is, not referring to a non-natural property) and subjectivist; it is *intrinsic-value-for-the-valuer* (p. 17). It is thus indexed to (and thus relativised to) an individual, and also to a time and to a possible world in which it is made. However, for Elliot, not just any attitude can be an adequate reference for the ascription of intrinsic value. The relevant attitudinal framework needs to be 'filtered' in various ways: it needs, for example, to be post-reflective, to meet certain standards of inference, and to be one that the holder would wish to persist into the future (thus countering to some extent concerns over ephemeralism).

Thus, Elliot supports a mind-dependent theory of intrinsic value, making it a relational property. But here he makes the seminal claim that while *meta-ethically* anthropocentric (for his subjectivism is both anthropogenic—no values without valuers—and indexed to the attitudes of individuals), it is not *normatively* anthropocentric, for the human mind can value things for themselves, for their own sake, as ends in themselves. Furthermore, in response to the concern over the fragmentation and insecurity of intrinsic value if it is conceived as dependent on subjective attitudes and the existence of valuers, Elliot argues that his subjectivist view of intrinsic value is *functionally* analogous to an objectivist view: it results in no practical difference to the assessment of value claims. He argues that whichever meta-ethical view one adopts, one would go through analogous procedures in debating and evaluating a claim—such as identifying and evaluating value-adding properties, checking the internal consistency of argument, referring to relevant empirical evidence, exciting and refining sensibility. That one participant understands this process meta-ethically in terms of comprehending moral facts and another as purely a matter of attitude adjustment makes no practical difference. The dynamics of the normative debate are basically the same—each participant makes the same dialogical moves. And if in the final analysis disagreement remained, this would be no easier to resolve on an objectivist account than it would be on a subjectivist account (pp. 23–41).

With regard to nature's intrinsic value, some value-adding properties to which environmental ethicists have drawn attention include the following: nature's beauty, diversity, richness, integrity, interconnectedness, variety, complexity, harmony, grandeur, intricacy and autonomy. But for Elliot the key property is that of being naturally evolved—the property of 'naturalness'. He surmises that it could simply be a brute fact about our attitudinal framework that this is why we value nature: 'At some point in the process of uncovering bases of value there will be a stopping point, beyond which nothing more can be said by way of accounting for the presence of value. Appeal to the property of being natural might be such a stopping point. But more can, I think, be said' (p. 59). Thus it is nature's otherness, its separateness and distinctness from creatures such as us, that is the basis of its intrinsic value. Nature is, in Stan Godlovitch's phrase, 'primordially non-artefactual' (p. 59). This can be crystallised in terms of the absence of intentionality in nature that stands it in opposition to the human world of culture and technology. This, combined with an appreciation of nature's aesthetic value that therefore also arises independently of intentional design, 'transforms the aesthetic value in question into the kind of aesthetic value that gives rise to moral value' (p. 61). I will return to the significance of the notion of nature being naturally evolved presently. First, since they would clearly have a bearing on the handling of discussion of nature's value in the educational context, I wish to identify some problems with Elliot's account of debates involving nature's intrinsic value.

Put simply, when someone says 'Wild nature has intrinsic value', she does not just mean that it has value for *her,* does she? She means *it* has value, and if someone else says it does not have value there is a substantive disagreement, not merely mutually bypassing expressions of preference that have to be reconciled only when some ulterior practical purpose, such as the need to formulate a common policy, requires it. The meaning of the intrinsicality of nature's value is part of understanding nature and of what would constitute an appropriate relationship to it. This is a crucial point for environmental education. Also, *contra* Elliot, one's meta-ethical view, however implicit, affects some aspects of the conduct of the debate; pursuit of truth is very different to conflict of subjective attitudes. The former involves a range of standards that reflect a certain humility before the facts; the latter is essentially a power struggle in which, therefore, a range of non-object-orientated strategies may legitimately be employed. In terms of the phenomenology of nature's value and the educational orientation it engenders, Moorean intuitionist objectivity seems a closer fit.

Furthermore, on a relational account such as Elliot's, are we not in danger of straying into the metaphysical magician's fallacy? We can only speak from within a form of life and it has been argued that within our form of life we experience nature and natural value as one, as self-arising. We may speculate that they are ontologically constituted by our personal attitudes, but we can no more experience them thus than we can experience a mountain or supernova as our construction, ourselves as their author. As with postmodernism, the founding distinction between the world and our response to it is in danger of being lost—which is not, of course, to deny that the world itself is relational and that we are bound up in it. What is the motive that provokes us to see everything as relational—that is, relational in such a way that *we set the agenda*? Might it again be the case that a language that reverberates with the will to power is holding sway here?

THE CONTINUITY OF NATURE AS A VALUE

I now return to Elliot's claim that nature as naturally evolved is central to our understanding of nature and its value. This clearly relates closely to the notion of nature's continuity as an aspect of nature as the self-arising, identified in the previous chapter.

In a discussion of the debate between environmental restorationists and conservationists, Elliot underlines the sense in which the *origin* of natural things can be an important element in our valuing of them (Elliot, 1995). He invites us to consider the argument often put up by those involved in resource extraction that they will be willing to restore the natural environment they destroy and that therefore no long-term loss of environmental value will result—indeed, it may be claimed that the restored environment may be an *improvement* on the original (for example, it may support greater biodiversity or be arranged in a way that is more aesthetically pleasing than the original). Clearly, this can present a strong challenge to conservationists who wish to defend an undisturbed natural environment. So what is wrong with it? Elliott argues that even if the restoration achieves all that it claimed (which empirically is hardly ever the case) there is an important element of value that will be lost: as he puts it, a special causal continuity with the past. He suggests that the policy of restoration involves the *faking* of nature, and that, in a way parallel to the discovery that what had been taken to be a Vermeer turns out to be a Van Meegaran, a loss of value is involved.

The central point is that the value of nature is not completely contained in what is sensibly present. *Origin* is an important consideration in the evaluation process and it certainly makes a difference to our feeling and valuing—even if the original were perfectly replicated—as to whether this woodland is actually a cunningly contrived ecological artefact in plastic replete with olfactory and other effects, artificially replanted following the destruction of the original, or the original stand which goes back hundreds of years. The element of direct contact with primeval nature unshaped by human hand—the element of authentic naturalness—is a value in itself, even though we sometimes have overriding reasons for destroying it. This neither denies that naturalness is often a matter of degree (there being little on the planet today that has not been affected by human activity in some way), nor does it require that we ascribe overriding value to everything that is natural (such as sickness and disease). It simply discloses that such naturalness is something we do in fact value, and that it is not irrational— or that it is no more irrational—for us to do so than to be concerned with the authenticity of a work of art.

Yet this argument may show that we value this quality of nature, it might be objected, but not that we are *justified* in doing so. But what sort of justification could be given here that did not turn nature's value into an instrumental value, or at least a substantially anthropocentric value as in ascribing to it aesthetic or 'spiritual renewal' value? That is to say, is not this requirement to give some further justification for a value that we do in fact hold another example of modern rationality exhibiting its own instrumental orientation—its inherent calculative motive? Why should we allow it to impose this orientation on our understanding of nature? Why should we accept its dictate that our valuing is inadequate if it cannot be formulated in calculative terms? This sort of humanist rationalist objection simply begs the issue at stake. All fundamental intrinsic values rightly are resistant to this requirement and properly demand that rationality be subservient to what they intuit—helping to reveal them more fully by working *within* their ambience. Not that rationality may not also be able to show up relationships (including conflicts) between different intuitions, but it only does this authentically when it works *within* the motives and meanings of the intuitions it claims to explicate, rather than imposing its own.

It seems to me that Elliot is right to point out that investigating just what would be involved in a *full* restoration could be seminal both in exposing the hollowness of the rhetoric of those who claim to be able readily to achieve it, and also in revealing how our appreciation of an environment can be enhanced by a deepened understanding of its history and of the subtlety and complexity (and maybe fragility) of the ecosystems it is habitat to. This has clear implications for environmental education.

To return now to the question posed at the beginning of this chapter: why should we feel that something valuable is lost with the human-caused destruction of the trout stream? An at least partial answer is now presented: nature's integrity, including its 'special causal continuity', is central to its intrinsic value. There is something ultimately 'true' or 'right' about it. We both recognise—feel—that the disappearance of the integrity of the self-arising is a loss and understand that, ultimately, this integrity also lies behind our sense of our own lives. Without this sense of an independent reality as a point of reference, our 'understanding' spins into the free-floating vacuity of a hyper-reality.

Thus, at a certain level and modulated in a certain way, Moorean objectivism rings true. In our everyday perception of things we do not understand them purely in terms of their physical (natural) properties. Phenomenologically, they have a meaning that is expressive of, and implicated in, a web of values that are part-constitutive of our form of sensibility, through which we have awareness of the real. In this sense, and *contra* Adorno, the notion of a thinking commissioned by things themselves is perfectly intelligible. If such a thinking is not politically innocent, neither need it be politically culpable. In their 'purely empirical' aspect, we can distinguish between descriptions and misdescriptions, and so here is a perfectly valid sense in which things 'commission' thinking (but do not determine it, since other valid descriptions are always possible). But also as participants in our grown form of sensibility—which I have argued to be non-optional and thus a source of non-arbitrariness—things proper are pervaded by values and these make a vital call on us. Speaking of 'the real presence of normative measures in nature', Joseph Grange suggests: 'Humans need to be encouraged to recover this sense of the normative measures embedded in their spatial surroundings. Without it they are truly without symbolic reference. They are effectively lost in space' (Grange, 1999, p. 101).

The issue of disposing ourselves so that we may be sensitive to such normative measures—that is to say, the issue of our epistemic stance—is the business of the next chapter.

Chapter 7. Nature and Knowing

We are nature seeing nature. We are nature with a concept of nature.
Nature weeping. Nature speaking of nature to nature (*Woman and Nature:
The Roaring Inside Her*, Susan Griffin, 1978).

In the preceding two chapters I have attempted to elaborate a sense of
nature that even though for the most part invisible—that is, not
foregrounded in modern consciousness—informs our understanding of
the reality to which we constantly make tacit reference in our everyday
intercourse with the world. As such, we would rightly expect nature in this
sense to have significant implications not only for how we regard our
relationship with it—a relationship that I have argued to be the pivotal
issue for environmental education—but also for the gamut of metaphysical notions in which I have previously argued education as a whole to be
embedded. It is now time to explore such implications with respect to one
of these notions, which, itself, frequently has been regarded as a central
goal of the educational enterprise: the acquisition of knowledge. I will
begin by providing a backcloth to this discussion in the form of a brief
sketch of three recent influential positions on the issue of knowledge in
education. I will then review some approaches to knowledge and knowing
that nature as the self-arising prompts, drawing comparisons with what
appears to be the current orthodoxy in education.

EDUCATION AND THE DECLINE OF KNOWLEDGE

For many years—say, from the late 1960s through to late 1980s—
philosophy of education was dominated by a liberal-rationalist paradigm
expressed in the very influential writing of thinkers such as Richard Peters,
Paul Hirst and Israel Scheffler. At the kernel of this orthodoxy was an
essentially Enlightenment conception of knowledge structured by what
was taken to be a universally applicable rationality. Thus, for example,
Peters characterised the proper stance of the rationalist thinker as that of
the 'generalised other', identity being 'as irrelevant as time and place' in
the rational estimation of things (Peters, 1974, p. 425). Controversially,
Hirst claimed that his rational 'Forms of Knowledge' were pivotal to the
articulation of all developed experience, and Scheffler developed a notion
of teaching that would respect the rationality of the (universal) student.
Throughout, and not withstanding the recognition in Hirst's 'Forms' of,
at one level, there being different kinds of rationality, an underlying monolithic rationality was in play—a rationality articulated around
publicly agreed standards and procedures for the acquisition and testing
of truth. Those forms of rationality in which these public standards and

procedures could be most clearly demonstrated inevitably enjoyed a higher status, and it was therefore no surprise that Peters regarded science as 'the supreme example of reason in action' and the physical sciences as 'perhaps the finest product that yet exists of the sustained and controlled imagination of the human race' (Peters, 1972, p. 211). And one of the great virtues of science on this view was its excellence in achieving that kind of transcendence of the present that is the *raison d'être* of rationality:

> The most obvious and all-pervading feature of reason is surely the transcendence of the this, the here and the now . . . Explanation, planning, justification, all share in common this obvious characteristic. They connect what is, what is done and what is to be done with the past and the future by means of *generalizations and rules* (ibid. p. 210).

Thus in his development of the genre, Charles Bailey (1983) entitled his exposition of liberal educational principles *Beyond the Present and the Particular: A Theory of Liberal Education*. To be sure, the heyday of such liberal education theory is now past, but it is not without continuing influence both in the sense that there remain those who continue to espouse it in some form and in that its legacy is still to be found in justifications for a broad rationality-based curriculum in Western democracies.

In previous writing I have criticised the rationalist valorisation of this motive to generalise—and to generalise in publicly agreed ways—from the perspective of the authenticity of the individual (see, for example, Bonnett, 1986, 1994). Presently, I will explore ways in which the view of nature developed in preceding chapters invites another set of reservations both with regard to the aspiration so to generalise, and the kind of education to which it leads. But first let me indicate the other two positions to be considered here.

There was a variety of causes of the (relative) demise of liberal educational theory, some philosophical, such as criticisms of its seeming premise of an ahistorical or universal rationality, others pragmatic. I will go into none of these here. Suffice it to say that another strand of Enlightenment metaphysics began to hold sway more powerfully in educational policy than the pursuit of rational truth for its own sake: the project of utility—and with it efficiency and productiveness. In the ever more competitive global market in which national and cultural barriers are eroded to the point of extinction, the education system takes on an ever more instrumental mien. And the educational curriculum becomes ever more technologised. This takes many interrelated forms ranging from educational institutions increasingly being structured and managed along quasi-industrial lines (itself something of a curiosity in a generally post-Fordist age) to the de-professionalisation of teachers as operatives whose sole area of discretion is with means not ends—and increasingly not even with the former.

In tandem with this runs an impoverishment of our conception of educational knowledge and what is involved in coming to know. Not only is the curriculum effectively narrowed around those subjects perceived to be of greatest economic utility compared with that breadth of knowledge sought by a liberal education: it undergoes a qualitative change. Sustained engagement with content becomes replaced with a preoccupation with abstract 'skills' and information-processing strategies, lent impetus by the transformations that ICT is making of the acquisition and understanding of knowledge in society at large and in education in particular. This emaciated—literally, abstract bones with little flesh—conception of knowledge lends itself to being fragmented into convenient learning modules structured according to pre-specified content and measurable objectives. Hardly much place here for a genuine engagement with the subtleties of unique situations and issues embedded in the rich contents of developed bodies of knowledge and understanding, or for listening to the call of what is incipient within the areas of thinking that they open up—intimations of the yet unknown that lead thought on, and a determination to follow wherever this leads. Elsewhere, I have argued that thinking, understanding and knowing in this demanding sense are quite left behind by a preoccupation with pre-formed and pre-ordering abstract thinking skills and strategies (Bonnett, 1995).

Finally, we have strands of an incipient postmodernism in education. While showing through increasingly strongly in educational theory, views associated with this stance of general incredulity over grand narratives have yet to be *self-consciously* taken up in practice to any marked degree. But, implicit in the above-mentioned trends towards modularisation of learning and content-independent skills, it may be possible to detect a certain utilitarian fragmentation and dispersal of knowledge grounded in grand narratives, and certainly the ascendance of ICT in education promises much in this respect. For example, Sherry Turkle, a great advocate of ICT, has argued that Internet experiences encourage 'models of psychological well-being that are in a meaningful sense postmodern'. She sees them as demonstrating the constructed nature of reality, self and other, and as leading to a view of ourselves as 'fluid, emergent, decentred, multiplicitous, flexible and ever in process' (Turkle, 1996, p. 263). And more explicit practical restructurings of education reflecting postmodernist views may be on the way. Of course as a theoretical position, post-modernism purports to be less a prescription and more a documenta-tion of what may already be underway in society at large—though these two aspects are likely to render mutual support. As we have seen (in Chapter 4), the basic position on knowledge to which postmodernism is drawn is to suggest that no one approach to it or version of it should be privileged because there is no description that can be checked against a reality that is not already mediated by other descriptions. Thus truth in the sense of revealing or reflecting underlying reality becomes illusory and the very idea of knowledge becomes questionable—claims to it acquiring a repressive, imperialist or chauvinistic countenance. Education becomes metaphysically pluralist and unrooted, the pursuit of truth becoming replaced by the pursuit of whatever sounds more interesting or facilitates coping.

In terms of the rough sketch given above, it may be fair to summarise the current position of state education—in the UK especially—as follows: it continues to pay a degree of lip service to the ideals of liberal education, implements utilitarian education and, despite a continued overt commitment to the rigour of traditional subject disciplines, increasingly reflects a postmodernist disdain for an education rooted in systemic beliefs in 'human nature' and the worth, or possibility, of enduring truths. All is increasingly made subservient to the ambition of remaining current in a constantly changing global market economy—to the delivery of relevant and often essentially ephemeral skills, techniques and attitudes, whatever these turn out to be. Thus—and not without a certain irony, given the claims of the 'knowledge economy'—on this brief sketch we are presented with a picture of a steady decline of knowledge in education. It begins with a degree of breadth and rigour but with a focus on disengaged generalisation, moves on to a further degree of abstraction and an increase in its utilitarian and technological character, and threatens to end in the abandonment of systemic human truths altogether in favour of the vagaries of whatever is 'more interesting' or 'enables us to cope', primarily in consumerist market economic terms.

How does nature as the self-arising position us with regard to these (rather starkly portrayed) views and the motives that energise them? Indeed, if we take nature as the self-arising how is it to be known authentically?

KNOWING NATURE

The orthodoxy in curriculum terms is that we come to know nature through science. For example, in the National Curriculum for England and Wales we encounter a wide range of statements relating to nature in the science programmes of study and virtually nowhere else. This is not to say that the possibility of learning about nature in other curriculum areas is excluded, but that science is clearly assumed to be the primary discipline that provides the natural home for such enquiry. Furthermore, reference to National Curriculum programmes of study makes it clear that the science envisaged from the beginning is based pretty much on the canons of classical (that is, modern, Enlightenment) science, which is preoccupied with causal explanations and measurement, and whose basic experimental interventionist character was enunciated by Francis Bacon. (See, for example, the programmes of study for Key Stages One and Two in the *National Curriculum Handbook for Primary Teachers in England*, Department for Education and Employment and Qualifications and Curriculum Authority, 1999, pp. 78 and 83.) The question arises then as to the appropriateness of this assumption that such science is an adequate vehicle for understanding nature. In the light of previous analysis a number of reservations spring to mind.

The first concern is its aggressive interventionist motives, arising from its history and the cultural milieu in which it was born, which viewed nature largely as something to be overcome, tamed and made servant to human purposes. These remain implicit in much *school* science as a set of inherent unexamined prejudices. Such motives are intimately connected to a rationalistic objectification of things and a preoccupation with causal explanations in universalistic abstract terms, terms that lead to a loss of cultural dimensions—the latter, as we shall see, being particularly significant in the context of environmental education. Perhaps most fundamental, and a powerful expression of its masterful instrumental motives, scientific accounts give abstracted snapshots in which, to use the vocabulary of a previous chapter, the 'things' of nature are transmuted into 'objects'. Thus the physical and biological sciences give a very partial knowledge both in this respect and in the fact that what is permitted to appear is heavily predetermined both by the scientific outlook in general and by the specific hypotheses or theories in operation in particular contexts.

It must be emphasised here that I am not arguing that science has nothing of importance to offer. On the contrary, it has become more important than ever in order to monitor the effects of human activity on the biosphere in ways and at levels that lie beyond what may be apparent to other kinds of knowing. And of course, our everyday as well as our more 'elevated' understandings of nature throughout are infused with scientific views. Rather, it is that learners need to be made aware of science's prejudices and its partiality in revealing nature when nature is presented from within a scientific perspective—including, where appropriate, the influence of vested government and commercial interests. Clearly, here, one must beware of simply indulging a wearisome re-iteration of criticisms that have a purchase only on a highly positivistic and instrumental caricature of science, but sadly much school science has the character of what Thomas Kuhn termed 'routine science'; it has yet to reflect more organic approaches, which, for example, rather than aspiring to the reductivism of a Grand Unified Theory or The Theory of Every-thing, see everything as, say, part of a fifteen billion year phe-nomenon in which, following the 'big bang', the radical unity of the original one is expressed in the irreducible diversity of the many. Put more modestly, it has, for example, yet to fully comprehend the deep artificiality of laboratory observations and the understanding of the natural world that they give.

The main point, however, in terms of the overall theme being developed is the following: how we know nature constitutes a highly significant aspect of the character of our dwelling and in order to take on the challenge of re-thinking this we need to consider the possibility of overcoming an essentially abstracted, disengaged approach to nature in education. This suggests that we perhaps need to rehabilitate the notion of 'knowledge by acquaintance' into the curriculum. But we must do this not in the manner of Russell's (1959) distinction between direct knowledge of sense-data and knowledge of conceptualised objects through descrip-tion, but rather in the way that a contrast can be drawn between *objects* and *things*, as previously characterised, and where the character of the acquaintanceship is more akin to the sense in which we may become acquainted with a person. Here the notion of acquaintance suggests not so much a knowledge of objectively verifiable truths about them (though it may certainly include this) but rather a direct, intimate, tacit knowledge that *affects* us—and that, perhaps, is closer to the Biblical sense of 'know' as a relatively unmediated experience of things. It follows that such knowledge may not be fully articulable because of its intense particularity and therefore non-generalisable features. In other words we seek an enriched, vitalised, sense of knowledge by acquaintance of nature, something of the essential poetic character of which is suggested by Henry Thoreau: 'Live in each season as it passes; breathe the air, drink the drink, taste the fruit, and resign yourself to the influences of each . . . Open all your pores and bathe in all the tides of Nature, in all her streams and oceans, at all seasons . . . Grow green with spring, yellow and ripe with autumn' (Thoreau, 1962, Vol. 1, pp. 394–395).

Undoubtedly science provides a certain access to nature, albeit of a reductionist kind, but there are reasons for not *privileging* the access it provides. For example, why should the knowledge of nature that it enables—a knowledge ever-increasingly articulated mathematically—be regarded as 'truer' or more authentic than, say, the knowledge achieved through the experience of helming a sailing boat in which one is acutely alert to, and in harmony with, the subtle nuances of wave and breeze? Here one *feels* directly the sheer power and sublime delicacy of nature. Perhaps a focus on such experience opens one avenue to the re-thinking of dwelling.

LEARNING FROM NATURE: A SPECIAL WAY OF KNOWING?

One interesting outcome of highlighting the need for a right relationship with nature is the view of knowledge and learning that follows from this. If nature is conceived as the self-arising, then dominant views of knowledge and learning that operate on the basis of essentially static representations of the world become inadequate. They occlude the ontological mysteriousness of nature and its essential fluidity.

One aspect of a kind of knowing that is more authentic to nature, so understood, is nicely illustrated by Rupert Ross' account of what was involved in an eleven-year apprenticeship as a fishing guide on a large lake in Northern Ontario (Ross, 1992, cited in Rogers, 2000). He describes how experienced guides were able to decide in which of the various locations on the lake the fish would be feeding on a particular day, but could only explain their knowledge in terms of 'hunches' and 'feelings'. They could not rationally elucidate their knowledge; it would permit of no reasoned backtracking, yet it allowed them reliably to *experience* (that is, not simply to predict) how things would be in different locations without being there. Ross describes this knowledge as a result of a very complex and condensed form of reasoning in which the memory images of previous experiences arise *in their own order* based on *their own emotional force and content*. The knowledge consists in a reliving of such experiences and the conclusions seem to create themselves such that: 'What had to be learned could not be expressed easily, if at all, in words; each person had to immerse himself in the enterprise and develop his own skills'. On this view, the sort of knowledge of nature provided by science is seriously distorting:

> With our quantifying science we have learned to see things, to understand things, as distinct from their constant change, from their *life*. We say 'the barometric pressure is X', when in fact we have frozen the life out of it for the purpose of measurement. It sits as a concept in our minds, separated from dynamism, from constant change. And thus we separate ourselves from feeling that life and from being able to know things through life (Ross, 1990, p. 82).

There are clear parallels here with Nietzsche's complaints of the ossifying effects of conceptual thought, and certainly knowing nature in the sense with which we are here concerned will be a complex, emotional, local, *dialogical* process. There is a long tradition of those who testify to the illumining effects on their thinking of entering into a more reciprocal relationship with nature. A recent example is provided by David Abram, who describes how he was held entranced by the web-spinning of small spiders at the entrance to a cave in which he was sheltering from the first storm of the Bali monsoon season:

> suddenly I realised that there were *many* overlapping webs coming into being, radiating out at different rhythms from myriad centres poised – some higher, some lower, some minutely closer to my eyes and some farther – between the stone above and the stone below.

> I sat stunned and mesmerized before this ever-complexifying expanse of living patterns upon patterns, my gaze drawn like a breath into one converging group of lines, then breathed out into open space, then drawn down into another convergence. The curtain of water had become utterly silent – I tried at one point to hear it, but could not. My senses were entranced. I had the distinct impression that I was watching the universe being born, galaxy upon galaxy (Abram, 1999, p. 34).

Is this merely some frivolous play of the imagination? In the spirit of Rorty's postmodernism, perhaps a 'more interesting description', but from the point of view of reality a worthless froth? Should experience of this kind form any part of serious nature education?

From such experiences Abram claimed to have learned of:

> the intelligence that lurks in nonhuman nature, the ability that an alien form of sentience has to echo one's own, to instil a reverberation in oneself that temporarily shatters habitual ways of seeing and feeling, leaving one open to a world all alive, awake, and aware. Its was from such small beings that my senses first learned of the countless worlds within

worlds that spin in the depths of this world that we commonly inhabit, and from them that I learned that my body could, with practice, enter sensorially into these dimensions (pp. 34–35).

As a result of such a transformation of perception he became a student of subtle differences and attended in a new way to natural phenomena such that, for example, the song of birds became 'no longer just a melodic background to human speech, but meaningful speech in its own right, responding to and commenting on events in the surrounding earth' (p. 35). And what do we *learn* from such engagement? It might be argued that we learn how to be in the world, to find a home in it.

Whatever else, here, at least, is a well-drawn example of an appreciation of the epistemological mystery, continuity and integrity of self-arising nature which the scientific mindset does not simply ignore, but attempts to invalidate. And thus the fundamental question is raised as to what nature 'really' is and how it should affect our perceptions and sense of underlying reality. On the face of it, it is less than self-evident that the interpretation of these issues implicit in modern science is either more true or more helpful in terms of developing an orientation of mind appropriate to burgeoning environmental issues. At any rate, it remains clear that the fuller engagement with nature exemplified above is only partly conscious and that it is largely, if not completely, occluded by abstract, discursive, conventionally academic discourse. Could such an account be suggestive not only of an educationally forgotten way of understanding nature, but of educational learning in a broader sense? As Jim Cheney puts this,

> Missing in modern conceptions of knowledge is a sense of active and reciprocal communication with the nonhuman world. On an older understanding, knowledge emerges from a conversation between world and person, and our human part in the genesis of knowledge in its most essential aspect, is to prepare ourselves ethically and spiritually for the reception of knowledge (Cheney, 1999, pp. 141–142).

How different is this orientation to that of Kant's judge and Bacon's inquisitor, where the active knowing subject interrogates what it has set up as passive objects determined by human interests, and where, essentially, the acquisition of knowledge becomes a monologue rather than a conversation—nature being required to put in an appearance in accordance with a set of categories that have been previously decided. From the current perspective, a curiously constipated exercise!

TRADITIONAL ECOLOGICAL KNOWLEDGE

Clearly there are strong similarities in the above account with aspects of what has been termed 'traditional ecological knowledge'. I have previously (Chapter 1) cautioned against thinking that we can assimilate the knowledge and understanding of non-Western culture into our own in a perfectly straightforward way. But it may be that elements of the character of indigenous knowledge can resonate with Western consciousness in a way that helps us to retrieve ways of knowing that we possess but which are now seriously underplayed, if not completely occluded in education. The various definitions of traditional ecological knowledge reveal certain strong interrelated features. (See, for example the definitions provided by Berkes, 1993; Grenier, 1998; Johnson, 1992; Studley, 1998; Warren, 1991, usefully gathered in Reid, Teamey and Dillon, 2002.) First, such knowledge is the result of an historical continuity in resource-use practices built up over generations living in close contact with natural systems. Second, it is unique and local, having developed around the specific conditions of a group of people indigenous to a particular bio-geographic area. It therefore contrasts with the international knowledge generated by universities, multinational business corporations, etc. Third, it is dynamic in nature, bearing the imprint of an ever-ongoing responding to the minutiae of local change. Fourth, it is integrative of the life of the community, forming the basis for natural resource management, agriculture, food preparation, health care, education and so forth. There are no *disparate* disciplines within it. Fifth, it is handed down by cultural transmission, often orally and through ritual, thus reflecting the knowledge of the body as well as the mind.

By definition then, because of its thoroughly local character, one cannot simply apply its content to other contexts—particularly to that of modern Western societies whose techno-economic situation is so different. But the conditions under which traditional ecological knowledge develops and the general values and qualities it expresses may be suggestive in other contexts, particularly in its approaches to learning and the kinds of knowledge that are given high status, as well as, of course, in its orientation towards nature. As we shall see, in some senses there are strong resonances with the 'action competence' approach to environmental education championed by the long-running European Environmental and Schools Initiatives (ENSI) programme to be examined later in Chapter 10.

Seminal to the present argument is the way that traditional ecological knowledge highlights a degree of identification with its object. This contrasts strongly with the disengagement both from its object and the subjectivity of the knower that is valorised by Western rationality. A view of knowing that celebrates subjective response and is directly experiential eschews the abstract perspective of the 'generalised other' and the consequent possibility of disciplines that atomise knowledge into discrete areas of enquiry that find it hard to speak to each other and that insulate facts from values. It asks us to consider the value of a knowledge that is existentially embedded in the social, cultural and moral tradition in which it arises; to be shaped by, and to express commitment to, a local ecological system over a sustained period of time; to exhibit patience and humility in the face of that which is both 'other' and intimately felt. In other words, a way of knowing that listens to what is near at hand, immediately before it, but not simply as some isolated occurrence, rather as *organically* embedded in (rather than abstractly related to) the rest of life and the environment which is its home. In other words, a way of knowing that senses the immanent in the particular.

ATTENTIVENESS

Something of the relationship to nature that this view reflects is to be found in Richard Smith's (1998) exposition of a notion of 'attentiveness'. His account suggests that the kind of attunement alluded to above is not altogether unfamiliar to the Western mind and need not involve high degrees of mysticism. Indeed it may be found to inhabit a wide range of everyday activities. For example—and in somewhat Heideggerian vein— he suggests it may be found in the activity of a craftsman who has developed a feel—in a certain sense, a love—for his material and works with it in a way which respects and responds to its own properties. He uses the term 'attentiveness' to denote that careful perception of things in which the demands of 'the insistent, selfish ego' are put aside, and in which we 'exercise patience, determine to see things justly, and refuse the consolations of fantasy' (p. 179). In such attentiveness the small contingent details of ordinary life and the natural world may be loved and respected. For Smith, this does not require a mystical neo-Romantic merging of mind with nature, but rather involves what he refers to as a sense of the standards implicit in self-understanding and self-mastery, testing one's actions against the internal goods of an activity and against what constitutes the genuine mutual flourishing of self and nature. In this way of relating to things we seek the good that we are able to realise *through* the action and not as a separate independently identifiable aim. Thus the good farmer does not cultivate his land with an eye only to short or middle-term profit, irrespective of harm done to wildlife. Greed would harm not only the land but also his soul, for it pulls against traditional agrarian virtues such as 'prudence, thrift, a certain steadiness – in terms of which he understands himself and his place in the world' (p. 175). And what can be said of the activity of such a farmer can be said of many another if approached in the right spirit.

But what are these 'standards' and from what exactly do they emanate? The problem here is that without some further characterisation of the reality in which they are taken to operate, notions such as 'seeing things justly', 'self-understanding', 'self-mastery', 'internal goods' and 'flourishing' become highly contestable.

Perhaps a paradigm case of such attentiveness would be the idealised relationship between mother and child in which high degrees of intuitive sensitivity to the needs of the infant are present and in which a certain reciprocity of feeling and satisfaction develop. Transferred to interaction with the world in general, the criterion of such attentiveness seems to be something like the mutual life-fulfilling quality of our working relationship with things. But is even this heightened notion of 'attentiveness' sufficiently qualified to sustain the kind of non-instrumental relationship with nature that Smith seeks to establish? Does the notion not gain much of its power from the assumption of certain unacknowledged values, values that remain hidden from critical scrutiny? For example, could not a farmer, say, display just such attentiveness, in terms of what Smith has so far made explicit, in the running of his battery farm? Could he not be constantly and responsively attending to the egg-laying potential of his chickens? He *need* not be motivated by greed (which it could be argued would not be compatible with his flourishing), but perhaps by an appreciation of the fitness for purpose of machinery and system, the beauty of its efficiency in contributing to a great enterprise of providing the population with high quality produce, the opportunities it provides for ingenious modifications and so forth. The question is: in what sense can 'nature' make demands on him and why should the farmer see himself as part of nature in *spiritual* terms? That is, why on this account should he attend to *nature*?

While from the perspective of the current argument Smith's account is helpful both in beginning to show how a transition from indigenous ways of knowing to modern Western contexts may be made and in raising the idea of attentiveness as a formal element in a rethought dwelling, it leaves the crucial issue of the substantial values that need to underpin the account unaddressed. That is to say that, notwithstanding its reverse intention, it is in danger of continuing to reflect that kind of disengagement and abstraction from particular realities that so characterises the rationality of Enlightenment humanism, leaving the important notion of 'attentiveness' open to appropriation by views to which one imagines Smith to be opposed.

At this point, however, I would like to refer to another of its strengths. Many of Smith's examples highlight a consideration that is too rarely addressed in the academically orientated (even if also highly instrumental) education of the West: the significance of the body in knowledge.

EMBODIED KNOWLEDGE

It is often overlooked, the knowledge that we possess through bodily contact with the world. In such awareness, knowledge of the self-arising may be particularly well preserved because here it is less susceptible to abstract generalisation and objectification. In our bodily intercourse with the world the abstract idea plays a less dominant role, we engage with the world less through an ordering cognition and more through a responsive *sensing*, as say when we feel the quality of the resilience of this piece of grass underfoot or the quality of resistance of a particular piece of wood to the chisel. It is constantly reflected in how we handle implements such as spade, paintbrush or fountain pen; in the casting of a fishing line, feeling just when to strike and how to play a fish; in leaning into a corner on a motorbike; in adjusting oneself to the rhythm of a cantering horse; in the setting of sails to catch a fickle wind. Here we have a vast realm of knowledge that is rarely reflected or respected in the conventional school curriculum, yet that connects us with what is self-arising in all that is around us. In John Passmore's words, 'Only if men [*sic*] can first learn to look sensually at the world will they come to care for it. Not only look at it, but to touch it, smell it, taste it' (Passmore, 1980, p. 189). The movement towards an intimate acquaintanceship with nature requires the development of certain feelings of mutuality towards it. It involves a deep appreciation of, and celebration of, the individuality of embodied things, an appreciation of the embodied by the embodied. That is to say both knower and known are implicitly understood as unique sites from which each is itself, as contrasted with a perception of generalised objects by a generalised viewer, the view from nowhere.

At its deepest level such knowing, which apprehends the other as truly other and not essentially as a vehicle to meet or oppose our desires, can rightly be construed as involving a kind of love. Thus Iris Murdoch has suggested that: 'Art and morals are, with certain provisos . . . one. Their essence is the same. The essence of both of them is love. Love is the perception of individuals. Love is the extremely difficult realization that something other than oneself is real. Love, and so art and morals, is the discovery of reality' (Murdoch, 1959, p. 51). In similar vein, Marilyn Frye's (1983) contrast between the arrogant eye and the loving eye expresses that transcendence of the self (which is yet an affirmation of the self) that is required if the reality of particular things is to be engaged:

> The loving eye knows the independence of the other . . . It is the eye of one who knows that to know the seen, one must consult something other than one's own will and interests and fears and imagination. One must look at the thing. One must look and listen and check and question . . . The science of the loving eye would favor The Complexity Theory of Truth . . . and presuppose The Endless Interestingness of the Universe (Marilyn Frye, in McFague, 1993, p. 52).

We have perhaps become more sensitive to the need for such a knowing in our relationships with other human beings, becoming more aware of a need to view individuals not simply as representatives of gender, race, or body type etc., but each as uniquely placed—experiencing the world through a unique body, uniquely sited. But there is still a long way to go, and often such sensitivity is overridden by convenient stereotypes. For us the challenge may be to extend this attitude towards the natural world as a whole, for the self-arising cannot reveal itself to the eye that primarily seeks to organise, to manage and to manipulate.

Yet all of this must, of course, be understood as occurring within a form of sensibility with its own horizons of significance. I am not implying a totally naïve—in the sense of unmediated—apprehension of some pristine reality. There is clearly a reciprocal relationship between human motives and the disclosure of otherness. This means that, *contra* the scientific materialism that, in A. N. Whitehead's words, sees nature as 'dull' and 'colourless', 'merely the hurrying of material, endlessly, meaninglessly' (Whitehead, 1985, p. 69), all things have value in that they are always encountered in a world of human significances, and in that they are condensations of that world that both gather it and open it up. The car that I drive and the mountain that I behold are instantiations—one might say 'nodes'—of an infinitely rich web of significances, and in observing, using and contemplating them, I gain entrance to, and participate in, that world.

As previously argued, from the beginning such a world of gathering things is imbued with values. In this sense value naturalism is true: everything comes with a value that is in a certain sense its own, for it belongs to it as the particular thing that it is, including when appropriate its instrumental function (but not *because of* its instrumental function). But this can still leave open the question of appropriate action, for this may require the weighing of different values in different contexts. In such circumstances the naturalistic fallacy stands: from the fact that something is the case, by virtue of that alone, one cannot necessarily infer that it ought to be the case. But often our direct intuition of a situation can decide the issue for us. Such is the nature of primordial human space. This is not to say that we should simply allow ourselves to be carried along by whatever happens to strike us at first glance, but that full and direct intuition of our situation should not be systematically overridden by generalising calculative inference. And natural space itself can welcome and it can forbid; it separates and it holds together. As an expression of the self-arising, it always has its own (subtly changing) *meaning*, such that, perhaps, as Joseph Grange notes: 'Surprise is the general reaction of the attentive walker in natural space' (Grange, 1997, p. 96).

Overall, this is suggestive of an understanding that is essentially a 'standing under'—a being held in the sway of—in a manner that is receptive-responsive, wondering and openly curious, that is celebratory, that intuits the wholeness of things in their many-sidedness and that stays with them in their inherent mysteriousness. That is to say a way of knowing, acquaintanceship, that allows itself to be vulnerable rather than seeking mastery.

And why—*in educational terms*—is such an intimate acquaintanceship with natural space significant? Because, in its awareness of the self-arising, it reveals the standard for the real and intimates what is involved in whole-hearted engagement. Educational learning and knowledge need to reflect this. They need to follow the contours of, and accept the demands of, that space that is primordial in our understanding of the world and ourselves. They must be sensitive to the invitations for engagement that it offers and therefore to the norms for valuing and understanding that it provides. Such an account reasserts the value of both direct intuitive engagement and understanding, and learning that is continuous and organic rather than modular and essentially atomistic—the latter being the common trend in the curricula of schools, further education and universities.

GLOBALISM THROUGH LOCALISM

It would in many ways be natural to assume that, given the picture that ecology presents of the biosphere as ultimately one ecosystem (that is, a vast web of interconnected and interdependent entities and phenomena), the kind of knowledge that will best equip us to understand our situation will be global. If we are to become aware of the consequences of our actions on the environment through their many ramifications throughout the web, we need a knowledge that is 'far reaching' both geographically and temporally. In contrast to the view developed above, this seems to assert the importance of knowledge of a basically abstract and theoretical kind, precisely such as that provided by international scientific enquiry. I have previously noted how this academic canon places emphasis on the discursive rationality of the scientific disciplines to show the way forward and represents the orthodoxy in the study of the environment in academic institutions. However, in the light of previous argument, it is no surprise to find that such a view has its opponents. They argue that such a global systems approach is defective both because it is impossible—the relevant matters are too subtle and complex to be adequately encapsulated by any theory—and because it underplays the value of, and stands in the way of, the regaining of an intimate relationship with our local context. Both of these objections relate closely to the argument that knowledge of nature as the self-arising requires a certain intimate acquaintanceship with unique situations and thus resists translation into abstract universals. Wendell Berry puts it thus:

> Properly speaking, global thinking is not possible. Those who have thought globally have done so by means of simplifications too extreme and oppressive to merit the name of thought . . . If we want to keep our thoughts and acts from destroying the globe, then we must see to it that we do not ask too much of the globe or any part of it. To make sure that we do not ask too much we must learn to live at home, as independently and self-sufficiently as we can (Berry, 1991, p. 61).

The problem that this school of thought identifies is the danger of exploiting, violating and oppressing areas of the globe that we do not properly understand because they are not—and in a profound sense, *cannot* be—part of our life-world. David Cooper (1992) suggests that the notion of 'environment' salient to this area of debate is not the 'global environment', nor even simply one's local physical or geographical environment, but the environment conceived as one's 'intentional field of significance': the web of entities and phenomena with which one has an unreflective familiarity and which form implicit and explicit points of reference for one's ongoing concerns and purposes. These are the things for which one has a 'feel', a sense of acquaintanceship from the inside, as it were, providing one's personal milieu. It is here that one *lives*.

However, from the perspective currently being developed, it might be objected that an individual's intentional field of significance so characterised could be a largely abstract domain divorced both from those things that are here being referred to as 'local' and from contact with nature. In an extreme case, for example, an individual might come to live a life increasingly preoccupied with various Internet spaces and virtual worlds. Here, the spirit of Heidegger's observation that today there is a danger of events from the other side of the globe becoming more familiar to us than the earth beneath our feet has some force. While some postmodernists (and others) have found such an idea risible in the context of modernity (even worrying because of associations with the philosophy of 'blood and soil'), there is an important sense in which ecologically we need to refocus on the immediate experience of nature. On the strength of previous argument only an intentional field in which nature is significant will be properly rooted in reality, and it is only care and involvement in *this* kind of environment that provides insight into what might be involved in sustainability and, importantly, in developing a fuller sense of and respect for what it means for others to care for *their* environments. Thus it can be argued that facing the environmental consequences of one's own actions in *this* milieu—eschewing assumptions that other parts of the globe can be exploited to relieve, for example, local depletion and pollution problems—brings a more direct aspect to our relationship with the environment. It brings it home, giving a personal cogency to the meaning of 'sustainability'.

Yet clearly this reassertion of the significance of knowledge by acquaintance alone holds the danger of insularity. However speculative and contentious some of the connections that are attributed to the biosphere may be, there are many that are now well recognised—for example, that various food webs can both maintain certain populations and also concentrate certain toxins. And it would be important, for example, to avoid the illusion of local, apparently sustainable, actions, that arises precisely because of ignorance about larger-scale consequences. Further-more, there are clearly problems already set in train, such as ozone depletion or oceanic depletion/pollution, which require global solutions. But even here, as Passmore has observed, the kind of knowledge most pertinent to environmental understanding is not a matter of high-level generalisations and abstract laws—of the sort implicit in the subject-based knowledge of many environmental education curriculum documents (see, for example, NCC Curriculum Guidance 7)—but a more intimate knowledge of particular organisms and ecosystems (Passmore, 1995, p. 137). Thus environmental education requires both local and global understanding, the one informing the other. But we have now established a priority here: for the global to achieve significance it needs to be affectively as well as cognitively rooted in the local. This means that what is at issue is no longer simply a set of international generalisations produced by disengaged rationality, but the carrying forward of an acquaintanceship with the local into the global. This would be a localisation of the global that, it has been suggested, has already occurred at another level with the broadcast of the image of the Earth viewed from space as a lone, fertile planet that is our home: an image made possible by science, but not fully comprehended by science.

Chapter 8. Towards an Environmental Ethos for Education

> The Spirit of Rio must create a new mode of civic conduct. It is not enough for man to love his neighbour; he must also learn to love his world . . . We must now conclude an ethical and spiritual contract with nature, with this Earth to which we owe our very existence and which gives us life (Boutros Boutros-Ghali, 1992, *Rio Earth Summit* closing statements).

Throughout this work it has been emphasised that the central issue for environmental education is that of our relationship to nature: what it is and what it should be. If previous argument to the effect that nature constitutes our primordial reality is correct, then how we resolve this issue has large implications for education as a whole. But returning for the moment to the focus of environmental education, clearly the attitudes that we engender towards nature are central to the whole enterprise, for while they do not always issue in behaviour, they provide the framework in terms of which behaviour is evaluated. And as with education in general, it is not, of course, that teachers and schools can avoid exhibiting some kind of attitude here, some set of values. To display 'neutrality' in debates on environmental issues is to display a value stance—revealed, for example, by contrast with the 'non-neutrality' displayed on other issues. So what should this stance be?

In the West, particularly with the growth of post-Enlightenment humanism, the dominant stance has been uncompromisingly anthropo-centric, placing a certain largely economic-materialistic conception of human welfare as the underlying goal of our everyday intercourse with, and explorations of, the natural world. This is clearly evidenced by the character of the great bulk of current scientific, technological and commercial activity. But, with the emergence of serious environmental problems taken to be the result of this attitude, this anthropocentrism has been challenged by a range of 'biocentric' and 'ecocentric' views broadly championed by the Green movement. Also, frequently intertwined with this debate, there is an issue about the aesthetic value of nature. Here, then, we have an area potentially rich in educational import. For convenience I will begin to explore it under the above topics of anthropocentric, biocentric and aesthetic relationships with nature.

ANTHROPOCENTRISM

In this context, I will take 'anthropocentrism' to refer to the view that environmental issues should be weighed in terms of what is in the long-term interests of human beings. Historically, this has been premised on the perception of a gulf between humankind and the rest of the natural world, nature being conceived of as something essentially alien. This has taken a number of forms, often mutually reinforcing, and it is worth noting the degree to which it is insinuated in the Western experience of the world. Much has been made of the claim that it has roots in Greek and Judaic thought where nature was experienced as profane, something to be conquered, or indeed, as 'put there' to serve humankind. Socrates in dialogue with Euthydemus saw the *telos* of things as serving human purposes; in Genesis 'man' is given dominion over nature. And there has been a long tradition, though one certainly not confined to the West, of orientating attention towards a care for the quality of a non-material inner life, and preparation for a non-terrestrial after-life, which has led to a neglect—indeed, sometimes an outright rejection of—the natural world as a source of concern, beauty or inspiration. By contrast—but offering to lead to a similar general conclusion—Darwinian evolution requires that the behaviour of each species must have as its prime function the success of its own species. While this supports neither the idea of nature as being there to serve *homo sapiens,* nor an ascetic indifference towards nature, it may be thought to lend legitimation again to a common underlying attitude of humans putting their own individual or species interests first.

Traditionally rationalism has been a powerful protagonist of the human/ non-human divide. For example, Aquinas articulated it in terms of the relative superiority of man, second only to the angels, in the Great Chain of Being in the approach to the perfection of Being found in God, though it is true that other versions of the Great Chain were less generous in their placement of man and emphasised the continuity and interdependence of its members. For Descartes it was the possession of incorporeal mind that separated man from the rest of nature, while for Kant it was the ability to contribute towards the achievement of a rational world. Again, for each, the conclusion was the same: the natural world should be subordinate to human purposes. It has no intrinsic worth, no intrinsic moral standing. As Kant put it with regard to sentient nature: 'Our duties towards animals are merely indirect duties towards humanity' (Kant, 1963, p. 239). That this general outlook prospered under the influence of the great flower of rationalism—modern (that is, 'classical') science—has previously been noted. When nature is projected as a vast machine ultimately constituted of inert atomic parts whose motion is the result of a variety of external mechanical forces, it is set up as essentially 'soul-less' and thus devoid of any intrinsic moral standing. It thus becomes legitimate for its laws to be extracted by highly interventionist and invasive experimental method if necessary—especially when enjoined by the Enlightenment vision of unimpeded human progress.

But the great divide has, of course, also been championed by those whom one would hardly characterise as rationalist. D. H. Lawrence (1934), for example, believed in a natural hierarchy in nature according to the degree of vitality or 'vividness' of experience an organism was capable of having, and (for him) its consequent ability to subordinate those below it. On this form of accountancy man naturally comes out on top again—and again, the upshot is that humankind is separated from the rest of nature, the latter becoming seen essentially as 'brute' and to be exploited as a resource for the furtherance of (higher) human purposes. Seemingly we have a naturalistic defence of the anthropocentric attitude. And given its underlying premise, it is little surprise that medieval man endured what Hegel termed the 'unhappy consciousness' involved in trying to reject the animal part of his own nature, or that certain Victorians, when not sentimentalising nature, were predisposed to regard it as 'red in tooth and claw', inefficient, profligate—to be kept at a distance and harnessed.

In addition to the above views of the natural facts of the situation, there is another now familiar consideration that can be taken to support anthropocentrism: the idea that 'nature' is a social construction. Some important senses in which this has been asserted and their implications have been discussed at some length in previous chapters, but it is worth reiterating the point here that to the extent that they are taken to be true, they can encourage the attitude of 'nature'—as a human artefact and therefore not foundational—being considered as somehow at the disposal of its 'authors', as with other artefacts.

Now all of the above can be presented as purely descriptive. What now seems to follow seamlessly from such descriptions is the conclusion that environmental concern should revolve around enlightened human self-interest. Such 'speciesism' would appear to be legitimated by a recognition of the mental superiority of the human species and the notion that in the absence of human consciousness there can be neither an environment as such to care for, nor anything to care (in the full intentional sense) for it. Furthermore, it has been argued, where ecological interdependence with all other aspects of nature is also acknowledged, this stance represents the best protection for nature as a whole. By connecting the long-term good of nature to the long-term good of humans, the appeal to human self-interest ensures the likelihood of environmentally friendly action. It also enables a defence of nature without making the contentious move of ascribing intrinsic moral—or other—value to nature.

The educational implications of this view are in principle straightfor-ward: essentially it results in a policy that is a more rationally rigorous version of the current humanistic utilitarian orthodoxy. Such rigour might well require that the timescale of consideration be extended to include future generations and that there be a move to include a consideration of a full range of human needs—and on a global rather than an ethno-centred basis—in deciding priorities over *whose* self-interest is to be served. The focus of environmental education would become to explore the consequences of actual and potential human activity, that is, to acquire empirical data and to discuss the balance to be struck between competing human interests. Clearly, such a discussion could hardly exclude broader moral and social/political issues to do with freedom and social justice, etc. Properly conceived, it would clearly lead to a recognition that environmental education demands more than the assimilation of 'neutral' facts and statistics; it will involve coming to terms with issues that are sometimes both highly speculative scientifically, and highly contentious morally and politically, albeit remaining within the parameters set by an underlying humanist utilitarian paradigm.

But if the human/non-human divide is factually correct in certain senses—and with our enhanced knowledge of the level of mental functioning of higher mammals, there are clearly problems in drawing sharp dividing lines on some of the criteria mentioned—in our present state of knowledge it is difficult to overlook the ways in which humankind and the rest of nature are very closely related. The burden of much research in ecology has been precisely to provide vivid illustration of this, and, as we have seen, there are a number of ways in which it is simply no longer tenable to maintain an *environmental* separation of humankind and nature. Quite the reverse: a high degree of interrelatedness with the biosphere—in both physical terms, and in terms of the development of our form of sensibility—seems undeniable. And of course, on another front, one of the central tenets of Darwinism is that we are not only ecologically, but *genetically*, related to the rest of nature, not to mention the fact that, on the Big Bang theory of creation, all of terrestrial nature is constituted of a common material, 'the ashes of dead stars'. And again, returning to a terrestrial level, some utilitarians such as Singer (1993) have wished to emphasise the degree of commonality between humankind and the rest of sentient nature in the capacity to experience pleasure and pain. Thus the notion that a human/non-human divide can legitimate anthropocentrism has its critics, and even if such a divide were accepted, proponents of the naturalistic fallacy would question the move from accepting the possession by humankind of qualities not found in the rest of nature to the speciesism of assuming human precedence in moral terms.

THE BIOCENTRIC CHALLENGE

Bio- (or eco-)centrism is a view that provides a radically different perspective on the issue. Basically, it holds that there is no great divide between human and non-human life, no privileged species. Humankind is intimately bound in with the rest of nature not just ecologically but *morally*. Indeed, on some versions, such as the 'Gaia hypothesis', the Earth as a whole is regarded as an organism with global feedback mechanisms that act to create conditions best suited for life as a whole (Lovelock, 1979), and it is this that comes to constitute the primary object of morality. There are clear echoes here of the Mediaeval/Renaissance experience of nature, and the notion that humankind is intimately bound in with nature both causally and morally is a prominent feature of Buddhist thinking. At a less-elevated level elements of this view have found expression in Albert Schweitzer's generalised 'reverence for life', which seems to express a widely felt intuition. Here, by way of illustration of some of its main tenets, I will examine two rather different recent but well worked through articulations of the position that seek to ascribe what I have previously termed inherent—that is, non-indexical—intrinsic moral value to nature. If successful, they would achieve a further Copernican revolution in our thinking whose consequences likely would have at least as great an impact on everyday life. To effect significant change in our relationship to nature is to effect significant change in our lives as a whole.

A Respect for nature

In his influential *Respect for Nature. A Theory of Environmental Ethics*, Paul Taylor sets out his argument for a biocentric outlook. It seeks to demonstrate an underlying unity encompassing the whole of living nature that would make moral differentiation in favour of humankind arbitrary. His basic tenet is uncompromising: there is a fundamental equality between all species of animals and plants such that 'None . . . is deemed more worthy of existence than another' (Taylor, 1986, p. 157). Taylor bases his case on what he takes to be a number of empirical 'facts' (pp. 156–158). First, we are biological creatures just as the rest are, and this gives us a 'oneness with the great Community of Life'. Second, we are functionally interdependent with every other member of this community. Third, through a heightened reality awareness (itself encouraged by a biocentric outlook) 'our awareness of the moment to moment existence of each living thing is sharpened and clarified', and we become aware that 'Like ourselves, other organisms are teleological centres of life . . . and the uniqueness of each organism, human or non-human, is made manifest in the particular way it carries on its daily existence in its given circumstances'. For Taylor, each organism can be seen to seek the realisation of its own good. There is a clear accord here with Rolston's view mentioned in Chapter 6, and elements of both seem to echo in the intuitions of nature evoked by Iris Murdoch's kestrel and Jim Cheney's spiders, described in the previous chapter.

However, given these 'facts', Taylor takes the argument a stage further:

> And just as we humans place intrinsic value on the opportunity to pursue our own good in our own individual ways, so we consider the realization of the good of animals and plants to be something that should be valued as an end in itself. As moral agents we see ourselves under an ethical requirement to give equal consideration to the good of every entity, human and non-human alike, that has a good of its own. When the good of one conflicts with another, we recognize the duty to be initially unbiased in our approach to a way of resolving the conflict. Since all are viewed as having the same inherent worth, the moral attitude of respect is equally due to each (p. 157).

Here, certainly, we have an unambiguous statement of a position that goes beyond Rolston in its demand for equality of consideration. But, put so plainly, it immediately confronts us with the following question: In what sense is it plausible for this rather Kantian stance of treating things as ends-in-themselves to be extended to nature in general? In some, perhaps many, cases such a view may seem to accord with some of our basic intuitions about nature. Some may share the sentiment expressed in Schweitzer's refusal to read at night in the African wild because of the moths that flew helplessly into the candle-flame and perished. It *does* seem somehow profane to fell a magnificent Californian redwood that perhaps has stood for several thousand years. It is hard not to feel remorse at the way the buffalo population of North America was reduced from 60 million to less than 500 in a period of a few decades. In the latter two cases this sense of loss and unease, it could be argued, is a sense not only of regret at potential benefits denied to humanity, but also of the way that such things communicate powerfully something of their own being—and destiny. We benefit from being in their presence in part precisely because we recognise their otherness and the respect that is its due. Something of this is expressed in Aldo Leopold's tribute to the crane in 'Marshland Elegy':

> Our ability to perceive quality in nature begins, as in art, with the pretty. It expands through successive stages of the beautiful to values as yet uncaptured by language. The quality of cranes lies, I think, in this higher gamut, as yet beyond the reach of words.
>
> This much though can be said: our appreciation of the crane grows with the slow unravelling of earthly history. His tribe, we now know, stems out of the remote Eocene. The other members of the fauna in which he originated are long since entombed within the hills. When we hear his call we hear no mere bird. We hear the trumpet in the orchestra of evolution. He is the symbol of our untameable past, of that incredible sweep of millennia which underlies and conditions the daily affairs of birds and men (Leopold, 1989, p. 96).

Our sense of awe, wonder, admiration or whatever, is a response to a worth that is independent of us and our aspirations, though there remains an ineliminable subjective element. I will return to this line of thinking presently. For the moment, while we may wish to acknowledge a certain resonance with some of our basic intuitions of nature, there are elements in Taylor's formulation that are less plausible, particularly the argument that he marshals to support his notion of *equal* worth.

Suppose, for the sake of argument, we accept that the empirical claims regarding 'our ecological situation' are correct—that is, we are to be understood in terms of biology and are located in the web of interdependent entities that constitutes the biosphere. So in this sense we are on a par with any other member of the biosphere. But while it is quite *consistent* with this to claim that humans and all other organisms are of equal worth, it certainly does not *follow*. This is partly because we may have additional characteristics that place us above the rest (traditionally, our rationality), but more generally because there seems to be a conflation here between *functional* and *moral* worth, which also overlooks some important ambiguities in the former notion.

By definition all organisms play some kind of functional role in maintaining the current state of the biosphere, indeed their existence and functioning *constitute* the current state of the biosphere. But this only offers a basis for attributing equal worth to them if that precise current state is better than other possible states. How would this be judged? Furthermore, with regard to treatment, distinctions need to be drawn here between an individual organism, a population and a species. Treatment that might be for the good of one of these categories may not always be so for the others—for example, culling, which is taken to benefit a population though at the sacrifice of certain individuals. And suppose, as seems likely, it were found that the functioning of some organisms (such as certain micro flora) was more pivotal to the well-being of the biosphere as a whole than the functioning of others (such as humankind)? On this argument would not those of more peripheral significance have less worth? These questions indicate that functionality issues are highly problematic for Taylor's thesis, that, at the very least, we need to separate moral worth arguments based upon the self-realisation of individuals from 'moral worth' arguments based upon the notion of interdependence, and that the idea of *moral* worth derives from the former rather than the latter. In which case moral worth would seem to attach to individuals rather than to populations or species since the notion of, say, a species 'self-realising' in the appropriate sense is deeply problematic.

But even if we suspend these reservations, whichever of the two strands that we take in Taylor's argument, it requires a further premise to justify the ascription of equal worth to all organisms. On the collectivist-organic argument his value premise is that broadly speaking (that is, allowing for some 'restoration') the current state of the biosphere should be preserved. This seems to be a widely held assumption, expressed clearly in Aldo Leopold's oft-quoted maxim: 'A thing is right when it tends to preserve the integrity, stability and beauty of the biotic community. It is wrong when it tends otherwise' (Leopold, 1993, p. 382). But there are many problems with this. For example, was it wrong to alter the (then) stability of the biotic community by inoculating against malaria? More generally why should any current state of the community be sacred, have more value than other potential states? There is also a conceptual issue: how dynamic is the notion of stability? How, for example does it accommodate on-going evolution? In terms of organisms, things are in a constant state of flux. On a *geological* timescale there have been, and will be, very different biotic communities. 'Natural' ecological history is characterised by small and large-scale upheavals that are the ultimate stimulus for the development of new species and equilibria. One wonders if ultimately it is not the stability of certain organism-transcendent processes that is being valued here— which again raises both the issue as to whether such processes can be moral objects and the spectre of 'eco-fascism'. Furthermore, on Leopold's view, could there not be a conflict between the pursuit of stability and the pursuit of beauty? And whose view of beauty should prevail anyway?

The point of such questions is to express a strong suspicion that scratching the surface of this sort of view rapidly reveals a strong underlying anthropocentrism—a tacit idealisation of the state of equilibrium that supports human flourishing and the view of beauty held by human beings. (Who or what else? Porpoises? Presumably, even on the basis of Taylor's 'heightened awareness' thesis, it would be far-fetched to attempt to interpret what would count as beauty for other organisms, even if we were to suppose that some of them were capable of experiencing it.) This then raises the fundamental question as to just how tenable it is to deny a special position to human beings. And if we grant that it is not tenable to deny them such a position, is it possible to resist the conclusion that they are thereby of some special—'extra'—worth?

With regard to the individual self-realisation strand in his argument, Taylor's *explicit* premise is a claim regarding a teleological aspect to every organism, which rational consistency then requires us to treat with equal consideration to the value that we as human beings place on pursuing *our* own good. But, again we seem to hit a problem. 'Rational consistency' can only operate upon relevant similarities. What are these in the case of the sense in which non-human organisms are teleological compared with human ones? This raises the question as to the intelligibility of speaking of, say, an amoeba (or a cabbage) striving for its own good. Such descriptions—even with regard to sentient organisms—hardly veil the anthropomorphism that vitiates the view. All such talk, if intended to exemplify self-realisation, requires not merely consciousness, but something akin to *human* consciousness, involving at the least a sense of agency and of the future.

The weight of such argument is to suggest that to speak of non-humankind as 'teleological' is to employ a metaphor that cannot support the conclusion of 'equal worth' that Taylor wishes to draw. Not now because, arguably, humankind is more influential (for good or ill) in the biotic community than any other species. (We have shown above how the issue of functional worth is an unhelpful distraction.) It is rather because it is only organisms of a certain level of conscious awareness—epitomised by human beings—that can entertain a world of significances, and hence are an essential condition of there *being* a significant world. They are teleological in the sense of being self-aware, and thus capable of having their own purposes and some conception of their own good. And it is having concerns in this sense that both lends their life a meaning and enables them to perceive meaning in the world around them. *Things matter to them.* It does not matter to an amoeba what happens to it. It may matter for the survival of its species, but this is a concern not felt by the amoeba, but only—and then only possibly—by humankind. We do children and nature no service if we encourage a false anthropomorphism in their understanding of non-human nature, which is by no means to deny that we should be alert to the levels of consciousness that other organisms may experience, nor, of course, to discount their susceptibility to pain, both physical and in some cases psychological.

But what we return to in the end is a recognition of the special place occupied by human beings as centres of conscious awareness in which the very notion of significance is located. This recognition transports us from the collectivist-physicalist perspective of 'man's place in nature' (or in the biotic community) implicit in the views of writers such as Taylor, the perspective that lends them any initial plausibility they may enjoy. It also follows that humankind is special in the moral sense not simply because it is truly teleological. It also has a special responsibility towards the ecosystem because, in addition to affecting it, it is the only entity that can experience responsibility, can *be* responsible. It is not, then, that the needs of, say, amoeba and humans should be judged impartially—neither being regarded as of greater worth. Rather, judgements have to be made from a sense of what is fitting within a world of significances that express the kind of acquaintanceship with nature of which only humankind or its psychological equivalent is capable. The development of this is an important task for education that will need to be acknowledged in its aims and instantiated in its methods and ethos.

But how are we to characterise this acquaintanceship? In the previous chapter I have explored notions of attentiveness and knowing that suggest part of the answer. Arguably, at the very least we should be seeking to enhance a way of relating to nature that does not *simply* reflect our self-referential practical needs, even when, and if, it is significantly coloured by them. The aesthetic attitude of a certain detachment or disinterest, to be discussed presently, may also be relevant here, and I have previously referred to the way our apprehension of a Californian redwood, etc., can be imbued with something akin to a feeling of deep respect. It is not uncommon for this to be evoked when we stand in the presence of many elemental aspects of nature. At the same time it is easy for this to be tranquilised through an overweening preoccupation with immediate practical gain. Thus Wordsworth's lament that:

The world is too much with us: late and soon,
Getting and spending, we lay waste our powers;
Little we see in Nature that is ours:
We have given our hearts away . . .

Yet even in our practical everyday commerce with nature it is possible to remain aware of its elemental qualities, and many indigenous cultures, such as Native American, Kalahari Bushmen etc., have enjoyed a reputation for doing precisely this. A way of life that is less insulating from the power and gift of nature would seem to be a prerequisite for a more open, that is, receptive and thus genuinely responsive, relationship to it. Examples given in the previous chapter suggest that one comes to know nature rather as one comes to know a person—not simply rationally, but intuitively and through a certain kind of intimacy that on occasion is capable of evoking astonishment and trepidation. This may well reflect something of Taylor's notion of 'heightened awareness'. It has significant educational implications, which we will explore presently.

But, from the ethical perspective, underlying all of this is a deeper issue: is there a special sense in which humankind is responsible for revealing, for celebrating, in a certain sense for *preserving* nature? At one level we might recall the Buddhist adage that man should utilise nature 'in the same way as a bee collects pollen from the flower, neither polluting its beauty nor depleting its fragrance'. At another, we might be led to reflect upon the nature and place of truth in human life—on the way that truth involves an openness to how things themselves are, an openness to the aspect of the self-arising in them, that is somehow intrinsic to all that we think and do. It is a primal source and point of reference, in the absence of which notions of—and the *experience* of—sense, understanding, reality, become incoherent. If this is accepted, then in our submission to such truth and in the consequent eschewal of wishful fabrication, human life is endowed with a sense of integrity and dignity that is definitional of it. This notion will be taken up in the following chapter when I develop the idea that sustainability is best conceived as frame of mind.

B Love of nature

Paul Taylor's view bears the imprint of a rational ethic of duty and obligation. By contrast, in her influential *The Ecological Self*, Freya Mathews (1994) modulates the biocentric perspective as an ethic of care. She does this by placing at the heart of our relationship with nature an attitude of identification with—and therefore affirmation of, and Eros towards—all other 'self-realising' entities that constitute what she terms the 'ecocosm'. In so doing she proposes a new extended sense of ourselves: the 'ecological self'. Thus, she endorses a position held in various ways by a number of Deep Ecologists that, by denying the required separation between us and the rest of nature, effectively circumvents the issue of whether non-human nature has intrinsic value or is an object of duty.

Developing the ecosophy of Arne Naess (1989) and others, which emphasises our embeddedness in nested, wholly interdependent ecological systems, she suggests that: 'When we recognise the involvement of wider wholes in our identity, an expansion in the scope of our identity and hence in the scope of our self-love occurs' (Mathews, 1994, p. 149). We find ourselves identifying with the rest of the 'ecocosm' and wish to affirm it as part of ourselves, properly conceived. But, of course, if the 'ecocosm' were itself essentially meaningless or even destructive, then our identification with it could only undermine our own sense of meaning and worth—or legitimate our own destructiveness. Such identification could hardly be a basis for love or conservation. So, Mathews claims, the ecocosm must have its own positive, creative *telos*. In this sense it must be a 'self', have a will to exist, which is its *conatus* and of which we are a part:

> It is in this human participation in the cosmic process that the meaningfulness of our relation to nature may be found: through our awareness of our interconnectedness with it we experience a love for this great self, a love which is actually constitutive of, or a tributary to, its own *conatus*, its own will to exist' (p. 155).

Central to this view, then, is the notion of the 'ecocosm', which is 'a self-realising system which is internally interconnected in an ecological—and therefore also in a topological and substantival—sense' (p. 147), where 'ecological' refers to a system in which individuals are seen to exist essentially as parts of a larger whole and in their interrelationship with other such parts. Thus we are held to flourish when we live in a way that affirms the ecosystem in which we are nested, in which we and all others flourish. This stance is based upon an underlying notion of substance monism which she argues is 'sanctioned' by modern (quantum mechanics) science—and thus represents a certain continuity with the dominant arbiter for thinking within the Western tradition.

Now clearly, such a thesis has extensive implications for how we conceive of ourselves and live our lives at every level, representing in the most comprehensive way the claim that our relationship with nature, in the sense of cosmic order, is the most primordial and formative. Thus for Mathews: 'The thesis that we, as human selves, stand in a holistic relation—a relation of 'oneness'—with the cosmos itself, promises more than a list of ethical prescriptions. It promises a key to the perennial questions of who we are, why we are born, what is our reason for living, etc. In short it promises to throw light on the *meaning* of life' (ibid.). On such a view, it is not simply that one should say that there are massive implications not only for environmental education but also education as a whole, but that at a fundamental level any such distinction is rebutted. Environmental education and general education coalesce when human flourishing and cosmic flourishing become one:

> A person will count as flourishing only if she is culturally as well as physically and materially well off. She is culturally well off if she is richly fulfilled in her emotional, imaginative, artistic, intellectual and spiritual life . . . *The culture that enables us . . . to flourish as human beings is precisely the culture that understands and represents our interconnectedness with Nature* (p. 156, emphasis added).

This view is appealing in a number of ways, perhaps not least in that it so thoroughly rehabilitates us into the greater order of things and gives us a 'home' in the world. Numerous commentators have suggested that our alienation from nature and its disenchantment (as briefly reviewed in Chapter 3) are the cause of a tacit sense of loss and rootlessness. Here, maybe, is a route back into the world, a conception of belonging that can both accommodate and surmount the humanistic/scientific world-view that has led us away from establishing our place *within* nature? But there are problems.

Take the sentiment of a unity of individuals with nature as the source of human flourishing expressed in the above quote. At first blush at least, this claim sounds highly stipulative and begs a host of questions concerning the centrality of closeness to nature to the good life. Such a sentiment would certainly not be shared for example by many pre-Romantics such as Dr Johnson, who saw wild nature as the antithesis of civilisation, the antithesis, therefore, of human fulfilment. Furthermore, it is at least arguable that if it is conceded that the individual has to be taken as the final arbiter of their own fulfilment, a person suitably orientated could derive all of the aspects of being 'richly fulfilled' listed by Mathews through a deep absorption in, say, the life of Formula One motor racing. The issue is raised as to what is the metaphysical basis of our relationship to nature. Is there any sense in which our ontology involves or requires a connection characterised by sympathy, empathy and identification? Or are such attitudes ultimately a matter of mere subjective inclination?

There seem to me to be three criticisms of the kind of view that Mathews espouses. I list them below in ascending order of magnitude.

First, her views about what is viable—and therefore what can be a component of human flourishing—only work, if at all, at the level of the species or the culture, not at the level of the individual. Despite her protestations to the contrary, it seems obvious that an *individual* could flourish, even in the terms prescribed by Mathews herself, in ways that are deleterious to the environment in the long term (for example, the Formula One devotee). And even at the species level, the issue is raised as to what is to count as deleterious—deleterious from what or whose standpoint? Clearly any particular state of the ecosystem favours some members more than others—and some not at all—namely those that are made extinct. As with Taylor's view, it is hard to suppress the suspicion that the semblance of genuine ecocentrism is a veneer that, when scratched, reveals a powerful, because disguised, anthropocentrism that prioritises those states of the ecocosm assumed to sustain human flourishing.

Second, and leading to a similar conclusion, her argument can constrain us to identify only with those parts of the greater whole that we perceive to support *us*. There is a plausibility in supposing that we could be moved to identify with the trees that recycle the atmosphere or with the Earth viewed as a lonely blue planet, but *not* with the malaria bacillus or with the HIV virus. But this essentially seems to return us to an anthropocentric position of a fairly conventional kind; aggrandised somewhat it is true, but sheer enlightened self-interest nonetheless. In which case we have to ask what Mathews' position offers the conservationist that is not offered as powerfully, but more simply, by straightforward enlightened self-interest as a motive? And shorn of its holistic pretensions, what does it offer to our understanding of our relationship with nature?

Third, her argument is viciously circular. She simply derives from human identification with the ecocosm values that she has previously overtly or covertly inserted in it. There is no convincing independent argument to show that it possesses these values.

So where does this examination of bio/ecocentric views leave us? It seems to me that ecocentric ideas have the considerable virtue of challenging us critically to examine unbridled conventional anthropocentrism, that they may be suggestive of important alternative attitudes, but that they lack the intellectual resources to replace it. (See, also, King, 1997, on this.) I wish to argue that ultimately they fail because they give too little credence to the special position that human consciousness has in the greater scheme of things. They ignore the significance of the way in which the idea of reality itself is human-related, that things only 'show up' (to borrow a term used by Taylor (1992) in this context) in the space that is consciousness.

However, there may be another way of preserving much that is cherished by biocentrism, yet that accommodates this element of human-relatedness.

NATURE AND AESTHETIC APPRECIATION

In the light of Petrarch's setting aside of aesthetic delight in nature as unworthy of the human mind, and Dr Johnson's estimation of Scottish scenery as 'a wide extent of hopeless sterility' that is 'quickened only with one sullen power of useless vegetation', experiences of which 'neither impregnate the imagination, nor enlarge the understanding', John Haldane rightly makes the point that 'there is nothing perennially obvious about the present-day reverence for nature and the elevation of its appreciation to the higher categories of human consciousness' (Haldane, 1994, p. 99). Yet today, one reason frequently encountered for preserving the natural environment is its beauty. Indeed, David Cooper is of the view that: 'Those in search of reasons of a non-utilitarian kind to care about the damage we do to nature, about the disappearance of natural landscapes and animal species, do well to cite the aesthetic depredation these entail' (Cooper, 1998, p. 100). Does this approach hold out the promise of articulating something of the essential concern of a biocentric ethic, for is not a concern for nature's aesthetic qualities a concern for something of transcendent value? Perhaps, but there are some problems. To begin with, as Haldane points out, in contrast to pre-modern aesthetics, which placed aesthetic objects as prior to aesthetic responses and attitudes, there has been a movement since the Enlightenment towards identifying the aesthetic *attitude* as prior, aesthetic experience resulting from the exercise of that attitude and aesthetic objects becoming objects as they are perceived in that experience. Such a subjectivist aesthetic is clearly in danger of reverting to an anthropocentrism, the apprehension of beauty being determined by the attitude of the beholder. Yet, the issue is more complex than this, for the aesthetic attitude was itself characterised by its original proponents, such as Kant, as one of detachment from theoretical and practical concerns—a disinterested contemplation—and thus one that would seem to reflect that very concern, previously expressed, of the need to transcend the instrumental attitude that dominates modern Western culture in our relationship with nature.

However, from the perspective of biocentric concern, certain reservations remain. For even if overtly instrumental motives towards nature are eschewed in aesthetic contemplation, surely it remains the case that human satisfaction rather than the intrinsic value of nature is the underlying value. It might be said that, if anything, the humanist motive has been extended, for now nature exists to please us as well as serve us— part of its value lying in its capacity to afford us aesthetic experiences. And as before, any value that nature is taken to have is a result of human evaluation—in which case, again, it is not 'intrinsic', but becomes an artefact dependent on its 'instrumental' contribution to something else.

With regard to the latter, David Cooper argues that to assume, *inter alia*, that human evaluation of things turns them into artefacts involves a fundamental confusion of conceptual dependency with causal dependency. It is true that the notion of values becomes unintelligible in the absence of actual or potential valuers, but to suppose that the 'formal anthropocentrism' of values requiring (human) evaluators implies that we *produce* such values is like 'imagining that, since things can only be described as loud or soft in virtue of their relation to creatures who are auditorily affected, it is therefore these creatures that 'produce' sounds or 'confer' them on a 'really' soundless world' (p. 102). 'Formal anthropocentrism' is silent about *why* we value things—instrumental or non-instrumental—and the focus would be better re-directed from reified values to the differing reasons we may have for valuing things, leaving open what weight is to be attached to the intrinsic qualities of a thing in particular cases. Thus, it would appear, genuine intrinsic value can subsist within the remit of an overarching formal anthropocentrism.

This, I think, is suggestive of an important point about human valuing. That worth and value can only be discerned by humankind in no way detracts from the sense of independent worth that things may have. Quite the opposite. Internal to the idea of *valuing* something, as against simply liking or desiring it, is a recognition of qualities—of, in the case of nature, perhaps, independence, diversity, subtlety, integrity, etc.—that are not simply the product of personal caprice, but that are somehow inherent in the thing itself. They meet a 'standard' that is independent of us in the sense of not simply being for us to *decide* (choose). Indeed, they, and we, become defined by the communicative relationship that arises between us. As I have previously noted, humankind has the capacity to entertain significances that are precisely *not* human-centred, even though they are necessarily articulated within a horizon that is inherently structured by human purposes. In bringing us into initial contact with nature, human-centred motives can heighten our awareness of non-human-centred aspects of the world. Through their modulations of, or resistance to, our activity, they stand out as 'other'. And this can be as true of aspects of our everyday practical equipment (such as Heidegger's peasant shoes) as of things that we do not think of in instrumental terms. Indeed in our modern preoccupation with ourselves, our awareness of things may be most powerfully provoked when their normal taken-for-granted compliance is withheld. Think, for example, of the sense of sheer inscrutable otherness that may be experienced when peering under the bonnet at a car engine that refuses to start.

Yet, in seeming contrast to biocentrism, Cooper states that the mere fact of the existence of a natural thing has no value implications, no implications for environmental practice and policy, for sheer existence has no intelligible bearing on what matters to us: 'If we are even to make sense of ascribing value to something on the basis of some qualities it has, we must be able to understand why something with those qualities should matter to us, how it might fit into the orbit of our concerns and intelligibly engage with some conception of a good life' (p. 103). Now this view, while ostensibly preserving a non-instrumental approach, nonetheless would certainly give rise to concern for biocentrists, a great deal hanging on the phrase 'fit into the orbit of our concerns', which seems to imply a 'causal', not merely a 'formal', anthropocentrism. Presumably, if this phrase were to be read as 'satisfy our concerns', this would not even meet the criterion of aesthetic disinterest. And even if some looser fit were intended, it clearly threatens to rule out the possibility of all life having *prima facie* value (perhaps because of a feeling of continuity within nature). For the idea to be interpreted in a way that is consistent with some generalised human regard for the self-arising, the notion of 'fit into' would need to be diluted to a point that makes it inappropriate.

But Cooper's responses to other objections to appeals to aestheticism in defence of nature are revealing. To the objection that aesthetic appreciation is too prone to variation and shifts in taste to form a secure foundation for such a defence, he counters that it is hardly obvious that other suggested foundations such as 'respect' or ascribing moral rights to natural objects will turn out to be less ephemeral than, say, aesthetic judgements on landscapes. But is this not, wrongly, to give the objection a causal/pragmatic rather than a conceptual interpretation? Could not the objection be not the empirical one that taste changes, but the *logical* one that taste is too subjective to do the required foundational work? The worth of nature cannot be a matter of our taste where this signifies something we can change, if in some significant sense it is to inhere in nature itself—albeit, in the 'formally anthropocentric' sense indicated above. It may be that issues of good and bad taste are not merely arbitrary, possessing a base of, perhaps, broad intersubjective agreement, but to conceive the worth of nature as a matter for human aesthetic *decision* would be to participate in an arrogance that is the equal of any instrumental approach.

Defending it against the charge of fragility, Cooper makes the point that aesthetic appreciation is not to be equated with pleasurable experiences, branding as 'philistine' someone who, say, looks to music only for the 'lumps in the throat' that it can produce. Rather, it appears, there is a seminal subject-transcendent characteristic of aesthetic appreciation illustrated in the finding of qualities of expression, form and meaning in the objects of people's taste in cultures removed from our own, such that we are able to see their aesthetic merit even when we do not share their experiences. But in *this* sense aesthetics is a relatively recent field of experience and is in high danger of being dominated by connoisseurship and a set of standards that are notoriously difficult to define and achieve consensus upon. It is also, presumably, unavailable to the untutored, and thus far removed from the kind of earthy receptiveness that biocentrists seek to reassert. What sense of such matters could, say, Heidegger's peasant woman have? And why should nature as the self-arising exhibit these aesthetic qualities as ably as artefacts such as paintings that are designed so to do? And where perhaps it does so, is the worth of nature—

say, the magnificence and significance of the heavens—to be measured according to such templates?

Cooper's positive thesis is interesting. He seeks to draw an analogy between experience of nature and the 'alternative worlds' opened up by great works of art, such as one enters into when reading a great novel. He suggests that natural environments, too, can 'constitute "alternative worlds" to explore with the full range of one's faculties. Sometimes a person who "goes into nature" is, somewhat literally, entering a different world from the city which is the milieu of his or her everyday, practically engaged existence' (p. 109). Citing Alan Goldman, he claims that (i) there is surely a value in entering other worlds for its own sake, of employing our sensory, cognitive and affective faculties in relative freedom from the pressing demands of life, and that (ii) a value of such entry is its refreshing effects on those faculties, and what it enables us to bring back with us into the 'actual' world.

At one level there is much here to be applauded. Engaging with nature in a non-instrumental way can be refreshing in the ways described and undoubtedly is of value. But the underlying tenor is dangerous. It sets nature up as something apart from ongoing practical life—yet, essentially, still a resource: something, therefore, likely to be too easily discounted when pressing practical demands and pressures re-enter the picture; and something unlikely to affect them, existing, as it is here being taken to do, in another 'alternative' world. In such a circumstance, experience suggests that the first of Goldman's points cited above will be heavily challenged, and that the second, clearly instrumental, point will slip down the list of other instrumental priorities. While important things *may* be taken back from the 'alternative world' of nature, this falls a long way short of meeting the need for the development of a kind of dwelling in which nature is present as the primordial reality. Though given our current cultural starting point, it may represent a contribution to such a retrieval.

Perhaps the fundamental reservation to emerge from this examination of the perspective that Cooper expresses is brought to a head in response to his conclusion that 'people without aesthetic appreciation of nature are stunted in spirit' and that it is 'hard to think of a more important reason for cultivating concern for our natural environments and for what is currently befalling them' (p. 111). While appealing, is this not in danger of standing matters on their head? The development of the human spirit is certainly central to education and aesthetic appreciation (in a certain sense) is an important aspect of the human spirit, but the view being developed in this volume suggests that a concern for natural environments is to be viewed less as a *consequence* of this demand and more as a *condition* of it.

The problem with allowing aesthetic appreciation to dominate—as against contribute to—an environmental ethos is that it is in danger of substituting the artifice of a humanistic connoisseurship for what might be termed the 'earthiness' of an authentic dwelling. This raises the possibility of intimidation by expert criteria and knowledge within an area of sensibility where direct personal intuition and a degree of spontaneity of response, befitting the befalling of nature as the self-arising, should be preserved. Here too, there is the danger of aesthetic fashions, such as modernism, that are antipathetic to the self-arising. Finally, what of aspects of nature that (depending on one's taste?) have little or negative aesthetic appeal, yet are essential to the functioning of the ecosystem? A less potentially prejudicial ethos must be sought.

Chapter 9. Education for Sustainable Development: Sustainability as a Frame of Mind

Is it not enough for you to feed on the good pasture? Must you also trample the rest of your pasture with your feet? Is it not enough for you to drink clear water? Must you also muddy the rest with your feet?

Must my flock feed on what you have trampled and drink what you have muddied with your feet? (*Ezekiel*, 34, verses 18–19)

In Chapter 7 I attempted to indicate some of the ways in which understanding nature as the self-arising not simply affects what might be involved in coming to know nature so understood, but also might invite the rehabilitation of currently overlooked—indeed, largely discredited—dimensions of knowing into education as a whole. I now wish to return to a topic that appears initially to belong within the focus of environmental education, but *inter alia* again to demonstrate that the issues it raises set off reverberations that affect education more broadly.

EDUCATION FOR SUSTAINABLE DEVELOPMENT

In recent years much of the discussion of environmental action and education has taken the idea of sustainable development as a key guiding notion. I have previously alluded to the fact that education for sustainable development is now an established part of the UK National Curriculum—as it is in most European and many Third World nations. And of course the notion has a much wider currency than as a guide to an area within education. It was first brought to prominence by the highly influential report of the Brundtland Commission, *Our Common Future* (Brundtland Commission, 1987), whose task was to address the broader political issues raised by the need for resource conservation and reduction of pollution on the global scale. It defined sustainable development in the following now well-known terms: 'a development that meets the needs of the present without compromising the ability of future generations to meet their own needs'. Not withstanding unresolved issues as to what constitutes 'needs' in this context, this sentiment was consolidated in the subsequent Rio Earth Summit's *Agenda 21* (UNCED, 1992), which, along with identifying various ecological commitments, set out specific proposals for the installation and treatment of sustainable development in the educational systems of signatory nations. Thus, in international terms undoubtedly, it has become the dominant idea in the area of addressing environmental issues. But how helpful is it to orientate thinking and policy around this notion, and how adequate a conception of environmental education does it promise? In pursuit of this question I will begin by examining its political attractiveness.

A large part of the appeal of 'sustainable development' is that ostensibly it brings into harmony two highly attractive but potentially conflicting notions. First, is the idea of conserving or preserving those aspects of nature that are valued but that are currently endangered through depletion, pollution and so forth. Second, is the idea of accommodating ongoing human aspirations to 'develop', that is, in some sense to have more or better, where this necessarily has implications for natural systems. Clearly this latter consideration has particular force in a situation where large parts of the global population are regarded as suffering from 'underdevelopment' and where it, therefore, seems both unjust and unrealistic to expect them to remain so. And even in 'developed' nations there is little sign of abatement of a continuing drive for *further* development, despite its known negative environmental impact. Indeed, quite the reverse is the case, which is not at all surprising where so much of the economic/ political/social system of 'developed' nations is prefaced on mass production and consumption. Thus there is a seductiveness in seeming to marry these two highly desired goals of sustainability and development, apparently bringing them into convenient harmony. However, with the growth of its appeal and influence there has arisen a suspicion that 'sustainable development' might involve a certain semantic sleight of hand that veils an undergrowth of ambiguities and tensions which are in danger of vitiating the notion and consequently any environmental policy that is based upon it.

Presently, and as a preliminary to seeing what can be salvaged from a notion that once seemed to promise so much, I will begin by examining some aspects of this problematic undergrowth. But first let me position sustainable development in relation to liberal theory, for even on the abstract interpretation referred to above, which couches the issue in terms of not compromising the ability of future generations to meet their needs, a range of issues is raised from the liberal standpoint. For example, Dirk Willem Postma (2002) has pointed out that Rawlsian liberal theory poses a number of conceptual problems with regard to the possibility of having a moral relationship with future generations. First, reciprocity is impossible. Second, we have no way of knowing in sufficient detail what the needs and desires of future generations will be. Third, given the above, intergenerational morality is in danger of becoming at best paternalistic and at worst repressive, since decisions made in the present are made necessarily in ignorance of the wishes of those affected, and therefore threaten to impose the present generation's ideals and values upon future generations and thus to deprive them of the opportunity to shape their own world. This would appear to betray the fundamental tenet of liberalism that each must be free to develop and pursue their own version of the good life.

Postma points out that the attempt by some proponents of sustainable development to avoid such problems, by couching the policy in terms of a negative morality that aims simply at minimising the effects of our current actions on the breadth of options open to future generations, seems doomed to conceptual failure. For this does not overcome the lack of reciprocity necessary to liberal morality, nor of course is it possible, indeed even desirable, not to shape the future world—including its cultural aspects—according to present understandings, values and ideals. Everything we do that will affect the future necessarily reflects the pre-judgements embedded in our current form of sensibility. Furthermore, in a liberal political context, such a negative morality leaves it open for the inevitable interpretation of sustainable development through the metaphor of the free market, a way of thinking inherent, so Postma claims, in every contract theory. It will thus come to embody an economic-distributive and anthropocentric perspective that, because of its location of environmental issues in the first order sphere of private morality, can never properly comprehend nor respond to environmental issues, which are ineluctably public in nature. Any normative implications of environmental concerns are also, for this reason, put beyond the remit of state-provided education. Environmental issues imply that what is needed is the development of the kind of enhanced sense of community that is occluded by liberalism—one in which *inter alia*, we recognise that, as Postma puts it, 'the idea of a virtual bond with past and future generations seems to be an anthropological *sine qua non* for humans to make sense of their life' (p. 54). Some important implications of this last point will be developed in Chapter 11. For the present, having indicated the kind of debate raised by the notion of sustainable development within a theory that is formative of the Western political outlook, I return to certain semantic issues.

SUSTAINABILITY

Notwithstanding their pivotal role in the discussion of environmental issues, the terms 'sustainable' and 'sustainability' seem frequently to be used as if their meaning were self-evident and somehow value neutral—almost as though they simply reflected a desire to preserve some readily identifiable underlying natural state of equilibrium. But of course this is far from being the case. To begin with there can be divergence over *what* is to be sustained. For example, while for some the focus has been on the *'balance of nature' or of an eco-system*, for others it has been sustainable *economic growth*. For others again it has been maintenance of a *culture*—for example, 'the ability of a community to create a way of life which is an expression of its values and aspirations' (Vandeburg, 1995)—or the capacity to satisfy *human needs*, as in the case of the Brundtland Commission statement, that has been the reference of sustainability. While related, each of these clearly gives a significantly different meaning to 'sustainability' and very different sets of policy implications, and there is no *prima facie* reason for supposing that they need be compatible with each other. Indeed, it has been pointed out—for example, by Gilbert Rist (1997)—that trading on such ambiguities has enabled the rhetoric of some policy makers to give the impression that they wish to do one thing (such as sustain natural ecosystems) while in fact attempting something quite different (such as sustain conditions for the continuance of their own economic growth).

Similarly, there seems sometimes to be a too easy assimilation of ecological sustainability with sustaining *democratic* culture. For example, John Elliott links the idea of a sustainable society with that of a democratic society and supports a conception of environmental education 'located at the centre of an educational change agenda designed to prepare the young in our societies for active citizenship in a participatory democracy'—albeit a democracy 'free of the ideological apparatus of economism' (J. Elliott, 1999, pp. 338—339). However, as discussion above made clear, this assumed interrelationship can be highly problematic, and I have previously referred to Ophuls' claim that, in the face of growing ecological scarcity, liberal democracy will need to be replaced by a completely new political philosophy and set of institutions (Ophuls, 1977, p. 3). Certain 'ecological imperatives', which are taken to derive from the fact that terrestrial nature, as a closed system, cannot sustain endless economic growth, conflict with the basis of liberal market policies. In addition, if these requirements are allied to the claim that nature has intrinsic value, a demand arises that may be regarded as taking priority over one grounded in merely contingent, instrumental value. The resulting 'imperatives' have been taken to include—for example, by Jonathan Porritt (1984, pp. 216–217): low consumption, local production for local need and labour intensive production. And for Ophuls there is one key question to ask of social policy: 'Is the way we organise communal life and rule ourselves compatible with ecological imperatives and other natural laws?' For 'how we run our lives will be increasingly determined by ecological imperatives' (Ophuls, 1977, pp. 7–8).

Clearly, *prima facie* this presents a serious challenge to any comfortable alliance between democracy and ecological sustainability, for if there are such ecological imperatives deriving from the laws of nature, then policies that are viewed as being in conflict with them are proscribed. Once identified, ecological imperatives not only are in effect removed from the arena of democratic debate but also set the parameters within which democratic debate can be allowed to function. Furthermore, insofar as such enframing is broad in scope, it is tantamount to defining a conception of the good life to which citizens need to be brought to conform, and thus it might be held both to run counter to the assumption within democracy of valuing diversity of view and to harbour the danger of peripheralising democracy as a contingent value—instrumental to achieving the public acceptance of these imperatives. There is, then, a basic value conflict between the absolute imperative—the authoritarianism—implicit in ecological imperatives and democratic procedures. (For further discussion of these issues, see Michael Saward, 1995.) The educational impact of this kind of conflict will be explored when we examine approaches to environmental education in the next chapter.

But perhaps the most significant general feature to arise from a discussion of sustainability at this point is the recognition of a value position inherent in the views of all who use the term. Not everything can be sustained and as soon as one seeks to clarify *what* is to be sustained, and at what level and over what spatial and temporal scales, one becomes involved in a selection that reflects a particular value or cultural position. In its broadest sense this returns us to one of the great axes of debate in the area of environmental ethics: the issue of anthropocentrism as against biocentrism, discussed in the previous chapter. Should we give priority to, measure policy in terms of, the satisfaction of (long-term) human needs, or the 'needs' of the biosphere (of which human beings are but one small part)? At one level generalised talk of 'sustainability' only cloaks the tension between anthropocentric and biocentric attitudes; it does nothing to resolve them. Yet at another level the term is generally used in a way that tacitly decides the issue, for notwithstanding the expression of concern for natural systems, its use is generally inherently anthropocentric in assuming the desirability of sustaining those natural systems that are conducive to *human* flourishing (however that is defined). But should we simply accept this as a given? Again, as we have seen, a number of writers have championed the worth and 'rights' of non-human aspects of nature—setting human needs strictly on a par with the needs of all other members of the 'great community of life' (Taylor, 1986), or go further and argue that, since humankind has been responsible for so much devastation, they should be subordinated to the well-being of the biosphere (see David Foremen, discussed in Attfield, 1994, pp. 228–229).

Finally, there is a set of thorny epistemological problems raised by the idea of sustainability. Put briefly, it has been claimed that even so-called stable systems remain predictable for relatively short periods of time, and the significance of contingency in any scheme of evolution—and the evolution of human-environment relations in particular (for example, what was there to predict that it would be Europe and not India or China that would develop into modern industrialism? (Simmons, 1995))—makes far-reaching prediction a hazardous business. But often it is precisely far-reaching effects (social, biological, climatic, etc.) that are of such importance in environmental matters—to wit, the cases of carbon-gas emission, nuclear power and genetically modified crops—and this general problem is only exacerbated by the extreme complexity of the systems relevant to environmental sustainability and the highly imperfect state of our current knowledge of them. It is not, of course, that we are not entitled to quite high degrees of confidence in our knowledge of some significant aspects of the environment (such as the ability of certain food chains to concentrate certain toxins or to maintain a certain population). The problem is that one of the great virtues of talk of sustainable policies is that it invites us to take a holistic, rather than an atomistic, view of consequences—so essential when dealing with a system of organic inter-relationships. It attempts precisely to eschew the tendency to externalise from the calculation relevant factors upon which reliable and complete information is difficult to obtain. As Paul Thompson points out, this is a particular danger when those making the calculations are not the ones who may have to bear the costs (Thompson, 1995, pp. 26–32 and Chapter 5).

But now, if we cannot predict the consequences of actions in these holistic terms, how can we decide what is truly sustainable?

This raises a further question: just what *kind* of knowledge will best illuminate, and equip us to deal with, issues of sustainability? For example, is it best conceived in terms of aspects of science and geography, as is the current policy in the National Curriculum of England and Wales? Where does this leave the moral, social, economic, aesthetic and spiritual dimensions of the issues that any adequate understanding of our relationship with our environment involves? In addition, we need to recall reservations about simply assuming the appropriateness of traditional subject domains as vehicles for pursuing environmental issues when historically many of their central motives were shaped in a cultural milieu preoccupied with subordinating and exploiting nature. Carolyn Merchant's discussion of how the gendering of nature as feminine seemed to legitimise an aggressive and invasive stance taken by modern empirical science at its inception is very much a case in point (Merchant, 1992, Chapter 2), and such considerations suggest that we cannot simply assume that the tacit values operative in traditional subject domains will accord with at least some versions of sustainability, nor that these domains themselves will facilitate the holistic—and therefore interdisciplinary—consideration of sustainability issues.

Clearly there is a need to acknowledge such problems and to work them through carefully if we are to achieve a coherent interpretation of 'sustainability' and its educational implications. This is certainly no less the case for the idea of sustainable *development*, to which I now turn.

SUSTAINABLE DEVELOPMENT

The melding of the idea of development with that of sustainability seems to provide a political 'dream ticket' in the area of environmental policy-making. But a number of writers have suggested that such a marriage has several problematic features, and inexorably reinforces a questionable anthropocentric stance. For example, Carl Mitchum (1997) suggests that the underlying motive of sustainable development policy is escape from scarcity and that this latter is defined by the modern Western world as the economy of subsistence. Yet, he suggests, it may turn out that the economy of subsistence and self-reliance is the only truly sustainable way of life. He also puts the point that, as a policy, sustainable development involves a subtle addiction to management, looking upon Earth as 'a spaceship in need of an operating manual'—no doubt to be penned by the politically powerful. For some, such an attitude is highly problematic not only for the political hegemony but in that it continues to express the kind of underlying arrogant superiority and instrumentalism towards nature that has been a prime contributor to present problems.

Again, Vandana Shiva (1992) suggests that in the Western mind 'development' can hardly escape connotations derived from the market economy and that thus situated, economic development is immediately interpreted as economic *growth*. Combining it with sustainability thus holds the danger of transmuting the fundamental motive to *conserve* into one of *finding substitutes* (for example, in terms of energy and materials, as original sources become depleted), which continues to express and feed the underlying motive for material growth and consumption. Indeed, from another perspective, this invites the view that if artificial recreations of nature such as plastic trees and virtual worlds increasingly can provide for human needs more cost-efficiently than nature itself, why should we bother to preserve the real thing (Krieger, 1973; Maser, 1988)? Shiva maintains that from the perspective of the market economy, sustainable development will inevitably be measured by—and therefore come to *mean*—the maximisation of profits and capital accumulation. To the extent that this occurs, it will override and denude the economies of nature and of people. For Shiva, true sustainability requires that development is not separated from conservation and requires that markets and production processes are reshaped on the logic of *nature's* returns. It requires a recognition that it is nature's economy that is primary, not the logic of profits. Far from bringing this home to Western consciousness, the notion of sustainable development is often used in a way that allows it to remain invisible. That the idea of sustainable development might function as part of a more general *simulation* of environmental concern in late modern society will be addressed in Chapter 11.

As things stand, sustainable development has become something that *everyone* can subscribe to without too much inconvenience, from enlightened captains of modern industry to subsistence farmers—the former concerned to create conditions for sustained economic growth, the latter concerned to survive into the future and perhaps better their material lot there. And what initially appears as massive consensus is in danger of breaking up and being revealed as so much empty uplift when pointed questions are put to it.

Yet there are others who are more sanguine about the prospect and value of marrying sustainability to development. For example, Robin Attfield has argued that developmentalism and environmentalism, properly understood, can be mutually supporting. If we see development as a moving away from 'underdevelopment', which he defines as 'a condition of society where several of the following factors reinforce one another: malnutrition, high infant mortality, low levels of literacy, relatively high morbidity among the young and the middle-aged, poor medical facilities, poor educational facilities, low levels of income per head and low levels of productivity per head' (Attfield, 1994, pp. 223–224, and pp. 223–233 *passim*), then we can see that not only does justice require such development where it is possible, but so too does environmentalism. For, according to Attfield, it is underdevelopment in the above terms that is an underlying cause of population growth and of ecological problems. Furthermore, the attitude of mind that sanctions the injustice of exploitation and oppression, whether it be towards other humans or nature, is essentially the *same* and is thus the common enemy of both developmentalism and environmentalism. (See also Katz, 1997.) While there are aspects of these arguments that require a good deal more supporting empirical evidence, the notion of the significance of an underlying frame of mind that is highlighted in this kind of account is one that I believe rewards further consideration and to which I will therefore return.

But notwithstanding Attfield's positive assessment, it is clear that the notion of sustainable development requires careful explication—and ultimately, I suggest, stipulative definition—if its use is not to invite confusion and perhaps a betrayal of the motives it was originally intended to express. Even then, depending on the as yet unknown realities of, for example, population growth and the sustaining power of ecosystems, its coherence may turn out to be chimerical. The great danger is that it simply becomes a term of political convenience used to mask or legitimate vested interests.

Let me now summarise the problematics of sustainable development. They fall into three categories:

  i) *Semantic.* It is possible for a society simply to interpret the term in ways that are congenial to it (for example, that involve minimum disturbance to its economic ambitions) and thus, say, for Western-style economies to use it to affect deep concern for the environment while pursuing sustainable economic growth in a way that shows scant regard for a more broadly conceived ecological perspective.

 ii) *Ethical.* Varying assumptions are being made about the rights and responsibilities of humankind in relation to the rest of nature and, for example, about whether any such underlying ethic should be anthropocentric, biocentric or something else altogether. This raises the fundamental issue of how any ethical dimension is to be grounded. There is also the issue of the nature of a moral relationship with future generations.

iii) *Epistemological.* Given the high degrees of complexity of the natural and social systems (and the sheer extent of the spatial and temporal dimensions over which they can operate) that are affected by human activity, and our current very imperfect state of knowledge of them, how are we to judge which actions will positively contribute to sustainable development? Even if the 'ends' of any policy were clear and regarded as unproblematic, are we in a position to judge the means? If not, how does one construct a policy in a situation where in practice it is impossible to avoid action that *might* have detrimental consequences for the environment—and for future generations, knowledge of whose needs is also problematic?

These seem to me to continue to represent very significant problems for the idea of sustainable development as a policy, meaning by this a strategy or course of action rationally devised in the service of some pre-specified goal. And, as several of the above mentioned thinkers predict, its assimilation to anthropocentric economistic interpretations is likely to be particularly true for modern Western culture, which is increasingly dominated by a set of motives that occlude the possibility of an approach to environmental issues that is genuinely open to nature. In such a culture, if a genuine responsiveness to the plight of natural systems is to occur, everyday values will need to be examined carefully and with a view to radical transformation. Yet, as I have argued previously, it is not that we can simply turn to some other culture, assumed to be more eco-sympathetic, to provide us with solutions, for such guidance will necessarily lack the 'internal' insight into Western culture's own peculiar capacities and problems and its horizons of significance for interpreting them. Nor, of course, is it that modern Western culture is completely devoid of the necessary intellectual and emotional resources to articulate and address the issues. As we have seen, there are, and have been for some time, obvious strands within it that advert to a considerable simpatico with nature. St Francis of Assisi, John Clare, Ralph Waldo Emerson, Henry Thoreau, Gerald Manley Hopkins, Albert Schweitzer and others may have been unusual, but they were not freaks. They expressed something that at some level we can all recognise.

SUSTAINABILITY AS FRAME OF MIND

In the first part of this chapter I have developed the point that sustainable development conceived as a policy, while in some ways a highly attractive notion in that it promises to meld aspirations for an improved standard of living with the perceived need for conservation, is also highly problematic in a number of ways. While it is not my position that progress cannot be made on such matters (and indeed, as indicated above, progress on the semantic front is underway), some of the ethical and epistemological issues remain so far from satisfactory resolution that one is invited to explore an alternative approach to the idea—namely, I suggest, sustainability conceived not as a policy but as *a frame of mind*. To adopt this approach is not simply to attempt to circumvent difficult issues but rather to refocus on a question that I have argued to be fundamental to any policy development—viz.: *what constitutes a right relationship with nature?* As previously noted, this raises a set of questions not only about basic understandings of, and motives towards, nature, but also about human identity and flourishing, which are also, of course, implicit in any proper understanding of sustainable development.

My intention in this section is to draw together a number of arguments, which have been deployed throughout preceding chapters, that may contribute to characterising such a frame of mind. But first, I need to clarify what I mean by this term. I intend the term 'frame of mind' to signify a general mode of engagement with the world through which the world as a whole is revealed to us, or, to use a Heideggerian expression loosely, it is a (more or less conscious) way of being in the world. This involves a certain cognitive/conceptual outlook, but also involves aspects of our sensibility that are not normally associated with 'looking', so characterised—a *sensing* of things that may occur as much through bodily contact as through more overt cognitive perception. Such an outlook also involves a gamut of affective, moral, aesthetic, imaginative and other receptions and responses. Thus I might equally well term it 'a mode of sensibility', and, relating this to a helpful analysis of possible interpretations given by Andrew Stables (2002), while characterising it in terms of 'mood' and 'disposition' has the attraction of emphasising a certain pervasiveness and possible non-cognitive features, it underplays the possible significance of cognitive elements. Furthermore, strictly conceived, I suppose an individual's participation in a mode of sensibility could be occasional or intermittent, particularly when competing modes are dominant socially and in this sense while 'frame of mind' in part certainly denotes how one is disposed towards the world at a particular time and carries connotations of fundamental orientation, this can fall short of its being one's 'default' disposition. But this *is* the aspiration, for as Iris Murdoch points out: 'We act rightly "when the time comes" not out of strength of will but out of the quality of our usual attachments and with the kind of energy and discernment which we have available. And to this the whole activity of our consciousness is relevant' (Murdoch, 1997, p. 375).

Next, it will be helpful to refer back to a definition of 'nature' itself. In the course of Chapter 3 I illustrated how 'nature' has many senses and showed that the idea has a long history in which it has been constructed and interpreted in a large variety of contexts. Here I wish to return to what I identified there as our current underlying sense of the term: 'nature' as a dimension of experience that apprehends the self-arising in the material/spiritual world of which we are a part, including the powers that sustain and govern it. Such aspects of the world are experienced as essentially *independent* of human will, but not *unaffected* by it. Thus, I made the point that even in the case of our own physical nature we can do things that affect the well-being of our bodies, but that what that well-being essentially consists in and the powers that it has to maintain itself—and with which we 'interact' for better or worse—are not things of which we are the authors.

To return now to the issue of sustainability as a frame of mind. Any view of how we should treat the environment expresses or assumes a certain frame of mind towards nature. Thus a straightforwardly anthropocentric environmental ethic that privileges enlightened human self-interest clearly does this, as, indeed, does the view that seeks to include *all* sentient life in a morality based on the maximisation of pleasure or happiness and the minimisation of pain (for example, Singer, 1993). These views can be seen as lying well within that constellation of ideas that constitute the current Western outlook and thus, when presented, require little if any disruption of what is taken to be common sense. Though Singer's view may require a degree of adjustment for some, it might be said to be quantitative rather than qualitative, the avoidance of the unnecessary infliction of pain being an entirely familiar motive.

However, as we have seen, there are other views that, while still rooted in aspects of the Western tradition, make greater demands on Western consciousness through requiring an increasing extension and depth of sympathy or empathy towards the flourishing of things beyond ourselves. Arguably, these amount to a *qualitative* change of outlook and ultimately lead to a transformation of what we take ourselves to be. For example, Paul Taylor's (1986) claim that, through a heightened awareness, we can perceive that all living beings are attempting to realise their own good, and that rationality requires that humans respect this in the same way that it requires respect for individual human beings seeking *their* own good, hardly resonates with current dominant Western attitudes. Similarly, transposing this idea from the context of a Kantian 'duty ethic' into the context of a 'care ethic', Freya Mathews' emphasis on the attitude of identification with—and therefore affirmation of, and Eros towards—an ecocosm of self-realising entities that constitutes a new extended sense of ourselves, an 'ecological self', requires a cultural and psychological leap.

But, whatever their differences and weaknesses, they both underscore a very important point: our relationship with nature, whatever its kind, is an important aspect of our own identity—and thus of our self-knowledge. The way we regard and treat nature—the whole that sustains us and of which we are a part—says a lot about the sort of beings we are as well as the sorts of beings we regard everything else to be. In this sense Heidegger (1998) was right in seeing that there is an important sense in which the idea of 'nature' that we hold defines our understanding of, and attitude towards, both the world and ourselves. This means, of course, that it will also set the contours of what can count as human flourishing. Thus it is apparent that the issue of sustainability as a frame of mind is not simply the issue of our attitude towards the environment but represents a perspective on that set of most fundamental ethical, epistemological and metaphysical considerations that describe human being. It is a perspective that is both theoretical and practical in that it is essentially concerned with human practices and the conceptions and values that are embedded in them. It thus requires a re-consideration of the metaphysics expressed in current Western attitudes, where by metaphysics is meant not the study of some highly abstract and abstruse realm that can only be known, if at all, *post hoc*, but, as argued in Chapter 2, the set of fundamentally orientating motives that are working themselves out in our time and that are expressed in, and form, the basic contours of our understanding and behaviour—that is, our form of sensibility.

Yet, if an adequate response to our environmental predicament in effect requires a metaphysical transformation, precisely because of this it must arise from within the horizons of significance with which our culture provides us—that is within the space opened up for us, made possible, by them. For it is our metaphysical horizons that fundamentally condition our sense of the real and, therefore, of what is possible, what is fitting and what is fantasy. Thus the transformation needs to be understood as a retrieval and re-generation rather than some external import or imposition.

In this vein, Charles Taylor refers to the pre-modern era in which our understanding of the order of things was bound up with our understanding of ourselves, because we perceived ourselves as an integral part of that order: 'And we cannot understand the order and our place in it without loving it, without seeing its goodness, which is what I want to call our attunement with it' (C. Taylor, 1983, p. 142). This sounds like a psychological generalisation rather than a strictly logical claim, and amongst other things it assumes that we love ourselves. Nonetheless, while formally it may be possible, for example, to despise one's origins and what sustains one, this seems an *empty* possibility that cannot be endorsed by those who have not somehow psychologically either separated themselves from their origins and what sustains them (which, arguably is precisely the achievement of modernity) or who have come to despise themselves. Of course, in a holistic understanding of our situation there is a level at which 'goodness' always means that which is in some way good for *us*: because conceived as part of a system, what is good for that system must benefit us. But, in contrast to Freya Mathews, this is not Taylor's real point. The issue here is less ontological and more about essential human nature in the sense of how things are *experienced*. I take it that Taylor is making the point that love is the natural human emotion towards what truly sustains us. Thus alienation from nature and from oneself are highly interrelated and key to our ability knowingly to despoil the environment. If we love ourselves, we will love what we believe supports us.

This view suggests strongly that part of education for sustainability as a frame of mind will be somehow to reconnect people with their origins and what sustains them, *and* to develop their love of themselves. But what is to be the underlying spirit of this 'reconnection'? What version of a 'reconnected' orientation towards nature should be sought? For example, both anthropocentric and biocentric attitudes are forms of connection. What is to be the source of non-arbitrariness in value judgements in this area?

Discussion of anthropocentric and biocentric views in the previous chapter suggested that both suffer problems: the first because of its essential oblivion to nature as the self-arising; the second because of its essential oblivion to the special character of human consciousness, and the consequent potential for ecofascism. This leads us to examine the possibilities of an approach that is neither anthropocentric in the conventional sense of seeing our relationship with the environment as properly orientated entirely around human interests or wants, nor ecocentric in the sense of subsuming us in, or subordinating us to, some greater whole. Such an approach would run along the following lines.

Taken as a theory of *meaning*, anthropocentrism points us towards an essential truth. Things—including 'purely natural' things—are always revealed to us in a context of human concerns and practices, and their reality is therefore always at some level conditioned by such concerns and practices. Notions such as care, sympathy, empathy, identification, responsibility, which fundamentally bring things close (and are celebrated by ecocentrism), are only possible for entities that operate at the human

level of conscious functioning—indeed, we might say that such qualities are partly *definitive* of it. Thus things show up—in a sense *become*
the things that they are—within individual and cultural horizons of
significance and in this sense are indelibly human-related. Heidegger's
portrayal of the ancient temple (discussed in Chapter 5) illustrated this at
the cultural level. At another, more specific level, the reciprocal
relationship between human motives and the disclosure of otherness is
nicely illustrated by certain artefacts, such as a sailing boat. Its hull and
sails are shaped by human purposes, but equally by the non-human
elements in which it is to perform. Indeed if it is a good boat it will be very
finely attuned to these, such that the non-human elements, through this
acknowledgement, are brought more sharply into relief: brought from
relatively vague and shadowy presence into the revealing light of mutual
appropriation to some human concern—as, for example, the qualities of
water displayed by the bows sheering through it and throwing it off in a
particular way. But the boat is also the embodiment of a wealth of cultural
motifs and personal associations—emotions, aspirations and fantasies. Its
'purely physical' properties only exist as an abstraction from this organic
gathering and their meaning and significance are implicitly bound in with
this.

So human beings are necessary participants in, but not in control of, the
showing up of beings. Human beings *enable*, but do not *produce* in the
sense of being 'sole authors'. And they are essentially themselves
precisely through participating in this disclosure of otherness. Thus, to
recognise that things are human-related in this way—and this is the truth
embodied in ecocentrism—implies neither that their meaning and
existence is purely a product of the mind, nor that our evaluative or
ethical stance towards them need be human-centred. In Chapter 5 I noted
that consciousness, alone, is not the author of things: it, itself, *is* only in its
relationship with things; things constitute consciousness as much as
consciousness constitutes things. That is to say consciousness *is* the space
where things show up, and the precise quality of conscious space at any
moment is conditioned by these things in their showing up (with all their
cultural significances).

On this account we are not the author, but, in Heideggerian vein, the
occasioner of things, and also of intrinsic value, in that only entities
functioning at our level of consciousness can discern such value; but we
are not the only *bearers* of intrinsic value. Thus it is perfectly
intelligible—and, for example, very characteristic of some aspects of
our experience of nature—to be deeply affected by the sheer otherness of
non-human things. Consider the feeling of deep respect that can be evoked
by the inscrutable massiveness of an ancient oak tree or, for that matter,
the delicate vitality of a ciliate protozoan in a drop of pond water viewed
through a microscope, not to mention the possible emotional impact of a
mountain, a galaxy or a god. With Iris Murdoch's caveat that we have
always to be alert to the disguised substitution of the self for the true
object of veneration, this is to reassert the significance of a *poetic*
dimension to human awareness. It suggests a broader, and more

demanding, conception of the contribution that the curriculum can make to environmental education than is sometimes recognised. Sustainability as an attitude of mind seeks openness to as many facets and significances of nature as possible—a receptiveness to the fullness of what is there— and thereby involves a certain basic simpatico with the non-human. It places humankind as neither the 'lord of beings' nor as something to be subsumed under some greater ecological whole, and although it can- not matter in the slightest to biophysical nature whether humankind survives—some equilibrium will always be established, with or without us—nature only has *significance* in that space that is human conscious- ness, or its equivalent.

How sustainability as a frame of mind is to be fostered in education is a topic for the next chapter, but here we need to note that the 'poetic' should not be equated with the 'passive'. We appropriate nature and ourselves not only through abstract reflection and aesthetic contemplation, but also in our making and in the intimate details of our sundry daily transactions with our environment. Some aspects of this point were developed in the discussion of the notion of 'attentiveness' in Chapter 6, but it also means that while the impact of particular—in a sense, elevated—experiences may be seminal, poetic response is also constituted by day-to-day prac- tices and actions that implicitly reflect the desire to disclose, conserve and safeguard things, to respect the intuitions provided by sensuous contact and properly to acknowledge natural rhythms and processes. It was to provide illustration of such sensibility in the process of building—what we might, therefore, call 'poetic building'—that reference was made to Heidegger's description of the old bridge and the Black Forest farmhouse. Such poetic receptive-responsiveness, of course, would be just as applicable to the building of non-material things such as interpersonal relationships and legal systems. Indeed, with regard to the former, such sensitivity and responsiveness to the other is a *sine qua non* of building a good personal relationship. (I have developed this idea in relation to the teacher–pupil relationship in Bonnett, 1996.)

An important feature of this view is that it locates the essence of sustainability in the space of human consciousness itself—that is, in the very event of being conscious at this level—and thus differs both from conventional anthropocentrism and ecocentrism, which can be regarded as veiling modifications of consciousness, the one legitimating an arbitrary narrowing of concern, the other advocating an arbitrary expansion. On this view, consciousness itself involves precisely—and primordially—that openness, responsiveness and responsibility towards things that are the essence of sustainability as a frame of mind. Thus, this argument roots the notion of sustainability in the notion of *truth* and its centrality to human being. Truth, as our awareness of things themselves in their manifoldness and mystery, and involving our sense of the fittingness of the language that both facilitates and expresses this disclosure (*le mot juste*), lies at the heart of human consciousness. In constituting an apprehension of what *is*, relatively unsubverted by external instrumental motives (though perhaps apprehending such motives, or arising in a context set by them and, of course, always occurring within our overall form of sensibility), the 'pure' sustaining nature of truth is also the essence of sustainability as a concern to let things be (as they are themselves)—to safeguard, to preserve, to conserve. This is clearly quite a different sense of sustainability to that which seeks to 'sustain', *in order* to have ready to hand, a resource required for some further development (such as might be taken to serve human material aspirations). This argument also implies a sense of sustainability whose denial would involve alienation from our own essence and therefore from our own flourishing. For authentic human being, the attitude of sustainability is not a bolt-on option but a necessity. It constitutes an element of our own good.

And by what warrant do I assert this? By the warrant of a descriptive metaphysical investigation—an attempt to retrieve sentiments deeply embedded in our form of sensibility. The veracity of its findings ultimately is to be measured by the reader referring them reflectively to his or her own experience.

One further point is worth emphasising here. This account takes issue with the notion of seeking a frame of mind that will *bring about* sustainability. This would be to revert to interpreting sustainability as a policy, and such an approach makes the frame of mind subservient to some highly contentious further goal—contentious now in the sense that it presumes to predict and to control the self-arising. Rather my argument invites us to consider that sustainability can *itself* be conceived as a frame of mind—and one that is of the essence of human being and, therefore, of human well-being. Obviously, this leaves it open to the criticism that we do not know whether the frame of mind advocated would in fact bring about *ecological* sustainability. There are two central points here. The first is that now posited as something external to us and pervaded by all the unknowables noted previously, ecological sustainability is not something for us to masterfully 'bring about'. Indeed, so presented, it is not even clear how we should define it. The second point is that if sustainability as a frame of mind is essential to human flourishing, its desirability is not ultimately dependent on whether it will lead to ecological sustainability somehow externally defined, though given its fundamental motive to reveal and safeguard things in their own nature, it is difficult to think that it would not be compatible with most versions. Rather, its achievement in some degree is what gives *point* to the achievement of any such ecological sustainability, and as such should define its character. Without it, 'sustained' human life would be so impoverished as to be of little worth—either to itself or in its revealing of nature.

Thus the possibility of education for sustainable development seen from this perspective involves a radical interpretation of the notion that retrieves non-instrumental conceptions of development and human flourishing and that, at the same time, recognises the special place that humankind has in the cosmos. While drawing on strands of thought central to the Western tradition, it clearly runs counter to many motives and values that are currently ascendant in Western society, and is therefore likely to be viewed as politically uncongenial. Prevailing values, and social, economic and political arrangements, determine what will appear as problems by directing attention away from their own problematic nature. If we are to enable pupils to address the issues raised by sustainable development rather than to preoccupy them with what are essentially symptoms masquerading as causes (for example, measuring pollutant levels and devising scientific 'remedies' rather than addressing the underlying motives and conceptions embedded in social practices that give rise to pollution), we must engage them in those kinds of enquiry that reveal the underlying dominant motives that are in play in society—motives that are inherent in our most fundamental ways of thinking about ourselves and the world. That such a metaphysical investigation will be discomforting for many seems unavoidable, but it promises to be more productive in the long term than proceeding on the basis of easy—because vague—assumptions about the goals of sustainable development, as though it were a policy whose chief problems are of implementation rather than of meaning and motive.

Chapter 10. Issues for Environmental Education

In Chapter 1 I sketched what I characterised as a tangled web of ideas and concerns that forms the backdrop to the issue of environmental education. I went on to identify a number of key questions that an adequate account of environmental education needs to address. At the heart of these was the question: What understanding of nature and our relationship to nature and the environment should we invite pupils to participate in? I suggested that this underpins the character of any ethic that should inform environmental education, the kinds of knowledge that best illuminate and promote a proper relationship with nature, the qualities of learning and the pedagogical approaches that would be consistent with this, and the character of the school as an institution and its relationship to the community. In subsequent chapters I attempted cumulatively both to explore some of the general issues relevant to a consideration of environmental education and to develop a basic orientation towards it. In preparation for a more direct focus on approaches to teaching, learning and the curriculum, which is the business of this chapter, I will review and draw together some key strands of the view that has emerged.

A BACKDROP TO ENVIRONMENTAL EDUCATION

From the outset, I suggested that a thorough exploration of the idea of environmental education leads us into the metaphysics of education—metaphysics here understood not as constructing a set of abstract categories, but as revealing primal motives that are working themselves out in our existence and thus that actively participate in and shape our lives in fundamental ways. We live in a certain metaphysical space. And so does education—in the way in which it is held in the sway of ideals such as those of truth, understanding, morality and personhood. These are powers that draw it forward into itself, to express its own characteristics. And intimately interfused with the draught of these powers is that of our understanding of nature: what we take it to be and how we interpret our position with regard to it conditions our understanding of ourselves and our place in the greater scheme of things. Indeed, I went on to argue that there is an important sense in which nature constitutes our primordial reality, even though in so many ways its visibility is occluded—for example, by an overweening motive for mastery and the character of the equipment with which this motive surrounds us.

This then raised the question: What is nature? Having acknowledged that the term has a multiplicity of meanings and that it often functions politically, I reviewed a number of powerful conceptions and senses that continue to shape our outlook. I argued that underlying the diversity remains an important unifying idea: nature conceived as the self-arising whose features furnish fundamental aspects of our metaphysical space, that is to say, our *reality*. I defended this notion against a set of objections, some of which I dubbed loosely 'postmodernist', where this can be interpreted as rejecting any such foundational reality. I accepted that our concepts of nature are socially produced, but not necessarily that they are all thereby rendered optional, arbitrary or function politically. And even when there are political implications, not all narratives of legitimation are narratives of power, there being such a thing as proper authority—though we need to be alert to the possibility of certain voices being expressed in ascriptions of nature and what is natural, and to recognise that any description of nature is partial. I argued that the idea of nature as the self-arising is deeply embedded in our form of sensibility, constituting one of its most fundamental meaning-enabling horizons, and that so understood it can rightly be experienced as real, valuable and non-ideological (in the pejorative sense), since at this level our form of sensibility is a condition of us having any meaningful experience whatever.

Moving on to delineating some of its important features, I suggested that the reality of nature as the self-arising exhibits the following: it is epistemologically mysterious; it possesses its own integrity as a spatially and temporally continuous whole; it is inescapable and everything that occurs within it is unique, cannot be 'replayed'; it has intrinsic value. Thus characterised, nature is that dimension of experience that, simply, we have to accept and that, because of its essential otherness, from which we can genuinely learn and be inspired, can save us from an essential stulti-fication. I argued that expressions of nature are best understood in terms of a metaphysics of open, infinitely-faceted, essentially mysterious *things* rather than stabilised, heavily categorised, intellectually possessed *objects*—things here also understood in the Heideggerian sense of arisings that gather a neighbourhood; through their inscrutable presencing a world of significances is opened up. It follows that if we are to know nature so characterised, we must learn to develop the receptive/responsive—that is to say, poetic—attitude that itself is a key characteristic of authentic dwelling, a dwelling that is in touch with what ultimately sustains it.

Thus we were brought up against the issues of nature's intrinsic value and of the kinds of knowledge appropriate to the apprehension of nature. Both of these constitute central elements in that 'right' relationship with nature that I have argued to be the prime goal of environmental education. While, amongst other things, this chapter will be concerned to explore some of the pedagogical implications of the ideas of knowledge, value and sustainability developed in the chapters that followed, by way of preliminary it is worth noting that an educational focus brings to the forefront an important general issue raised by the analyses that led up to nature as the self-arising: how is it discerned?

At various points previously, I have acknowledged that it can be misperceived, that, for example, it can be faked, that what is essentially a matter of optional convention can be presented as a matter of irrefutable nature. To take an innocent example, a young child might take a string puppet to be a living animal. She is enthralled, perhaps, by the naturalness of its movements and in this she may be right: if the artistry of the puppeteer is sufficient, an element of the natural will be present, contributing to the significance of the experience. But a time will come when she needs to be brought to see the strings and *their* significance. So it may be for many areas of experience. Discerning the self-arising then requires careful attention that, where there is cause for concern, may include calculative rational investigation but primarily involves consulting our experience in a broader sense—including, through a communicative rationality, that of others—if ideological and other impostors are to be detected. We may need to explore how something looks and feels from a wide range of vantage points within our form of sensibility and to be open to the intuitions that they offer. Much of what we so come across—a harebell in the grass, a hatching baetis fly nymph in the stream—is clearly natural in not bearing the imprint of human intention. But there may be other cases where we have cause for suspicion concerning the extent to which something presented as purely natural truly is so, such as gender characterisations and roles, or versions of what constitutes a proper equilibrium in nature. Ultimately, in such cases, we may need to contemplate how a thing sits within our form of sensibility in its many modes and nuances, which range from direct sensuous contact to science, art and poetry.

Thus, in educational terms, sensing nature as the self-arising and understanding our relationship with it will require a broad and rich curriculum in which a receptive-responsive rather than rational-assertive thinking holds sway. I attempted to elucidate this underlying stance in terms of sustainability as a frame of mind, arguing that ontologically, human consciousness is neither the author of things, nor a contingent spectator, but the 'occasioner' of things—it is the space (world) where meaning and value is discerned, there being no significant things without consciousness and no consciousness without things. Therefore, disposing ourselves so that things can show up as they are in their epistemic mystery and many-sidedness—sustaining them in the sense of letting them be what they are themselves, rather than, say, what they are in terms of their use or as defined objects—is not some peripheral and dispensable luxury, but constitutive of our essence. It is through such a disposition that we may truly come home. Recognition of the respectful, other-sensitive, receptive-responsive or 'poetic' thinking that this involves—and that is expressed as much in making as in perceiving—leads to interpreting sustainability as both necessary to authentic human being and as eschewing the overweening instrumentalism and mastery tacit in policies of sustainable development, such motives constituting the currently dominant metaphysics that has brought us to our present environmental situation of alienation and irresponsible dependence. So understood, sustainability as a frame of mind is perhaps an example of what Iris Murdoch once termed a 'virtuous consciousness', a way of thinking that strives to apprehend things freed from 'the anxious avaricious tentacles of the self' and 'sees the pointlessness of virtue and its unique value and the endless extent of its demand' (Murdoch, 1997, p. 385).

As she also pointed out, 'It is a *task* to see the world as it is' (p. 375). By way of opening up the issues raised for environmental education, I will now address the question of what might be involved in developing such a frame of mind in which revelation rather than manipulation is the aspiration.

DEVELOPING SUSTAINABILITY AS A FRAME OF MIND

Previous argument has made it clear that essentially we are concerned with a gradual change in how we apprehend the world at a fundamental level—that is, the growth of a different metaphysical basis to education. Amongst other things, this means that, as a priority, we need to reconsider what counts as the knowing and learning appropriate to education. For example, we need to ask what projects towards the world different kinds of knowledge and learning express. Clearly the inherent mystery and fluid integrity of nature conceived as self-arising—the world of open, infinitely faceted 'things'—is not susceptible to an engagement that is preoccupied with intellectual (and other) possession and that is articulated exclusively through systematised conceptual schemes. Self-arising facets of the world are simply occluded by teaching that has this orientation. More intimate, intuitive, often sensuous and 'non-logical' encounters with things must be admitted. Participation, celebration, accommodation to the strange and willingness to be affected must displace an overweening drive to disengage from the immediately present so as to set it to order, to control it, to be 'effective'. And certainly, on this view, conventional science would cease to hold the privileged position that it currently enjoys as arbiter of our understanding of the natural world. Whatever unity nature possesses, it is diverse and complex beyond the compass of any systematised understanding—from our perspective, always in part a shadowy and inchoate unity. Here then, the issue of environmentally adequate knowledge and its curriculum organisation is raised: Should it be subject-based and if so, what kinds of subjects? Should it be a holistic, integrated curriculum, and, if so, according to what structural principles? These and related points will be taken up presently.

First, it is important to note that a frame of mind that is in some sense adequate to nature as the self-arising will constantly evolve: as its elements develop they refine one another, enable new interpretations, apprehend new relationships and hierarchies, and so begin to reflect the ever-changing countenances of things. Discussion in the previous chapter acknowledged that a frame of mind *per se*, while inclining towards something enduring, could be intermittent, even transient. This reflected the fragility of a sustaining frame of mind in a culture in which countermanding attitudes have become solidified in dominant social structures. Yet the fundamentality of orientation involved in sustainability as a frame of mind suggests strands that will neither rapidly arise nor dissolve. A steady disposition is required. What, therefore should be its ethical basis? Should an explicit environmental ethic of respect for natural things be taught in a way that parallels the teaching of a basic human ethic of respect for persons?

This focus on an evolving frame of mind, rather than on the acquisition of the pre-specified knowledge and behaviour content that tend to be emphasised by a 'delivery' model of the curriculum, suggests that the issue is not exclusively—perhaps, not primarily—one of formal curriculum content and pedagogy but rather a matter of the general culture of the school (and, of course, of society). The underlying versions of human flourishing and the good life that are implicit in the ethos and practices of the school as a community both invite direct participation in—and therefore tacit commitment to—ways of relating to the world and condition the spirit in which the formal curriculum is taught and received. Therefore, they too will need to reverberate to a metaphysics—open up a space—that celebrates those kinds of experience of the presence of nature in which the power and subtlety of otherness and the elemental is felt and allowed to matter, whether directly experienced or mediated through literature, art and craft. A space, too, where essentially natural produce—including such produce incorporated into artefacts—can be experienced, at least partly, as a gift rather than simply as a function of demand.

Such a perspective will translate into questions concerning the status accorded to different activities, relationships and versions of 'being successful' in life. Following C. A. Bowers (1995), we might be very worried if an audit of school life revealed that, however implicitly, ultimately 'success' is portrayed in terms of the values of market production and consumption, if the projected sense of community embraces only humankind, science and technology are accorded high status in the curriculum and their advances are represented not only as synonymous with progress but also as chief in setting the limits to human endeavour, and if the needs of the present and near future are countenanced as overriding. Also we might be alerted to the way that, for example, a classic children's author such as Philippa Pierce sometimes portrays animals as essentially objects to satisfy human emotions (*A Dog So Small*, *The Battle of Bubble and Squeak*), or to the way an overtly 'nature-centred' novel such as *Tarka the Otter* uses animal situations as a vehicle for conveying human perspectives (on beauty, for example). It might sensitise us to an implicit advocacy of exuberant outlooks and lifestyles that ignores their energy requirements and their cost in terms of environmental pollution and depletion, to the relative emphasis on the value of time devoted to aesthetic and spiritual activity as against economic 'productivity', to the kind of talk of 'Our world' that does not problematise what 'we' includes, and to the use of fables that are often (but not always) emblematic of hierarchical power rather than interdependence (Whitley, 1996).

SUSTAINABILITY AND THE CURRICULUM

So how might developing sustainability as a frame of mind best be approached in terms of the school curriculum? In response to a previous articulation of my view on sustainability, and looking at the curriculum as a whole, Andrew Stables and Bill Scott (2002) have argued that it would be a mistake to attempt to erect sustainability as an additional cross-disciplinary element based on some holistic conception of an appropriate frame of mind and its developmental needs. They prefer a more piecemeal, 'postmodern' approach that eschews any such implied grand narrative in favour of developing sustainability *within* the differing perspectives that existing school disciplines have to offer. They point out that as we are not in a position to regenerate the education system (particularly teachers' expertise and attitudes) from scratch, this would also seem to be more far more realisable in practice. Such a view provokes a number of important points.

First, to advocate the development of sustainability as a frame of mind is not to be committed to some totalising cross-curricula alternative to the disciplines. Not only would this carry with it the danger of a certain ecofascism, it would overlook the following facts: that (a) on the view I have developed, sustainability is neither to be hived off into some discrete theme, nor to be given some independent, detailed, pre-specifiable content to supplement or replace the disciplines (there is a sense in which it is best construed as a way of teaching rather than another subject or theme); and that (b) in day-to-day experience many eco-related issues (including our understandings of nature) occur in a piecemeal way, there being no obvious overarching objective logic to link them. This is entirely consistent with an underlying reality experienced as the self-arising, and I have pointed out that genuine openness to situations is not enhanced by seeking to impose all-embracing systematic conceptualisations. Precisely the opposite. Nonetheless, a certain underlying posture, frame of mind, is required that can lend such piecemeal understandings and actions a certain organic consistency. There is a certain *ethical* holism in the way that they can be sensed as somehow fitting and compatible—as, say, in the case where anger is felt at both the assault of a young child and the vandalism of a tree; just as there is a converse ethical holism involved in anthropocentrism—exemplified in extreme form by the Nazi goal of dominating both humans and nature (see Katz, 1997). So, under current mainstream curriculum organisation, part of the development of sustainability as a frame of mind will necessarily occur in the context of a traditional subject curriculum, expressing, as it does, presumably, enduring strands of our form of sensibility.

However, at the same time, certain questions will need to be raised of a 'within discipline' approach. First, might not this approach be susceptible to an unhelpful conservatism? Proper account will need to be taken of the danger of motives inherent in a discipline (including its own critical procedures), which may be covertly hostile to self-arising nature and, therefore, set up eco-problems in a way that conceals their own contribution to them—remembering that many disciplines have their roots in a cultural milieu whose dominant aspiration was and is to conquer and exploit the natural world. *Contra* the defence that is sometimes put up, this problem will hardly be exposed by reflexive techniques *within* that discipline. There is a sense in which the primary agenda of a discipline sometimes may need to be amended—as may its presumptions concerning how much of the story it is able to tell and the primordiality of its account.

Second, in the light of the above, does not the supposed practical advantage attributed by Stables and Scott to a within-discipline approach trade on an ambiguity? Its plausibility rests in playing to the established loyalties and strengths of practitioners within the disciplines, but 'examining . . . the various ways in which each discipline construes, and has construed, the human-nature relationship' sounds to have more the character of a *meta*-disciplinary examination. This is likely to be just as unfamiliar and uncomfortable for 'subject-loyal' teachers as an external education for sustainability framework. It is, of course, an interesting point as to how far a particular discipline may incorporate its own meta-enquiry, but I suggest that this is rarely a feature of disciplines as taught at school. This has pretty obvious and highly important implications for the professional development of teachers, which includes the need for all teachers to acquire a broader cultural understanding of the material of their subject in order that they may convey something of its rootedness in their pedagogy. It also raises again the desirability of pupils' being invited to locate the claims to knowledge made by the disciplines against a broader backcloth of metaphysical understanding. This might enable them to challenge any unjustifiable, currently dominant assumptions concerning the superiority of approaches to knowledge that tend towards abstraction and that disengage pupils from their own intuitions of the real. This is just one way in which the importance of authentic discussion needs to be highlighted in the teaching of environmental issues, as does the need to accept and explore different vocabularies for articulating understanding and issues. This line of thinking further suggests the value of a certain kind of open *conversation* in education—meaning by this a form of dialogue that is less goal-orientated or pre-focussed than discussion is usually taken to be. For example, it would not be concerned to solve some pre-specified problem or explore some delineated issue, but rather, as it were, to follow its own path, achieving a certain rigour by attending carefully to whatever occurs on its way and feels significant. This could hardly be part of the formal curriculum, but again intimates the signifcance of the wider life of the school.

Such issues concerning the generation, legitimacy and 'ownership' of knowledge in the educational context are nicely illustrated by the ideas that have arisen in a long-standing international programme exploring the ways in which environmental concern should impact on educational practice: the Environment and Schools Initiative (ENSI) programme initiated in 1986 by the OECD. It is evident that those involved in this project see the impact as being radical in a range of ways that, taken together, would certainly transform the nature of schooling as it is commonly practised in Western Europe and elsewhere. In his account of the project's evolution, John Elliott describes it as having arrived at an agenda that transgresses many traditional boundaries enshrined in educational systems: between the school and the university as the traditional site of knowledge production; between subject specialisms; between childhood dependency and adult responsibility, between formal learning inside schools conceived as warehouses and informal learning in real-life social and community contexts; between insiders and outsiders; between institutions/organisations; between knowledge producers and knowledge users; between teaching and educational research; between teaching and learning; between knowing and acting; between 'global' and 'local' knowledge; between facts and values, etc. (Elliott, 1999, p. 330).

These 'transgressions' arise from the recognition that an adequate educational response to environmental concern requires the development of individuals who are prepared to participate in 'shaping the social and economic conditions of their existence in society' and transforming the manifold ways in which the school as an organisation interacts with and impacts upon the environment. As Peter Posch puts it, there must be a shift of priorities from

the prevalence of learning tasks structured by systematic knowledge to a focus on complex, real life unstructured situations which raise controversial issues . . . and from passive learning of facts, rules and principles to the active generation of knowledge by pupils and teachers in the local contexts of action, to a pro-active shaping of the environment, to promoting a critical reflective attitude towards given stocks of knowledge (Posch, 1999, p. 342).

This approach clearly represents a radical departure from traditional environmental education as 'environmentalism', which essentially seeks to transmit from above predetermined environmentally 'good' attitudes and behaviour. There are two strong underlying themes in this 'new generation' environmental education:

i) Because engagement has to be local and communal and because there are so many unknowns, teachers and learners must have the autonomy to identify and decide issues in the light of local contingent circumstances.

ii) Because what lies at the heart of environmental concern is the need for action, central to learning is the notion of knowledge as *action competence*—being effective in the real world. Crucially, this involves not just factual and theoretical knowledge, but the understanding, capacities and attitudes necessary to working communally to bring about change.

In its desire to transgress old boundaries and roles, in its repositioning of actors and institutions in the generation, transmission and application of knowledge, the ENSI programme raises fundamental issues about the nature of the knowledge that is important in education similar to those posed by my own position. For example, is its character and truth to be determined through the application of standards said to be inherent in the academic disciplines or through the life experience of those grappling with the many-sided but organically interrelated issues that confront them in the immediacy of their life-world? Is what counts as knowledge to be determined by authorities and experts or through open democratic debate? What remains of the traditional distinction between facts and values? Are they not inherent in each other, their apparent separation being the product of false dualisms between perceiver and perceived, perceiver and purpose? The way we develop such questions and the answers that we give have huge implications for the reality of the process of education as a whole.

Yet, while at one level the aspiration of ENSI to oppose the imposition of environmentalist attitudes ('environmentalism') is to be applauded, its advocating that, in place of this, pupils exercise their own rationality through practically addressing local environmental issues in collaboration with their local community—thus developing 'action competence'—raises its own problem: the faith put in rationality. This arises at two levels. First, can environmental education afford to be procedurally neutral when so many other powerful influences in modern Western society—including some within education itself—are not? In a social, economic and political climate that privileges consumerism and the 'free market' and in which (as I have argued) a certain violation of nature is systemic, how open is the rationality of pupils and other agents in local decision-making likely to be? Second, in the light of the critiques by Heidegger and others, which show that modern rationality is itself not neutral but expresses certain aspirations towards the world (notably to classify, explain, predict, assess, control, possess and exploit it), such motives embedded in rationality of this kind will condition the perception and evaluation of environmental issues. It has been argued that it is precisely the ascendancy of such rationality that has led to our current environmental predicament, and thus ENSI's highly democratic strategy holds the danger of installing a set of antipathetic motives at the heart of environmental education—a position in which they may remain invisible and inviolate. One of the most frequently encountered sentiments in the official literature of environmental and sustainability education—both in Europe and North America—is that students be helped to make 'informed and responsible' choices. It is of the highest importance that the parameters of thinking within which they are invited to arrive at such choices are exposed and evaluated.

The bottom line here is that today it seems naïve to suppose that immersion in either traditional subject disciplines or locally grounded action will engender the frame of mind being sought. A degree of reconstruction of both is likely to be required. But, in the context of teaching, such 'reconstruction' should not take the form of an ordering imposition on pupils but rather of invitations to engage in an orientation that is exhibited as valuable in the thought and action of those with whom they rub shoulders and in the practices of the institutions in which they live. In parallel with this there would need to be an encouragement to identify and critically to examine the metaphysics that orders current social practices—uncomfortable as that will be for all involved. Bearing in mind the view of metaphysics that I have taken, this will be best accomplished not through abstract general speculation but cumulatively through reflection on experiences and practices in which students participate, or that impinge on their concerns, through specific case studies that reflect related but different contexts, and through literature and art that display human motives and the powers in play in enveloping life contexts. Here the emphasis would be on identifying underlying motives that energise current practices and, through such engagement, allowing the curriculum of environmental education to emerge. Therefore, in addressing the issue of curriculum integration, it will be in terms of such emergent engagements that the unity of the curriculum will need to be conceived—a unity, therefore, not exclusively of pre-formed academic interdisciplinary connections, but of developing, consciously-felt demands, of calls to thinking that arise from ongoing engagement with the currently unknown. (I have developed these ideas more generally in terms of their implications for teaching in Bonnett, 1994, 1995.) From this it will be clear that the 'rubbing shoulders' advocated above should not be interpreted as some totally uncritical osmosis: rather it advocates an opportunity for pupils to experience what it means for such values to be expressed in a life and in a community as a basis for questioning. Teaching is more than telling, and on the account I have given the domination of nature and the domination of humanity are expressions of the same underlying motive. A teaching that attempts to *impose* a view of a relationship with nature and the good life on pupils is simply self-defeating in terms of the development of sustainability as a frame of mind. Proper authority—be it of nature, value, view or person—has to be *recognised*, has at some level to be freely consented in. Hierarchies that reflect this do not dominate but facilitate.

With the above in mind and in keeping with previous discussion, education for sustainability as a frame of mind would seek to encourage a personal interest in and love of nature, both through direct experience of aspects of nature in which sensuous knowledge could be experienced and acquired, celebrated and reflected upon, and through a more disinterested understanding and appreciation. Here, while science—taught in a certain way—will have a place, art and poetry may be especially edifying in the way that they can invite a thinking and engagement that, while intensely personal, is not self-assertive. As Murdoch puts it, the instinctive appreciation of beauty found in both nature and art can lead to a change in the quality of consciousness, affording us the possibility of 'a pure delight in the independent existence of what is excellent . . . totally opposed to selfish obsession . . . a perfection of form which invites unpossessive contemplation and resists absorption into the selfish dream life of the consciousness' (Murdoch, 1997, p. 370).'We surrender ourselves to its *authority* with a love which is unpossessive and unselfish' (p. 372).

Many have attested to the ability of great art and literature to challenge us to rise above habit and to see things afresh and in some sense for themselves. Indeed, for many this is definitional of great art. In thus disrupting our absorption in the current, they may spur us to comprehend our metaphysical situation in such a way as to indicate a path beyond it— not, again, primarily through some grand orchestration, but through the various and intimate minutiae of our everyday transactions, so that cumulatively they come to reflect a steady and durable simpatico with what is other. This could rightly be termed a frame of mind or way of being that is democratic in the additional sense that it includes nature as a contributor to and recipient of any interaction: a voice to be heard. In this regard, it is particularly important that nature is not primarily set up by education as some essentially abstract system, potentially to be separated (precipitated) out and wholly comprehended by objective (that is, disengaged) rational analysis. Such objectivity—something abstracted from human life—is precisely not what its otherness consists in.

In this sense educational practices that reflect traditional—that is, Cartesian—dualisms of self and world, knowledge and action, will need to be reviewed. As previously argued, it is not that there are no important distinctions to be made in these areas but that, until education communicates just how much we as unique embodied consciousnesses are in nature, and just how much nature is in us (that because of our physical, emotional and spiritual interdependence nature is not to be understood as some potentially disposable asset or dispensable object), a proper orientation to the self-arising will remain elusive. We are not tourists: the Earth is neither hotel nor theme park; it is home. From this perspective there will be much to be said for the democratisation of the school as an institution so that *all* members of its community develop a sense of belonging. (For two short case studies of 'eco-schools' that developed this approach, see Eder, 1999 and Breidler, 1999.)

In the sense both of seeking a poetic response to the epistemologically mysterious and of accommodating the ongoing concerns of individuals, groups and communities in the search for wisdom in relation to their environment, the curriculum of environmental education will be essentially and continually emergent. In its attendance on the manifoldness of nature as the self-arising, diverse and traditional hierarchies of status within and across subjects are likely to be overrun—science taking its place beside poetry and music in revealing nature, and expressing and evoking its significance. Kevin McCarthy (1995) posed the question: Why is it considered more scientific to study plants in a laboratory in monochrome technical diagrammatic cross-section than in an artistic drawing, produced outdoors in full colour from first-hand observation? If we are interested in the truth of the plant, should we not want to know it in its natural environment, its particular posture in relation to its neighbours and the movement of air, its hues in relation to subtleties of lighting—that is to say, aspects of its multifarious *being* in the world? The media through which we attempt to communicate the truth of nature need to be carefully considered with respect to their adequacy to the fecundity of the self-arising. For example, the predominance of the printed discursive text and technical diagram may need to be reviewed so as to make room for the interweaving of fact and value in narrative and for the spontaneity of the oral and the gestured. Origin myths and other mythic-poetic narratives, which are powerful primal conditioners of our conscious space, and, therefore, provide a certain underlying interpretative basis for the findings of rational disciplines, need to be allowed to make their contribution and to be brought into a relationship with such findings. The stories we can hear and weave can provide a residence for theories, reflecting back to us our tacit intuitive apprehensions of the world and restoring a holism to our understanding of nature. The synoptic and enlivening power of the imagination is key here, and it should on no account be placed in opposition to truth and understanding; as the Romantics realised, it is essential to achieving a dialectical relationship with the objects of our knowledge.

In Chapter 3 the role of the imagination as facilitating some sort of entry into the world of non-human nature was raised. This was developed to some degree in Chapter 7, raising among other things the possibility of trans-species experience and the notion of some kind of solidarity with nature. While emphasising the essential otherness of nature, the thesis I have developed says nothing against, for example, the possibility of there being certain sensations such as pain and its abatement that we have in common with some aspects of nature, or against the idea that, through the use of imagination, we can have some notion of the good of things in nature—of what would count as their well-being and fulfilment. However, *contra* Rolston and others, this does not require us to suppose that other organisms that, as far as we know, have no self-awareness and sense of agency themselves somehow have any sense of, or 'care' about, their own fulfilment. On occasion though, our imagination may encourage us to ascribe more self-awareness to non-human species than formerly, and it may be important that in so doing it thus prevents us from resting too complacently in what may be currently assumed as scientific fact. And, of course, imagination is essential for any appreciation of the epistemic mystery of things: of what is inchoate in the now but is past or not yet, or perhaps never—that is to say, the particular but infinite possibilities of things. Given an undergirding understanding of the intrinsic value of the self-arising, the use of the imagination can both enable us to identify with what sustains us and enliven our feeling for what might count as the self-fulfilment of the essentially other of natural things. It can develop, for example, our sense of what it would be to let them be and of the nobility of working with things so as to bring out their world-enhancing natural qualities: to consider seriously, through an open sensing rather than a purely calculative ordering, what this might involve would be an important aim of education. Thus grounded, education should constantly pose the question of what is valuable in life and so develop a philosophy of wisdom rather than simply one of power and mastery.

In sum, the development of sustainability as a frame of mind is essentially a matter of coming to apprehend that which lies always beyond our authorship, analyses and management and yet is closest to us—a reciprocator in all our perception and interaction. It is the recognition of this reality that liberates us from stultification and that spiritually sustains us, and it is thus this reality that we have a special personal and cultural responsibility to reveal. Therefore, any environmental ethic that we seek to convey to pupils must be one in which perception and action become apt to things themselves: an ethic not of rules but of receptive response, where discernment is given priority over definition. Education needs to help pupils to live in such a way that they can flourish in an authentic— that is, poetic—relationship with the self-arising. To do this—and harking back to the discussion of Charles Taylor's view in the previous chapter—it in turn needs to help them to learn properly to love themselves so as not to be prepared to sell themselves cheaply to a global economism that will require them to be ever on call and ready to consume. At the very least this would suggest a reassertion of the Romantic values of particularity, diversity, harmony and spontaneity in education. It would also issue a challenge to those centres of learning in the West whose high status is bound up with the dissemination of a knowledge whose genius has been largely to increase power by disrupting harmony and annihilating particularity. In more general terms it might also suggest a certain appropriateness in retrieving the mediaeval metaphor of nature as mother and so pose the question of how her (Western) offspring might be educated out of a particularly truculent adolescence into a new and mature rapport with a battered parent.

PLANETARY CONSCIOUSNESS

A number of Green thinkers emphasise the importance of developing some form of 'planetary consciousness', and it is clear that, while genuine engagement with the self-arising in their immediate environs is pivotal, pupils will in some sense need also to be encouraged to transcend the horizons of their immediate neighbourhood. For example, their sense of identity, their loyalties and their sense of unity must be brought to extend beyond the purely local if there is to be a wise and just basis for addressing global problems. Writing immediately before the turn of the twentieth century, Holmes Rolston III suggested that

> In the next millennium, as we already realize, it will not be enough to be a good 'citizen', or a 'humanist', because neither of those terms has enough 'nature', enough 'earthiness' in them. 'Citizen' is only half the truth; the other half is that we are residents on landscapes. Humans are Earthlings. Earth is our dwelling place. From here onward there is no such thing as civic competence without ecological competence (Rolston III, 1999, p. 134).

He notes how a powerful planetary consciousness was the virtually unanimous experience of some two hundred astronauts from varying cultures. Their awe at their first sight of the Earth as a whole was expressed, for example, by Edgar Mitchell as 'a sparkling blue and white jewel . . . laced with slowly swirling veils of white . . . like a small pearl in a thick sea of black mystery'. Or again by Michael Collins, who said: 'I remember so vividly what I saw when I looked back at my fragile home—a glistening, inviting beacon, delicate blue and white, a tiny outpost suspended in the black infinity. Earth is to be treasured and nurtured, something precious that *must* endure' (p. 108).

Such a consciousness would clearly be an asset in bringing about a refocusing, away from short-term material wants that are known to damage this Earth and towards a more long-term holistic perspective for the evaluation and valuing of human activity. It would seem to sit well with the notion of sustainability as a frame of mind, providing a poetic intimation of the larger picture and our place within it. It brings home not only the important instrumental points that for all practical purposes, and for the foreseeable future, the Earth is our only home, and that if we are to survive we have no choice but to live in harmony with its ecological systems, but also the fact that psychologically and spiritually we are bound up with the fate of Earth. In the educational context this could surely on occasion be a good starting point for addressing many of the environmental problems that we presently confront, encouraging students to ask not simply what is good for an individual or local community but what is good for the planet—*and to begin to appreciate the relationship between the two*. I have previously argued that appreciation of the global requires an affiliation to the local.

Impressed by the pace of globalisation, there have been those, however, who have suggested that humanity needs to develop a global view of reality that is not so much one precipitated by a seminal confrontation with the 'home planet' in its otherness and beauty, as one produced by the possibilities for global communications provided by modern technologies, particularly the Internet. Here there has been talk of developing a 'global brain', a 'collective consciousness' (Russell, 1983), that will form the basis of the solidarity needed in addressing global problems. At this point, and from the perspective I have been developing, a range of reservations arise, particularly regarding the danger of resurrecting an impoverished universal rationality as a basis for understanding and unity. For example, harking back to the discussion of traditional ecological knowledge in Chapter 7, there should be serious concerns over what would be the fate of such essentially local understanding. Could it be made 'Internet compatible' without loss? How would it fare in competition with a homogenised international knowledge? And is the Internet a suitable vehicle for conveying the rich and essential particularities of knowledge that, it has been mooted, are characteristic of an awareness that is true to nature as the self-arising? Put another way, the crucial question arises: What *sort* of global community does the Internet facilitate? Can the otherness of different cultures be truly preserved? What quality of unity and broader citizenship does it engender? It is my view that such issues are of sufficient importance as to warrant the fuller attention that would locate them in a wider metaphysical framework. I turn to this, amongst other things, in the next chapter.

Chapter 11. Education for a Post-Humanist Age: the Question of Human Dwelling

> The Perfectibility of Man! Ah, heaven what a dreary theme! The perfectibility of the Ford car! The perfectibility of which man? I am many men. Which of them are you going to perfect? I am not a mechanical contrivance.
>
> Education! Which of the various me's do you propose to educate, and which do you propose to suppress?
>
> Anyhow, I defy you. I defy you, oh society, to educate me or suppress me according to your dummy standards (*Benjamin Franklin*, D. H. Lawrence).

An underlying theme running through this volume, and one that is implied in any consideration of how we should relate to nature, is the question of authentic dwelling: How, today, should we be in the world? This question remains a challenge, and some avenues for making a start on re-thinking certain current tacitly accepted responses to it have been suggested. Implicit in posing matters in this way is a reservation about humanism as a guide to human being and, therefore, as a basis for education. Humanism, of course, is a rich and varied tradition of thinking that has brought many benefits yet that it would be easy to caricature. But there are certain motives within it—or to put it another way, there is a certain version of it—that gives rise to concern when viewed from the environmental perspectives developed in this volume. These motives will need to be overcome if the relationship to nature that I have argued to be essential both to human well-being and to meeting the sources of environmental concern is to be achieved. So what do I mean by humanism and what are the offending motives?

ELEMENTS OF HUMANIST METAPHYSICS

By humanism I refer to that broad perspective that assigns to human beings a special place in the greater scheme of things, setting their nature and interests at the centre of study and policy. Metaphysically, its considerable achievement has been both to release humanity from a radical dependence on and subservience to some divine, supernatural order and at the same time to resist the assimilation of humanity into some natural order that would put it on a par with other living organisms. If medieval thinkers 'philosophised on their knees' and in the idiom of devotional Church Latin (though even here it was the salvation of the human soul that was their central concern), the humanistic mood encouraged humankind to rise to 'full stature' and contemplate its own possibilities and power, its own progress and perfectibility in its own languages, which articulated its own worldly concerns. Commenting on one of its great luminaries, Iris Murdoch puts it thus:

> Kant abolished God and made man God in His stead . . . Kant's conclusive exposure of the so-called proofs of the existence of God, his analysis of the limitations of speculative reason, together with his eloquent portrayal of the dignity of the rational man, has had results which might possibly dismay him. How recognisable, how familiar to us, is the man so beautifully portrayed in the *Grundlegung*, who confronted even with Christ turns away to consider the judgement of his own conscience and to hear the voice of his own reason (Murdoch, 1997, p. 365).

She continues: 'The centre of this type of post-Kantian moral philosophy is the notion of the will as the creator of value. Values which were previously in some sense inscribed in the heavens and guaranteed by God collapse into the human will' (p. 366).

Thus, while in many ways liberating, its aspiration for humankind to assert its own will—to seek mastery and to endeavour to take control of its own destiny—ultimately orientated it towards exalting the active over the contemplative life. And the unchallenged end of moral action becomes human welfare and the establishment of human authority. Its consequences for the characterisation of human culture are made explicit by the neo-Kantian, Ernst Cassirer, in his *An Essay on Man*. He concludes: 'Human culture taken as a whole may be described as the process of man's progressive self-liberation. Language, art, religion, science, are various phases in this process. In all of them man discovers and proves a new power—the power to build up a world of his own, an "ideal" world' (Cassirer, 1970, p. 228).

Now of the several motives inscribed in humanism as described above, environmental concern as explored in this volume leads us to pay particular attention to two interrelated themes. The first is the issue of the differentiation of humankind from the rest of nature. The second is the epistemology that follows from it. That a certain differentiation is necessary is not in dispute—extreme ecological naturalist accounts that posit humans as completely at one with nature would mean that they are no more able to modify their current environmentally harmful behaviour than can a cat killing birds. This certainly raises the issue of human nature itself as important for environmental education. For example, if at some deep tacit level we understood ourselves as ineluctably selfish, aggressive or competitive, perhaps tainted with some original sin, if, that is, we came to regard such motives as structural to our constitution, the consequences for environmental policy would be considerable, though, of course, not necessarily straightforward. From the perspective of this volume, the significant point is whether we are supposing humankind to be qualitatively different from the rest of nature in either the other-oriented sense of having special capacities and responsibilities towards nature or in the self-assertive sense of an entitlement to master nature and bring it into the service of self-given human purposes and desires. In what follows, I will mean by 'humanism' that modernist version that emphasises the latter motivational orientation. This essentially interprets progress as increase in power and, as I have previously noted, surfaced most explicitly with the birth of modern experimental science, the utilitarian-rational precepts of the European Enlightenment and the associated ascendancy of modern technology, conventionally perceived as a human product and servant.

A key feature of this attitude of mind is a transformation of nature as underlying reality through that movement towards the mathematisation of science powerfully heralded in Newton's *Mathematical Principles of Natural Philosophy*. From this standpoint, science as arbiter of the ultimate reality of nature, once persuaded to see itself as fundamentally mathematical, that is, to see its fundamental descriptions and explanations as essentially mathematical, comes to understand nature itself as governed by the laws of mathematics. 'Ultimate' nature is subsumed under mathematics. Now for such mathematically redolent science to describe and explain things, increasingly it has to set them up as knowable in advance—as instances of pre-defined categories—and in so doing it annihilates the particularity of the individual thing. Not only this: in order to produce general explanations, it needs to locate them in a uniform space-time continuum that similarly effaces the particular character of individual locales. In this way, all is set up as knowable in principle. There need be no mysterious remainder in a system of uniform objects whose motions are governed by external forces that are mathematically describable. Individual things do not have their *own* nature, for example, a motion that is intrinsic to them as the thing that they are, as on the preceding Aristotelian model. As Heidegger puts it: 'Nature is now the realm of the uniform space-time context of motion, which is outlined in the axiomatic project [of mathematicised science] and in which alone bodies can be bodies as a part of it and anchored in it'. Such bodies have 'no concealed qualities, powers and capacities. Natural bodies are now only what they show themselves as within this projected realm' (Heidegger, 1978, p. 268). In his exegesis of Heidegger on these points, George Pattison notes how Heidegger relates this now customary way of seeing things to that great motif of modernist humanism, Kant's concept of *pure* reason, which, again, is something very different to the rationality of man as 'the rational animal' of previous centuries:

> Pure reason bespeaks the mathematical predetermination of the realm of knowable things. 'What is a thing must be decided in advance by the highest principle of all principles and propositions, i.e., from pure reason, before one can reasonably deal with the divine, worldly and human' [Heidegger, 1967, pp. 110-111]. On this basis, Heidegger concludes that Kant is not concerned with 'the question of the thingness of the things that surround us' but with 'the thing as an object of mathematical-physical science [p. 128]' (Pattison, 2000, p. 94)

One is strongly reminded here of the ontological inversion suggested by Nietzsche when he claimed that the 'last evaporating fumes of reality' have been placed at the beginning of metaphysical understanding rather than at the end (referred to in Chapter 2), and as far as the underlying reality of nature is concerned, the upshot, again, is a preoccupation with it as an abstract schema—a preoccupation that, because it always looks past things themselves, leads to a sightless transparency and a constipation of thinking—this precisely, and perversely, as with great ingenuity it sets everything up to be manipulated and exploited for the human good. To refer back to Cassirer's characterisation of humanism as aspiring to an 'ideal world', here, indeed, we find ourselves confronted by a 'nature' shaped by human ideas and ideals rather than reflecting and respecting anything that nature may have to offer of itself, in its self-arising: a world, indeed, that is in one sense 'empirical' but only allowed to put in an appearance in terms of a set of systematised projections placed upon it. Thus orientated, we find ourselves inhabiting an essentially uniform mathematical space-time world in which, ultimately, the shining of the blueness of the sky becomes transmuted into a mere wavelength, and distances of unimaginable traverse and toil are readily accounted for in 'light years'. Under the universalising motive of humanism, this is the character of the world that assumes the countenance of the 'really real'.

MODERNIST HUMANISM AND THE ENVIRONMENT

Similarly, the humanistic focus on the will and the interests of humankind can lead to an eclipse of those aspects of the world that are not, from this perspective, intrinsically related to such interests—namely, precisely the self-arising. To take one important example: our relationship with the land as such is to a significant degree occluded because this is assumed to be of a certain (utilitarian) kind that needs only acknowledge nature's own structures and boundaries when their reluctance or refusal to support human aspirations becomes manifest. Indeed, nature only registers in this reality as obstacle or opportunity. Such an orientation thus uproots us by undermining an intimate relationship with and commitment towards any particular piece of land recognised as possessing its own independent individual character and value. Psychologically we become itinerants, tourists, spectators, essentially homeless beings to whom the uniqueness of particular locations has been reduced to their ability to satisfy generalised desires—desires super-ordinate from the point of view of a particular location. We perhaps for a while require a peaceful location and look for one that 'fits the bill'. But when we have found this, perhaps by searching various databases in which they are conveniently stored, commitment to this particular location remains essentially limited to its ability to satisfy our demand; if our desire changes or its ability to meet our desire fails, we are inclined to look elsewhere.

Essentially in this relationship to the land, our responsibility is to ourselves not to the land; self-fulfilment of a singularly self-centred kind is in play. From its perspective—and especially when conjoined with a susceptibility to being heavily impressed with the richness and importance of human society and the chatter that swells into the great social and political issues of the moment—to exhibit or defend an absorption in and a commitment to a particular geographical region can appear as a provincialism (or worse) that stands unfavourable comparison with a seemingly outward-looking, knowing and elevated cosmopolitanism. It is assumed that to belong to, to tarry in, the same place is stultifying, that, because there is now little awareness of the constant subtlety of the particular and the intimations of the universal that may lie immanent within it, breadth of experience is superior to depth of experience. For the detached, spectatorial self is insatiable in its appetite for novelty and 'news', and, having abstracted itself from fidelity to the particular and become tranquillised to the call of its infinite depths and nuances, the invitations to participate in them as both stranger and friend, it has little else to draw upon for sustenance. Yet, as George Eliot observes in *The Mill on the Floss*: 'What novelty is worth that sweet monotony where everything is known, and *loved* because it is known?' And such knowledge, love and fulfilment do not suddenly spring up at first acquaintance: they are *grown*; they are the achievement of an intimacy that develops dialogically between experiences over the years:

> We could never have loved the earth so well if we had no childhood in it—if it were not the earth where the same flowers came up every spring . . . the same hips and haws on the autumn hedgerows, the same redbreasts that we used to call 'God's birds' because they did no harm to the precious crops . . . These familiar flowers, these well remembered bird-notes, this sky with its fitful brightness, these furrowed and grassy fields, each with a sort of personality given to it by the capricious hedgerows—such things as these are the mother tongue of our imagination, the language that is laden with all the subtle inextricable associations the fleeting hours of our childhood left behind (Eliot, 1994, p. 38.).

In contrast, the humanistic motive to focus on the self and its perfectibility expresses a metaphysical *dissatisfaction* that infects our relationship with nature. The world is not good enough as it is; we need *progress*—humanly organised and increasingly modulated through mathematisation as economic growth. Nature can be annulled or improved upon in the pursuit of such progress, and our experience of time becomes ever more linear to provide the space within which such progress is to occur and may be measured. The natural, cyclical, rhythms of the self-arising become a quaint sideshow and the knowledge of elders an anachronism. The past is thoroughly understood as what *is* no longer—mere 'history'—in the sense of being disposed of, left behind, as a disengaged rationality indifferently culls what it wants from the increasingly flat standardised world that it has itself ingeniously placed at its disposal.

One small but illuminating current example of this orientation is provided by the growing phenomenon of the 'flying winemaker'.[1] Such 'winemakers' visit vineyards around the globe advising local growers on how to produce their wines more economically and to make them more universally palatable—that is inoffensive—and thus compatible with attracting supermarket contracts. Advice is given on standardised production procedures to achieve consistency of taste and yield and to eradicate idiosyncratic tastes that might not find immediate favour with the mass market and so might need to be 'acquired'. Short cuts to achieving certain qualities that are in demand are also suggested, such as introducing oak chipping or extract into the wine to avoid having it standing 'idle' for years in oak casks, and so forth. Here then, we have a universalistic, rationalistic, economically driven approach that achieves good value, consistent wines, carefully designed to meet the demands of a pre-specified public taste. And what is wrong with this? Is it simply snobbery or archaism to rue the emptying out of the particularities of wine-growing locales or 'terroires' and of the historically grown practices that give each wine its own character and that are intimately entwined with a way of life? Does it matter that the pride in production of those who understand themselves as upholding traditions born of a long, intimate working relationship with local vine, soil and weather, and that the pleasure in consumption of those for whom such a history is an important part of the experience of drinking wine are destroyed by the loss of traditional local methods? Are the pride and the pleasure misplaced? I argue not. In this instance (unlike in the production of, say, medical vaccines), 'inefficiencies' and susceptibilities to an inconsistent product are not defects but virtues, for they inspire on the part of grower and drinker an openness to the nuances of nature as the self-arising, an appreciation of subtle diversity and the on-going cultivation of practice and taste. From this perspective, the flying winemaker is to a degree an Enlightenment agent dealing in universals to the cost of a sense of place and its gift.

It needs to be emphasised here that the embeddedness extolled in the above example is not to be read as a defence of parochialism, but rather as enabling a certain transcendence. Only through such rootedness and, therefore, experience of deeper allegiances can one, with the exercise of imagination and perhaps the stimulation of new ideas, apprehend the immanent in the particular and truly empathise with others in *their* locales and situations. Though dangers of insularity and oppression by rigid tradition are not to be underestimated, such 'rooted transcendence', where it occurs, often contrasts with the shallow, if vocal, free-floating, abstract, intellectual and political 'solidarities' that tend to dissolve and re-form with passing expediencies. Such embeddedness can also be an aid to the vigilance and steadiness of purpose required to recognise and address the often slow gathering of environmental problems that continues long after they may have fallen out of the news and gossip of a larger public.

In terms of broader political positions, and with such considerations in mind, it is clear that the conventional association of Green thinking with liberalism and the political Left comes up for question, since it can be argued that both of these positions embrace articulations of progress and knowledge that celebrate motives that occlude such a steady intimacy with nature as the self-arising. This affiliation of Green thinking with Left politics gains an added currency when the Right is associated with unbridled free-market economics. But, as commentators such as John Gray point out, this web of associations deserves closer scrutiny, especially in the light of the catastrophic despoliations of nature that occurred under the institutions of the former Soviet Union, consideration of which, he argues, leads to the conclusion that 'unlimited government has been the greatest destroyer of the common environment in our age' (Gray, 1999, p. 282).

But wait! Is an implied assimilation of modernist humanism—in the terms in which I have defined it—with Soviet style institutions defensible? I believe that in *metaphysical* terms it is. The underlying motives of a knowledge of rationalistic universalism, of unbounded instrumentalism and utopianism, of central planning and social/natural engineering, and of the total mobilisation that to a significant degree they reflected, are the purest expressions of such a humanism—as may be capitalism, in a different way. Given such a stark claim, it is perhaps worth emphasising that I refer here not to humanism as a whole, but to a particular version of it that reaches its completion in a highly instrumental or calculative rationality, a rationality whose essential motive is unfettered mastery. I am of course aware that there are those who would see themselves as working within the Enlightenment tradition more broadly conceived and who are equally critical of such a motive. I have previously alluded (in Chapter 2) to the communicative rationality of Habermas, and within the recent history of rationalist philosophy of education itself the example of Richard Peters' concern with activities that can be shown to have intrinsic worth springs to mind. However, it remains the case—or so I would argue—that what I have termed 'modernist humanism' can be seen to be a working through of certain Renaissance and Enlightenment humanist motives and that they have achieved a certain ascendancy during modernity—indeed, such that in many ways they may be taken to characterise it.

GREEN CONSERVATISM

So what can conservatism contribute to the idea of a dwelling that reflects a right relationship with nature as the self-arising? In social terms, Gray suggests that bulwarks against certain inherent features of centralised planning are required: 'environmental despoliation on a vast scale is an exorable result of industrial development in the absence of the core institutions of a market economy, private property and the price mechanism. This is a vital truth as yet little understood by Green theorists, even though it is all too plain in the post-communist countries' (p. 281). Thus, he argues that it is not the market and private property that are the enemy, but the project of promoting maximal economic growth. He recommends a *considered* place for free markets in an ecologically sensitive economy, arguing that market institutions can have positive ecological functions—for example, in registering subtle, sometimes inarticulable, shifting patterns of resource-scarcities expressed in price information available to all that unavoidably is not available to central planners. This allows some measure of rationality in decision-making—although it also has some serious ecological limitations such as an inability to signal the onset of a cumulative public bad such as global warming and an indifference to global markets decimating local trades and modes of production. In addition, and in the light of previous discussion, I would point out that the market mechanism installs a high degree of subjectivism in the registering of nature's value—the influence of the transient, the uninformed, the unreflective and maybe the downright selfish weighing on at least equal terms with the more informed, contemplative and receptive-responsive. To the extent that previous argument in support of nature's value as deeply and subtly embedded in our form of sensibility is accepted, such an indiscriminate market mechanism provides a wholly inappropriate arbiter.

But perhaps a more powerful strand in Gray's argument is the claim that: 'Competition for natural resources, living or otherwise, in the absence of property rights in them, spells inexorable ruin for such resources' (p. 283). For in such a situation no one has an incentive to adopt a long-term view of the utilisation of resources. Indeed, quite the reverse. While this raises the question of whether property rights are the only or the best way of giving people a long-term interest in the natural environment—and invites, for example, consideration of organisations such as the RSPB that are highly protective of bird life without there being such rights—more fundamental to the position that has been developed in the present argument is the issue of the motives that inform the sense of belonging involved in property rights. A sense of belonging to the land, and in that sense having a home, and the notion of the land belonging to an individual as property are related but significantly different notions, the latter suggesting something that is at one's disposal. Implicit here is a kind of possession and commodification that lends itself to motives of mastery and exploitation that, for example, could lead to asset stripping of various kinds. Arguably, this is illustrated by modern farming techniques that have slowly destroyed the structure of what Aldo Leopold once called 'that dark laboratory that we call the soil', such that it has now either eroded or has constantly to be supported by artificial additives. Such harm will all be inscribed in, but not revealed by, any price information ascribed by the market.

Given the political and social realities of our time, it may be that private property and free markets can be better than some of the alternatives in preserving nature, but clearly we must beware a simplistic eulogising of these aspects of conservatism as, at the same time, we note its possibilities and its closer associations with ecological concern than modernist humanism. For there are other promising relationships between conservatism and ecological thinking that are worth noting. In particular, the multi-generational orientation of conservatism and the pivotal notion of the embeddedness of the individual in a larger whole have strong parallels with ecological notions of historical and temporal interdependence that are aspects of the continuity of the reality of the self-arising. As Gray observes, in conservatism the common life is accorded a certain primacy—the good life presupposes embeddedness in communities— and it is less individual rights than forms of life that are viewed as most in need of protection. Clearly the dangers of fascism and of unthinking adherence to, or cynical upholding of, an unjust *status quo* need to be kept in mind, yet there is here a timely warning about the opposite danger, the allure of novelty, especially in the form of large-scale social and technological experimentation—and also an invitation to examine modernist assumptions about the nature of progress as ceaseless centrally initiated change and infinite growth. Gray is surely right to point out how this preoccupation may suppress awareness of mystery and tragedy in human life and a sense of the importance of the individual lives (and environments) that are overlooked or sacrificed in the interests of such progress. There is also the point that improvements in one sphere are often accompanied by new evils in others and that so-called measures of progress often gloss over what are incommensurables in human terms— for example, the reassurance of security as against the excitement of adventure, the gaining of analytic power as against direct instinctive involvement.

In the context of the easy assumptions concerning progress that litter public debate, it may be salutary to consider the proposition that progress as something engineered and imposed is not so much debatable as incoherent, the modern conception being a symptom of a hubristic humanism. As Gray points out, it is not that conservatism seeks to arrest all change. This would be to confuse a certain stability, which consists in ongoing changes that are responsive to the play of rhythms and the shifting particularities of life in its relation to the environment, with fixity. But risk-aversion is recognised as the path of prudence, and proper consideration needs to be given to the legitimacy of a steady-state society that attends to deeper sources of allegiance (such as reclaiming a sense of place, local culture and history) as opposed to those motives elevated by scientific fundamentalism allied with liberal humanism.

Clearly there are significant educational implications here. But they are *not* a matter of aiming simply to maintain the *status quo*. In the current age of strong modernist humanist influences, radical reform—albeit auto-chthonous rather than simply instrumentally and centrally fabricated—will be necessary. Such conservatism seeks not to conserve any *status quo* but to discern, retrieve and develop those aspects regarded as expressive of a properly rooted dwelling—thus, for example, the critical examination of current school curriculum subjects recommended in the previous chapter. Furthermore, insofar as it should not conceive of the school community as essentially to be governed by some central hierarchy constructed by a universalistic rationality, this strand of conservatism also might encourage the development of an organic community more spontaneously and tacitly responding to its members, to their situations and aspirations. It thus emphasises the importance of the *ethos* of the school and raises the possibility of teacher-pupil relationships as having a poetic person-to-person rather than commodified character. The quality of mutual listening instantiated in such relationships would be wholly in keeping with the development of sustainability as a frame of mind described in the previous chapter.

A POST-HUMANIST DAWN?

Andrew Stables and Bill Scott (2001) detect what they feel to be certain post-humanist trends abroad today. They instance the renewed debate about animal rights and the trade in pollution permits that valorises the non-human by assigning value within the capitalist market to natural resources such as the rainforest 'on the basis of what they give us, even if we leave them alone'. Such shoots of hope are certainly to be sought, but we must be wary of reading too much into them in terms of the degree of non-anthropocentrism that they are taken to exhibit. In many ways a capitalist market assigning monetary value to aspects of nature is the antithesis of poetic receptiveness—both in the kind of value that it is given and in the assumed commensurability of this with economic development values it remains highly instrumental. If some recognition of the longer term is to be welcomed, and if some kind of accommodation to capitalism is a pragmatic requirement today, we must, at the same time, not lose sight of the fact that there are severe dangers inherent in this kind of recognition of nature. Education for a post-humanist age will need to be alert to the metaphysical implications of such pragmatic compromises and to help students keep their eye on the ends that such means are intended to serve. (As I shall argue presently, this applies especially to certain aspects of current life that have become most ubiquitous, such as ICT.)

Something of the character of the difficulties and dangers here is exemplified in what Ingolfur Bluhdorn (2000) has referred to as the arrival of a 'post-ecologist constellation', which characterises late-modern society, not simply as one of its faults but as an essential feature. This constellation includes seeing nature as a heavily contested social construction, the de-ideologisation of eco-politics and the loss of its specific identity through integration into other fields, and the reformulation of ecological issues as economic issues and issues of efficiency. He argues that, in a society that reflects this constellation, unsustainability is inherent and tacitly accepted—it is an indispensable feature of late-modern consciousness, and hence 'its social and ecological unsustainability cannot be regarded as a curable fault of contemporary society or a flawed frame of mind that could be rectified through appropriate education' (Bluhdorn, 2002, p. 65). Thus, the problem becomes one of how to manage unsustainability and its implications rather than its removal and key to the political management of unsustainability are strategies of simulation that enable society to reassure itself that it still upholds modernist and ecological ideals. Such strategies operate through a combination of reflexive redefinition of these ideals in ways congenial to the new constellation and ostentatious emphasis in public discourse on political renewal and economic greening. Indeed, in its ability to override environmental considerations in reality while signifying environmental concern in public discourse, the concept of sustainable development might itself be regarded as a post-ecological invention whose use contributes to continuing unsustainability. Thus, on Bluhdorn's analysis, 'we may conclude that the discourse and policies of ecological modernization and sustainable development function to simulate the possibility and desirability of environmental justice and integrity without genuinely aiming to address, let alone reverse, the fundamental unsustainability of late-modern society' (Bludhorn, 2002, p. 66). He concludes that since this is a *societal* rather than an individual self-deception, viable alternatives are not available: it is difficult to identify any subject to whom it would appear *as* a deception and society itself would not be prepared to accept the revelation of its own barbarism were its motive to be undisguised. If we do not accept this bleak conclusion, we may certainly recognise elements of the strategy he describes and be sensitive to the size and nature of the obstacles to be overcome. We may also be sober in our evaluation of signs of post-humanism breaking out.

THE RISE OF ICT

It seems to me that a particularly powerful way in which modernist humanism asserts itself culturally is through the promotion and use of computers. Here the motives of mastery and control, abstraction and universalisation, and disengagement from the sensuous and the truly given are capable of achieving a new ascendance. Here the notion of the immediacy of the given is transmuted into the immediacy of being on call—a self-purposefully erected world readily accessible at the press of a key. So motivated, in education and elsewhere the cultural understandings and values reinforced by computer use can be seen as antithetical to a celebration of nature as the self-arising. By way of example, in what follows I will examine two aspects of this 'social computerization' that pose a serious challenge to the reality of nature, that is, to a reality in which nature as the self-arising remains a positive power. This examination has a particular cogency in the light of the many pressures both to incorporate computer and Internet-based learning into the school curriculum, and to conceive of the Internet as a vehicle for the free sharing of ideas, enlisted, as it has been by some, as a facilitator of the planetary consciousness sought by many environmentalists.

Take the growth of online and other computer-mediated virtual realities. These bid to become a supreme expression of modernist humanism. Of particular concern from the current perspective is the fact that, with varying degrees of success, they present a reality rather than a *view on* reality—and it is a reality whose every feature has been calculated by someone (often anonymous), the author's structures and values being invisibly as well as visibly embedded in it. Furthermore, actors entering such realities—which they can replay or escape from at will—are released from properly rooted moral sentiments and, therefore, become essentially irresponsible. This is very different from the space opened up by great art and literature whose chief quality, I would argue, is to create an ambience or perspective that is essentially evocative rather than invocative. Great art does not aspire to *re-create* reality but to *explore and reveal* reality, including its ethical dimensions. It aspires to create a space where this can occur afresh. Virtual reality does precisely the opposite. The speed of technological advance suggests that any current poverty of the sensuousness of virtual reality is likely to be a transitory problem. But even when the technology can produce high degrees of sensuous experience (and is therefore no longer exclusively screen based), this experience will still be of a certain pre-calculated kind—that is, it will be neither self-arising nor revealing of the self-arising in the manner of great art, but will rather be like the carefully controlled artificial aroma of rising bread meted out at some supermarket 'bakeries'. Such realities promise to become increasingly compelling by occluding essential aspects of nature and making any moral involvement at best optional. Of course, all computer (and other) models and simulations do this, but properly presented, they do not purport to *be* reality. Nevertheless, these too, in reducing understanding to abstract models, strip nature of many essential dimensions (such as its sensuous presence, manifoldness, contingency and epistemic mystery) and, therefore, must not be set up as providing some privileged understanding.

But, it might be objected, is there a *necessary* qualitative difference between 'natural' spaces and, say, online space? Indeed, might it not be possible to create 'natural' spaces online? For the reasons given above, the fact that the Internet can host multifaceted realities through an increasingly subtle melding of text, images and sound says nothing on this. But the idea has been pursued by David Kolb in relation to Heidegger's notion of 'the fourfold'. The idea here is that the central qualities of true human dwelling may be characterised as a 'fourfold' of 'earth', 'sky', 'divinities' and 'mortals', where these are to be understood as primal dimensions of dwelling that enable us to live with the rich presence of things and to be authentically related to nature and time. On conventional interpretations, these qualities stand opposed to those elevated by technological awareness. Kolb suggests, however, that we should view Heidegger's fourfold in an anti-foundational way such that 'Earth and sky can gather and we as mortals can be open to the gods whether we are with jet airliners and computers, or the wine jug that Heidegger describes' (Kolb, 2000, p. 125). According to Kolb:

> Heidegger's four dimensions do suggest ways in which truer places may be constructed online. For an online site to be a place, it needs to be more than a static block of data. It needs 'earth', objects to interact with that have some independence and thickness of their own; it needs 'sky', times and changes, so that it is not always the same but varies according to its own rhythms; it needs 'gods', ideals and aspirations and calls to what we might become; it needs 'mortals', a sense that choices are meaningful in finite careers, that time makes demands and is not unlimited in amount.

This sense of opening possibilities and an identity being offered and forwarded puts more 'there' there (p. 124).

And, no doubt, as we find ever-increasingly sophisticated ways of connecting with cyberspace, which allow more and more of our sensory and executive capacity to be engaged, so, it would seem, it will become increasingly difficult to distinguish such 'places' from 'natural' places. Indeed, if this process were complete—that is to say, if cyberspace could be so engineered and we could be wired up to it in a way that enabled states of consciousness no different to those achievable in the equivalent 'natural' space—what could the distinction consist in? Only this: *one would be derivative and a fake*.

It seems to me that any such account presupposes some more adequate place for the 'there' *that provides the standard for recognising what it can be*—for how else could the idea of 'more there' be understood? It is clear that, on Kolb's account implicitly, this point of reference is a natural place in the sense of a place where all the senses are in play in inextricable response to that which is self-arising at some level. Though this latter may be 'faked', it *matters* if it is faked: first, because, as Robert Elliot (1997) has pointed out, provenance is critical to the way we perceive the world; second, because the fake is subject to an essential generative poverty. Only contact with the genuinely self-arising, the authentically 'other', can prevent the eventual constipation of thought and stultification of the human spirit. The truth about ourselves and the world in which we live does not spring from someone's constructed reality, however sophisticated and compelling. Though such realities may on occasion represent or illustrate limited aspects of it, truth about ourselves and the world is grounded in our experience of the self-originary, those intimations that we receive of things that lie *outside* what we have self-purposefully erected.

Similarly, there is an issue concerning the general organisation of material on the Internet. In many ways it is entirely random, possesses no organic unity and is accessed through essentially algebraic means. For example, the 'natural' patterns of association that can become established by hypertext links through frequent use and ease of flow (Standish, 2000), possess neither the principle of coherence, nor the authorial sense of responsibility, of a unified text. They speak of a reality—a 'nature'— whose values are either non-existent or essentially casual, especially when we consider that hot links refer us to sites that may be constantly changing in ways that are quite arbitrary in relation to any original logic of the link. There is no qualitative inherent reciprocity as there is in a natural system. Furthermore, there is the concern that, as Michael Heim (1993) has argued, the reality of the Internet—which is largely interrogated through Boolean search logic—involves a move away from Aristotelian logic based on direct statements/propositions (which itself is already at a remove from the sensuous intuition of things themselves) to an abstract, system-oriented symbolic logic based on algebra. With this mindset, systemic consistency becomes more important than the direct reference to things addressed in our experience. And when system precedes intrinsic significance, the way is cleared for the primacy of a 'knowledge' atomised by modularisation into standardised units in order to be suitably manipulable and accessible to such a logic. In distinctly Heideggerian vein, Heim makes the point that: 'In its intrinsic remoteness from direct human experience, Boolean search logic [facilitates] a gain in power at the price of our direct involvement with things . . . Placing us at a new remove from subject matter, by directing us away from the texture of what we are exploring' (in Lankshear *et al.*, 2000, p. 31).

All web searches (including question searches) make use of logics that, even if not strictly Boolean, assume a realm of pre-defined entities with fixed characteristics—that is, *objects*. This is a key difference with the ontology of nature and it brings us back to the previously explored central metaphysical dichotomy of *objects* and *things*. Thus, in the context of the remorseless promotion of ICT in education—itself largely generated by modernist humanist motives of efficiency and control (not to mention vested corporate interests)—we are forced to confront the possibility of an educational environment developing where many defining aspects of nature will be routinely suspended. Assured of the manifest benefits of some forms of ICT use, education risks slipping into spaces where natural integrity and, therefore, true contingency and spontaneity are absent; where full sensuous, mysterious presence and unique identity and responsibility have fallen away; where, as participants, it is possible for our own identity to remain fluid and covert as we anonymously live through different personas acting in a range of online places. The learning spaces that to varying degree are bidding to supersede conventional classrooms and schools may increasingly have the character of places where the terms of existence itself are under human control and, as has been previously argued, intrinsic or ethical value has been neutralised or greatly attenuated. There is a danger, then, that if and when educational practice migrates into these spaces, the quality of learning may come to be measured in terms of ability to access and produce pastiches from the modularised content of databases (of whatever form and level of sophistication) and to act successfully in simulations or computer models, rather than sense what is on the move—what calls to be thought—in a face-to-face encounter with the subtle, spontaneous and ever-changing cadences of the human and natural world, and the developed (as against atomised) narratives that can capture this.

Several of these themes are echoed in C. A. Bowers' cautions concerning the cultural amnesia that results from equating computer use with the latest stage in our evolutionary development:

> The widespread translation of cultural life into digitally based simulations and data bases has now made such words as 'wisdom' appear irrelevant. It has also substituted the words 'data' and 'information' for the more complex phenomena that we previously called 'knowledge'. In the past knowledge was associated with a deep understanding of the patterns and relationships that were refined over generations of experience (Bowers, 2001, p. 3).

This last reflected, amongst other things, an ongoing relationship with and understanding of local nature.

Bowers argues that the growing influence of computers and the cultural epistemology upon which this influence is based are marginalising the variety of mytho-poetic narratives or root metaphors that serve as a schema for making sense of information and, in contrast, are setting language up as a mere conduit for the transfer of objective information. In reinforcing the idea of a universalised (and thus abstracted) autonomous individual as the basic social unit, these factors sustain and advance anthropocentrism and ignore the way in which individuals are embedded in social systems that are in turn embedded in natural systems. Being part of the larger ecology of interacting patterns of cultural and natural systems is not part of the cultural experience that accompanies computer-mediated experience (p. 5). Extracted from his or her cultural experience of time and place, everything becomes determined from the vantage point of the individual's immediate experience. As one commentator puts it: 'Computing is not about computing anymore. It is about living . . . As we interconnect ourselves, many of the values of a nation-state will give way to those of both larger and smaller electronic communities. We shall socialize in digital neighbourhoods in which physical space will be irrelevant and time will play a different role' (Nicholas Negroponte, in Bowers, 2001, p. 7).

Whatever its overstatement, this expresses the kind of commodification of human and community relationships in which computer use can be imbricated. This is further illustrated by the vital role that computers play in co-ordinating global economic activity—participation in such 'development' requiring the sacrifice of local cultural traditions that in turn are attuned to local ecosystems. Here, as Bowers notes, we are led to the issue of a high status knowledge that involves a messianic spreading of the process of commodification into every aspect of individual and community life, computers being the principal technology that now promotes the globalisation of such knowledge and the elite groups who benefit from it (p. 10). Given this milieu, it becomes inevitable that those who would challenge this hierarchy appear archaic and peripheral because they speak from the position of what is now defined as low status knowledge, of non-commodified community relationships and traditions.

In sum, and put starkly, the question is raised as to whether extended participation in certain forms of modern ICT—which, I have argued, is itself a developed expression of modernist humanism—has the potential to encourage an attitude towards the world that undermines the ground for an authentic relationship with nature and with ourselves. 'Cyberspace' is not just a socially constructed concept but also a socially manufactured reality. No matter how sophisticated a computer simulation of a field trip or a computer modelled aspect of nature may be, there are no messy intrinsic moral constraints upon the kinds of intervention that might be attempted. *It is not that kind of reality.* As they exist in this kind of space, things are stripped of intrinsic and ethical value and exist only to be manipulated. Now, clearly, considerations of this kind apply to many motives and spaces that pre-date the ascendance of computers, but the power and influence of the reality that modern ICT facilitates—its potential accessibility, its highly interactive and engaging qualities, and its pervasiveness as a (increasingly *the*) medium for the broadcast, exchange and perhaps formation of knowledge and thought—place it in a new league. And the danger is that, so endowed and so positioned, it may contribute to establishing a frame of mind that may be both re-applied to other kinds of 'nature' and diminish their perceived relevance.

HUMAN FLOURISHING

It is clear that one of the issues raised by the above critiques of expressions of modernist humanist impulses is that of a notion of human flourishing that is neither exclusively human- (self-)centred, nor *simply* a human construction and therefore optional. How plausible is it to suppose that there is in this sense a non-human-determined human essence that, if expressed in the way we live, constitutes our well-being, constitutes authentic dwelling? This is a large question. But even Sartre, one time proponent of unbounded freedom and an inspiration for Rorty's rejection of essences, says that we are *condemned* to be free—the ontological fact of our freedom is not a matter of choice, even if how we respond to it always is. While this issue of human essence is certainly raised by the thesis I have been developing, a full examination of it lies beyond the scope of the present text. However, there is a strand in it that we are in a position to pursue—namely, the implications of taking a right relationship with nature as the self-arising as an important aspect of authentic dwelling. The argument has been put that an open responsiveness to things themselves, as they inhabit natural space in which values are embedded, is deeply constitutive of our historically grown form of sensibility. In this sense such responsiveness is an aspect of our essence. If such an argument is accepted, it raises a number of reservations for accounts of human flourishing that define it in terms of desire satisfaction, for currently dominant modernist humanist motives cultivate and prioritise desires that subvert such responsiveness. But the issue is not, essentially, one of a proper approach to understanding human flourishing coming to the 'wrong' answer, but rather of the subjectivism of the approach itself. Even if the desires are in some sense informed and autonomous, on the account that I am giving they need to be premised on an understanding and an underlying ethos that are not matters of choice. There are ways of relating to nature as the self-arising that are fitting (and therefore revealing of it) and ways that are not. This does not mean that one can, therefore, provide some objective definitive list, applicable to all, of what the fitting responses would be in varying circumstances, but it indicates a realm in which a listening to the other so as to reveal, sustain, and celebrate it is the appropriate response. As for how individuals respond within this ambience, these are matters largely of spontaneity and contemplation (the two now understood as closely related), and in significant part also matters of chance and proclivity.

If this receptive celebratory element in the relationship with nature and, therefore, human well-being clearly stands in contrast to modernist humanist notions of progress and perfectibility, it perhaps nods towards a forgotten and politically unfashionable human ideal: contentment. Unfortunately in an age mesmerised by perpetual decisive action and a constant flow of new initiatives, this can connote a certain mental torpor and complacency, a lack of ambition, and perhaps an apathetic resignation and acceptance of one's lot or that of others. If lack of ambition and acceptance are interpreted as lack of self-promotion and an acceptance of certain bounds on one's desires and sphere of influence, they are indeed related to contentment, but this is hardly to concede any objection of mental torpor. Thankful listening, in the senses previously elaborated in this book, is truly challenging and rewarding. Discerning things themselves in their uniqueness—human or non-human, and finding the fitting response, be it word or action, can be a challenge of the highest order, as can be resisting the many and powerful pressures to do otherwise. Recognising the other—its authority—and attempting to do justice by it and have justice done by it, is no dummy of life, but its vital core.

Here we are brought up against the issue of the necessary subjectivism of valuing so much deprecated by Heidegger (1978, p. 228). His objection that, in valuing, everything is subject to human estimation and thus becomes object of a valuing subject is well taken if the valuing is anthropocentric. Here the thingness of things is destroyed, and indeed it is true that the 'bizarre effort to prove the objectivity of values'—as a way of enhancing their status—'does not know what it is doing' (p. 228). As also Iris Murdoch points out 'Good' 'is not a mere value tag of the choosing will' (p. 376). But there are other kinds of valuing that are not, I think, to be dismissed in this way. As self-aware agents, humankind must (that is, cannot avoid), and has a positive responsibility to, 'estimate' things, but now in an ecocentric sense of evaluating them in their relationship to the whole, and must do this spontaneously-contemplatively in poetic response to things themselves. This itself reveals another problem with anthropocentrism from the perspective of environmental concern. It restricts the realm of moral obligation to those who can enter into some kind of social contract, that is, rational agents. And while it can be argued with a good deal of plausibility that an enlightened viewing of the rest of nature as there to satisfy human desires, a viewing that takes proper account of our dependence on natural systems, brings with it a high regard for nature and also a high degree of protection, this essentially instrumental relationship remains deeply unsatisfactory from the point of view of human dwelling developed in this volume. This—not least because it impacts upon the human need to find a home in the midst of the growing homelessness brought on by the humanistic impulse for mastery, where again this is not itself conceived as human in the sense of humanly contrived, but rather as something non-human that is working through us, has requisitioned us—holds us in its sway.

In some ways, and from the perspective I have developed, humanism, insofar as it is the name that has come to call up such motives, could be seen as a massive misnomer. It names many motives that are the antithesis of being fully human. On the other hand, there may be some who would incline to the view that the position I have set out is 'pre-humanist' rather than post-humanist. For example, there are those, such as Haraway (1991) who would associate post-humanism with an age of machines or cyborgs, and who would indeed claim that, with our machine and computer metaphors of body and mind and with the growing use and prospect of machine implants, this is an age into which we are entering. In respect of her own view she writes: 'I am making an argument for the cyborg as a fiction mapping our social and bodily reality . . . By the late twentieth century . . . we are all chimeras, theorized and fabricated hybrids of machine and organism . . . The cyborg is our ontology; it gives us our politics' (p. 150). And, according to Haraway, we should welcome the fact because, as a founding metaphor, it promises to confound old dualisms of body/mind, of nature/machine, and to liberate us from the constraints of 'the natural'.

My response is that while such an age could be construed as biophysically post-humanist, metaphysically it would be quite the reverse. Insofar as such machines turn out to be more efficient means of expressing motives of disengaged mastery, they promise to deliver us ever more completely into the iron cage of technical rationality. The loss of pre-humanist innocence with its recognition of the special place and character of human consciousness within the cosmos is irrevocable. Post-humanism as here espoused, and as advocating a certain recognition of the authority of nature, does not reduce humankind to the servitude of the medieval or Renaissance view, but recognises that human beings have accumulated profound power, choices and responsibilities. It simply reasserts aspects of the human situation that are occluded by modernist humanism (as I have defined it) and that are necessary for the exercise of wisdom. It does not deny our power but acknowledges its limits and recommends that we refrain from using it in ways essentially destructive to ourselves in nature. While environmental concerns are not the only ones to raise the possibility of such a post-humanist perspective, they represent a particularly important and powerful impulse in this direction.

NOTE

1. I am grateful to Ian Frowe for suggesting this example to me.

Bibliography

Abbs, P. (1996) *The Polemics of Imagination* (London, Skoob Books).

Abram, D. (1999) A more-than-human world, in: A. Weston (ed.) *An Invitation to Environmental Philosophy* (Oxford, Oxford University Press).

Achterberg, W. (1995) Can liberal democracy survive the environmental crisis? Sustainability, liberal neutrality and overlapping consensus, in: A. Dobson and P. Lucardie (eds) *The Politics of Nature* (London, Routledge).

Adorno, T. (1986) *The Jargon of Authenticity*, trans. K. Tarnowski and F. Will (London, Routledge & Kegan Paul).

Attfield, R. (1994) *Environmental Philosophy: Principles and Prospects* (Aldershot, Avebury).

Attfield, R. (1995) Ethics and the environment: the global perspective, in: B. Almond (ed.) *Introducing Applied Ethics* (Oxford, Blackwell).

Bailey, C. H. (1983) *Beyond the Present and the Particular: A Theory of Liberal Education* (London, Routledge & Kegan Paul).

Baudrillard, J. (1988) *Selected Writings*, M. Poster (ed.) (Cambridge, Polity Press).

Beck, U. (1992) *Risk Society: Towards a New Modernity*, trans. M. Ritter (London, Sage).

Beck, U. (1994) *Ecological Politics in an Age of Risk* (Cambridge, Polity).

Berkes, F. (1993) Traditional knowledge in perspective, in: J. Inglis (ed.) *Traditional Ecological Knowledge: Concepts and Cases* (Ottawa, International Development Research Centre).

Bernstein, J. M. (1992) *The Fate of Art: Aesthetic Alienation from Kant to Derrida and Adorno* (Cambridge, Polity Press).

Bernstein, R. J. (1991) *The New Constellation* (Cambridge, Polity Press).

Berry, T. (1988) *The Dream of the Earth* (San Francisco, Sierra Club Books).

Berry, W. (1991) Out of your car, off your horse, *The Atlantic Monthly*, February 1991.

Blake, N., Smeyers, P., Smith, R., and Standish, P. (1998) *Thinking Again: Education After Postmodernism* (Westport, Connecticut, Bergin & Garvey).

Bluhdorn, I. (2000) *Post-Ecologist Politics: Social Theory and the Abdication of the Ecologist Paradigm* (London, Routledge).

Bluhdorn, I. (2002) Unsustainability as a frame of mind – and how we disguise it: The silent counter revolution and the politics of simulation, *The Trumpeter*, 18.1, pp. 59–69.

Bonnett, M. (1986) Personal authenticity and public standards: towards the transcendence of a dualism, in: D. Cooper (ed.) *Education, Values and Mind* (London, Routledge & Kegan Paul).

Bonnett, M. (1994) *Children's Thinking* (London, Cassell).

Bonnett, M. (1995) Teaching thinking and the sanctity of content, *Journal of Philosophy of Education* 29.3, pp. 295–309.

Bonnett, M. (1996) 'New' era values and the teacher-pupil relationship as a form of the poetic, *British Journal of Educational Studies*, 44.1, pp. 27–41.

Bonnett, M. (1997) Environmental Education and Beyond, *Journal of Philosophy of Education*, 31.2, pp. 249–266.

Bonnett, M. (1999) Education for sustainable development: a coherent philosophy for environmental education? *Environmental Education, Sustainability and the Transformation of Schooling, Cambridge Journal of Education. Special Issue*, 29.3, pp. 313–324.

Bonnett, M. (2000) Environmental concern and the metaphysics of education, *Journal of Philosophy of Education*, 34.4, pp. 591–602.

Bonnett, M. (2002) Education for Sustainability as a Frame of Mind, *Environmental Education Research*, 8.1, pp. 9–20.

Bonnett, M. and Williams, J. (1998) Environmental education and primary children's attitudes towards nature and the environment, *Cambridge Journal of Education*, 28.2, pp. 159–174.

Bonnett, M. and Cuypers, S. (2003) Autonomy and authenticity in education, in N. Blake, P. Smeyers, R. Smith and P. Standish (eds) *The Blackwell Guide to the Philosophy of Education* (Oxford, Blackwell).

Bowers, C. A. (1995) Toward an ecological perspective, in: W. Kohli (ed.) *Critical Conversations in Philosophy of Education* (London, Routledge).

Bowers, C. A. (2001) Computers, culture and the digital phase of the industrial revolution: expanding the debate on the educational use of computers, *The Trumpeter*, 17.1, pp. 1–16.

Breidler, I. (1999) Two primary schools on the way towards ecologisation, *Environmental Education, Sustainability and the Transformation of Schooling, Cambridge Journal of Education. Special Issue*, 29.3, pp. 367–377.

Brundtland Commission (1987) *Our Common Future* (Milton Keynes, Open University Press).

Butt, J. (1963) *The Poems of Alexander Pope* (London, Methuen).

Capra, F. (1975) *The Tao of Physics* (Berkeley, Shambhala).

Capra, F. (1982) *The Turning Point* (New York, Simon & Schuster).

Cassirer, E. (1970) *An Essay on Man* (New Haven, Yale University Press).

Cheney, J. (1999) The journey home, in: A. Weston (ed.) *An Invitation to Environmental Philosophy* (Oxford, Oxford University Press).

Clarke, B. (2002) *The Stream* (London, Black Swan Books).

Coleridge, S. T. (1973) *Biographia Literaria Volume One*, J. Shawcross (ed.) (Oxford, Oxford University Press).

Cooper, D. E. (1992) The idea of environment, in: D. Cooper and J. Palmer (eds) *The Environment in Question* (London, Routledge).

Cooper, D. E. (1998) Aestheticism and environmentalism, in: D. Cooper and J. Palmer (eds) *Spirit of the Environment* (London, Routledge).

Connelly, J. and Smith, G. (1999) *Politics and the Environment* (London, Routledge).

Dearden, R. F. (1968) *The Philosophy of Primary Education* (London, Routledge & Kegan Paul).

Derrida, J. (1981a) *Dissemination*, trans. B. Johnson (Chicago, University of Chicago Press).

Derrida, J. (1981b) *Positions*, trans. A. Bass (Chicago, University of Chicago Press).

De-Shalit, A. (2000) *The Environment. Between Theory and Practice* (Oxford, Oxford University Press).

Eder, E. (1999) From scepticism to the urge to take action, or from daily frustration to a solo initiative, *Environmental Education, Sustainability and the Transformation of Schooling, Cambridge Journal of Education. Special Issue*, 29.3, pp. 355–365.

Eliot, G. (1994) *The Mill on the Floss* (London, Penguin).

Elliott, J. (1995) The politics of environmental education: a case study, *Curriculum Journal*, 6.3, pp. 377–393.

Elliott, J. (1999) Sustainable society and environmental education: future perspectives and demands for the educational system, *Environmental Education, Sustainability and the Transformation of Schooling, Cambridge Journal of Education. Special Issue*, 29.3, pp. 325–340.

Elliot, R. (1995) Faking Nature, in R. Elliot (ed.) *Environmental Ethics* (Oxford, Oxford University Press).

Elliot, R. (1997) *Faking Nature* (London, Routledge).

Fleischman, P. (1969) Conservation, the biological fallacy, *Landscape*, 18, pp. 23–27.

Foreman, D. (1993) Putting the Earth First, in: S. Armstrong and R. Botzler (eds) *Environmental Ethics* (New York, McGraw-Hill).

Froebel, F. (1967) *Fredrich Froebel: A Selection from his Writings*, I. Lilley (ed.) (Cambridge, Cambridge University Press).

Frowe, I. (1992) Persuasive forces: language, ideology and education, in R. Andrews (ed.) *The Rebirth of Rhetoric: Essays in Language, Culture and Education* (London, Routledge).

Frowe, I. (2001) Language and educational practice, *Cambridge Journal of Education*, 31.1, pp. 89–101.

Frye, M. (1983) In and out of harm's way: Arrogance and love, *The Politics of Reality* (Freedom, CA, The Crossing Press).

Garrard, G. (1998) The Romantics' view of nature, in: D. Cooper and J. Palmer (eds) *Spirit of the Environment* (London, Routledge).

Geldard, R. (1995) *The Vision of Emerson* (Rockport, MA, Element Books).

Giddens, A. (1994) *Beyond Left and Right* (Cambridge, Polity Press).

Glacken, C. J. (1967) *Traces on the Rhodian Shore. Nature and Culture in Western Thought from Ancient Times to the End of the Eighteenth Century* (Berkeley, University of California Press).

Goodin, R. E. (1992) *Green Political Theory* (Cambridge, Polity Press).

Grange, J. (1997) *Nature. An Environmental Cosmology* (New York, State University of New York Press).

Gray, J. (1999) An agenda for Green conservatism, in: M. Smith (ed.) *Thinking Through the Environment* (London, Routledge).

Grenier, L. (1998) *Working with Indigenous Knowledge: A Guide for Researchers* (Ottawa, International Development Research Centre).

Griffin, S. (1978) *Woman and Nature: The Roaring Inside Her* (New York, Harper & Row).

Haldane, J. (1994) Admiring the high mountains: The aesthetics of environment, *Environmental Values*, 3.2, pp. 97–106.

Haraway, D. J. (1991) *Simians, Cyborgs, and Women. The Reinvention of Nature* (London, Free Association Books).

Heidegger, M. (1967) *What is a Thing?* trans. W. Barton and V. Deutsch (Chicago, Henry Regnery).

Heidegger, M. (1975) *Poetry, Language, Thought*, trans. A. Hofstadter (New York, Harper & Row).

Heidegger, M. (1976) *The Piety of Thinking*, trans. J. Hart and J. Maraldo (Bloomington, Indiana University Press).

Heidegger, M. (1977) The question concerning technology, in *The Question Concerning Technology and Other Essays* trans. W. Lovitt (New York, Harper & Row).

Heidegger, M. (1978) *Martin Heidegger Basic Writings*, D. Krell (ed.) (London, Routledge & Kegan Paul).

Heidegger, M. (1998) *Pathmarks*, W. McNeill (ed.) (Cambridge, Cambridge University Press).

Heim, M. (1993) *The Metaphysics of Virtual Reality* (New York, Oxford University Press).

Hertzberg, A. (1998) Religion and nature: the Abrahamic faith's concepts of creation, in: D. Cooper and J. Palmer (eds) *Spirit of the Environment* (London, Routledge).

Hillier, J. (1998) Paradise proclaimed? Towards theoretical understanding of representations of nature in land use planning decision-making, *Ethics, Place and Environment*, 1.1, pp. 77–91.

Jantzen, G. (1984) *God's World, God's Body* (London, Darton, Longman & Todd).

Johnson, M. (1992) *Lore: Capturing Traditional Environmental Knowledge* (Ottawa, International Development Research Centre).

Kant, I. (1963) *Lectures on Ethics*, trans. L. Infield (London, Methuen).

Kant, I. (1970)) *Critique of Pure Reason*, trans. N. Kemp Smith (London, Macmillan).

Katz, E. (1996) *Nature as Subject* (Lanham MD, Rowman & Littlefield).

Katz, E. (1997) Nature's presence: reflections on healing and domination, in: A. Light and J. Smith (eds) *Space, Place, and Environmental Ethics* (Lanham, Rowan & Littlefield).

King, R. (1997) Critical reflections on biocentric environmental ethics: is it an alternative to anthropocentrism?, in: A. Light and J. Smith (eds) *Space, Place, and Environmental Ethics* (Lanham, Rowman & Littlefield).

Kolb, D. (2000) Learning places: building, dwelling, thinking online, *Enquiries at the Interface: Philosophical Problems of Online Education, Special Issue Journal of Philosophy of Education*, 34.1, pp. 121–133.

Kovel, J. (2002) *The Enemy of Nature: The End of Capitalism or the End of the World* (London, Zed Books).

Krieger, M. (1973) What's wrong with plastic trees? *Science*, 179.

Lankshear, C., Peters, M., and Knobel, M. (2000) Information, knowledge and learning: some issues facing epistemology and education in a digital age, *Enquiries at the Interface: Philosophical Problems of Online Education*, Special Issue, *Journal of Philosophy of Education*, 34.1, pp. 17–39.

Lawrence, D. H. (1934) *Reflections on the Death of a Porcupine and Other Essays* (London, Martin Secker).

Lawrence, D. H. (1973) Benjamin Franklin, in: J. Williams and R. Williams (eds) *D. H. Lawrence on Education* (Harmondsworth, Penguin Books).

Leopold, A. (1989) *A Sand County Almanac* (New York, Oxford University Press).

Leopold, A. (1993) The land ethic, in: S. Armstrong and R. Botzler (eds) *Environmantal Ethics. Divergence and Convergence* (New York, McGraw-Hill).

Light, A. (2002) Contemporary Environmental Ethics: From Metaethics to Public Philosophy, *Metaphilosophy*, 33.4, pp. 426–428.

Lively, J. (1966) *The Enlightenment* (London, Longmans).

Lovelock, J. (1979) *Gaia* (Oxford, Oxford University Press).

Lyotard, J-F. (1984) *The Postmodern Condition: A Report on Knowledge*, trans. G. Bennington and B. Massumi (Manchester, Manchester University Press).

McCarthy, K. (1995) 'Science: power or wisdom?', *School Science Review*, 76.2, pp. 7–14.

Marshall, P. (1995) *Nature's Web* (London, Cassell).

McFague, S. (1993) *The Body of God. An Ecological Theology* (London, SCM Press).

McKibben, W. (1989) *The End of Nature* (New York, Random House).

Maser, C. (1988) *The Redesigned Forest* (San Pedro, R. & E. Miles).

Mathews, F. (1994) *The Ecological Self* (London, Routledge).

Merchant, C. (1992) *Radical Ecology* (London, Routledge).

Midgley, M. (1995) Duties concerning islands, in: R. Elliot (ed.) *Environmental Ethics* (Oxford, Oxford University Press).

Milton, K. (1996) *Environmentalism and Cultural Theory* (London, Routledge).

Milton, K. (1998) Nature and the environment in indigenous and traditional cultures, in: D. Cooper and J. Palmer (eds) *Spirit of the Environment* (London, Routledge).

Mitchum, C. (1997) The sustainability question, in R. Gottlieb (ed.) *The Ecological Community* (London, Routledge).

Murdoch, I. (1959) The sublime and the good, *Chicago Review*, 13.3, pp. 42–45.

Murdoch, I. (1997) The sovereignty of Good over other concepts, in *Existentialists and Mystics* (London, Chatto & Windus).

Naess, A. (1989) *Ecology, Community and Life Style*, trans. D. Rothenberg (Cambridge, Cambridge University Press).

National Curriculum Council (1990) *Curriculum Guidance 7: Environmental Education* (York, National Curriculum Council).

National Environmental Education Advisory Council (1996) *Report Assessing Environmental Education in the United States and the Implementation of the National Environmental Education Act of 1990* (Washington DC, US Environmental Protection Agency).

Nietzsche, F. (1990) *Twilight of the Idols*, trans. R. Hollingdale (Harmondsworth, Penguin).

Oakeshott, M. (1962) Rationalism in politics, in: *Rationalism and Politics and Other Essays* (London, Methuen).

Oakeshott, M. (1972) Education: the engagement and its frustration, in: R. Dearden, P. Hirst and R. Peters (eds) *Education and the Development of Reason* (London, Routledge & Kegan Paul).

Ophuls, W. (1977) *Ecology and the Politics of Scarcity* (San Francisco, W. H. Freeman).

O'Riordan, T. (1999) Ecocentrism and Technocentrism, in: M. Smith (ed.) *Thinking Through the Environment* (London, Routledge).

Orr, D. (1992) *Ecological Literacy* (Albany NY, SUNY Press).

Orr, D. (1994) *Earth in Mind: On Education, the Environment and the Human Prospect* (Washington DC, Island Press).

Palmer, J. and Neal, P. (1994) *The Handbook of Environmental Education* (London, Routledge).

Passmore, J. (1980) *Man's Responsibility for Nature* (London, Duckworth).

Passmore, J. (1995) Attitudes to nature, in: R. Elliot (ed.) *Environmental Ethics* (Oxford, Oxford University Press).

Pattison, G. (2000) *The Later Heidegger* (London, Routledge).

Peters, R.S. (1972) Reason and passion, in: R. F. Dearden, P. H. Hirst and R. S. Peters (eds) *Education and the Development of Reason* (London, Routledge & Kegan Paul).

Peters, R. S. (1973) The justification of education, in: R. Peters (ed.) *The Philosophy of Education* (London, Oxford University Press).

Peters, R. S. (1974) Subjectivity and standards, in: *Psychology and Ethical Development* (London, Allen & Unwin).

Plumwood, V. (1995) Nature, self, and gender: feminism, environmental philosophy, and the critique of rationalism, in: R. Elliot (ed.) *Environmental Ethics* (Oxford, Oxford University Press).

Porritt, J. (1984) *Seeing Green* (Oxford, Blackwell).

Posch, P. (1999) The ecologisation of schools and its implications for educational policy, *Environmental Education, Sustainability and the Transformation of Schooling, Cambridge Journal of Education. Special Issue*, 29.3, pp. 341–348.

Postma D. W. (2002) Taking the future seriously: on the inadequacies of the framework of liberalism for environmental education, *Journal of Philosophy of Education*, 36.1, pp. 41–56.

QCA (1999) *The National Curriculum. Handbook for Primary Teachers in England. Key Stages 1 and 2* (Qualifications and Curriculum Authority, London).

Rawles, K. (1998) Philosophy and the environmental movement, in: D. Cooper and J. Palmer (eds) *Spirit of the Environment* (London, Routledge).

Reid, A., Teamey, K. and Dillon, J. (2002) Traditional ecological knowledge for learning with sustainability in mind, *The Trumpeter* 18.1, pp.113–136.

Rist, G. (1997) *The History of Development: From Western Origins to Global Faith* (London, Zed Books).

Rogers, T. (2000) In search of a new space where nature and culture dissolve into a unified whole and deep ecology comes alive, *The Trumpeter*, 16.1, pp. 1–11.

Rolston III, H. (1997) Nature for real: is nature a social construct?, in: Chappell, T. (ed.) *The Philosophy of the Environment* (Edinburgh, Edinburgh University Press).

Rolston, III, H. (1999) Ethics on the home planet, in: A. Weston (ed.) *An Invitation to Environmental Philosophy* (Oxford, Oxford University Press).

Rorty, R. (1994) *Philosophy and the Mirror of Nature* (Oxford, Blackwell).

Rorty, R. (1989) *Contingency, Irony, and Solidarity* (Cambridge, Cambridge University Press).

Ross, R. (1990) *Dancing with a Ghost* (Markham ON, Octopus Publishing Group).

Rousseau, J. J. (1970) *Emile For Today: The Emile of Jean Jacques Rousseau*, trans. W. Boyd (London, Heinemann).

Russell, B. (1959) *The Problems of Philosophy* (London, Oxford University Press).

Russell, P. (1983) *The Global Brain: Speculations on the evolutionary leap to planetary consciousness* (Boston MA, Houghton).

Saward, M. (1995) Green democracy?, in: A. Dobson and P. Lucardie (eds) *The Politics of Nature* (London, Routledge).

Scruton, R. (1994) *Modern Philosophy* (London, Sinclair-Stevenson).

Shiva, V. (1992) Recovering the real meaning of sustainability, in: D. Cooper and J. Palmer (eds) *The Environment in Question* (London, Routledge).

Simmons, I. G. (1995) *Interpreting Nature* (London, Routledge).

Singer, P. (1993) *Practical Ethics: Second Edition* (Cambridge, Cambridge University Press).

Smith, M. J. (ed.) (1999) *Thinking Through the Environment* (London, Routledge).

Smith, R. (1998) Spirit of middle earth: practical thinking for an instrumental age, in: D. Cooper and J. Palmer (eds) *Spirit of the Environment* (London, Routledge).

Smithson, I. (1997) Native Americans and the desire for environmental harmony: challenging a stereotype, in: P. Thompson (ed.) *Environmental Education for the 21st Century* (New York, Peter Lang).

Solomon, R. C. (1980) *History and Human Nature* (Brighton, Harvester Press).

Soper, K. (1995) *What is Nature?* (Oxford, Blackwell).

Soule, M. and Lease, G. (1995) *Reinventing Nature: Responses to Postmodern Deconstruction* (Washington DC, Island Press).

Stables, A. (2001) Who drew the sky? Conflicting assumptions in environmental education, *Educational Philosophy and Theory*, 33.2, pp. 245–256.

Stables, A. (2002) On the making and breaking of frames in pursuit of sustainability, *The Trumpeter* 19.1, pp. 49–57.

Stables, A. and Scott, W. (2001) Post-humanist liberal pragmatism? Environmental education out of modernity, *Journal of Philosophy of Education*, 35.2, pp. 269–279.

Stables, A. and Scott, W. (2002) The quest for holism in education for sustainable development, *Environmental Education Research*, 8.1, pp. 53–60.

Standish, P. (2000) Fetish for effect, *Enquiries at the Interface: Philosophical Problems of Online Education, Special Issue Journal of Philosophy of Education*, 34.1, pp. 151–168.

Strawson, P. F. (1964) *Individuals* (London, Methuen).

Studley, J. (1998) *Dominant Knowledge Systems and Local Knowledge*, Mtn Forum On-line Library Document, http://mtnforum.org/resources/library/stud98a2.htm Accessed August, 2001.

Taylor, C. (1983) *Philosophical Papers Two: Philosophy and the Human Sciences* (Cambridge, Cambridge University Press).

Taylor, C. (1991) *The Ethics of Authenticity* (Cambridge, MA, Harvard University Press).

Taylor, C. (1992) Heidegger, language and ecology, in: H. Dreyfus and H. Hall (eds) *Heidegger: A Critical Reader* (Oxford, Blackwell).

Taylor. P. (1986) *Respect for Nature: A Theory of Environmental Ethics* (New Jersey, Princeton University Press).

Thompson, P. B. (1995) *The Spirit of the Soil* (London, Routledge).

Thoreau, H. (1962) *The Journal of Henry David Thoreau*, B. Torrey and F. Allen (eds.) (New York, Dover Publications).

Turkle, S. (1996) *Life on the Screen: Identity in the Age of the Internet* (New York, Simon & Schuster).

UNCED (1992) *Agenda 21* (New York, UNCED).

Usher, R. and Edwards, R. (1994) *Postmodernism and Education* (London, Routledge).

Vanderburg, W. H. (1995) Can a technical civilisation sustain human life?, *Bulletin of Science, Technology and Society*, 15.

Warren, D. M. (1991) *Using Indigenous Knowledge in Agricultural Development.* World Bank Discussion Papers, No. 127. (Washington, DC, World Bank).

Whitehead, A. N. (1985) *Science and the Modern World* (London, Free Association Books).

Whitley, D. (1996) Aesop for children: power and morality, in: M. Styles, E. Bearne and V. Watson (eds) *Voices Off* (London, Cassell).

Wissenburg, M. (1995) The idea of nature and the nature of distributive justice, in: A. Dobson and P. Lucardie (eds) *The Politics of Nature* (London, Routledge).

Index

Printed in Great Britain
by Amazon